PLAY YOUR WAY TO
GOOD
MANNERS

Play Your Way to Good Manners

CompanionHouse Books™ is an imprint of Fox Chapel Publishers International Ltd.

Project Team
Vice President–Content: Christopher Reggio
Editor: Amy Deputato
Copy Editor: Colleen Dorsey
Design: Mary Ann Kahn
Index: Elizabeth Walker

ISBN 978-1-62187-185-9

Library of Congress Cataloging-in-Publication Data

Names: Naito, Kate, author.
Title: Play your way to good manners : getting the best behavior from your dog through sports, games, and tricks / Kate Naito, CPDT-KA, MS and Sarah Westcott, CPDT-KSA.
Description: Mount Joy, PA : CompanionHouse Books, an imprint of Fox Chapel Publishers International Ltd., [2019] | Includes bibliographical references and index.
Identifiers: LCCN 2019018844 (print) | LCCN 2019019395 (ebook) | ISBN 9781621871866 (ebook) | ISBN 9781621871859 (softcover)
Subjects: LCSH: Dogs--Training. | Dogs--Behavior.
Classification: LCC SF431 (ebook) | LCC SF431 .N355 2019 (print) | DDC 636.7/0835--dc23
LC record available at https://lccn.loc.gov/2019018844

Fox Chapel Publishing
903 Square Street
Mount Joy, PA 17552

Fox Chapel Publishers International Ltd.
7 Danefield Road, Selsey (Chichester)
West Sussex PO20 9DA, U.K.

www.facebook.com/companionhousebooks

We are always looking for talented authors. To submit an idea, please send a brief inquiry to acquisitions@foxchapelpublishing.com.

Printed and bound in China
22 21 20 19   2 4 6 8 10 9 7 5 3 1

PLAY YOUR WAY TO
GOOD
MANNERS

GETTING THE BEST BEHAVIOR FROM YOUR DOG
THROUGH SPORTS, GAMES, AND TRICKS

KATE NAITO, CPDT-KA, MS
SARAH WESTCOTT, CPDT-KSA

CONTENTS

MEET THE AUTHORS

Stroll down 21st Street in the quiet neighborhood of South Slope, Brooklyn, and you'll find that it looks nearly identical to the other tree-lined streets. That is, except for the surprising number of dogs being walked up and down this particular block. That's because it's home to the Brooklyn Dog Training Center, where every kind of urban canine, from chubby Corgi puppy to muscular Pit Bull mix, comes to learn both manners and sports.

Walk into the center, and you're likely to be greeted by **Sarah Westcott, CPDT-KSA,** the founder of both Doggie Academy and the Brooklyn Dog Training Center. On any given day, you can find her on the sidewalk with a handful of cheese and a leash-reactive dog; on her hands and knees, puppy-proofing someone's home; or at the training center, giving both private and group lessons in agility and rally obedience. When she's not teaching, Sarah actively competes in several dog sports, but agility is her primary focus. Her young Border Collie, Fever, competes at the Masters level in agility and has traveled to the Border Collie National Specialty. Fever also has titles in dock diving and tricks, and she enjoys their disc dog league. Sarah's other dog, Hank, an eleven-year-old Labrador Retriever/ Redbone Coonhound mix, is still competing in agility. Hank also has several titles in rally obedience and tricks. At the Brooklyn Dog Training Center, Sarah applies sports techniques and trick training to all kinds of situations, whether it's teaching a puppy manners or helping a dog overcome a behavior issue. Her knowledge of trick training has come in handy in other ways, too: Sarah works as an on-set animal trainer, and you may have seen Hank and Fever on TV shows and in commercials!

Kate Naito, CPDT-KA, is the Manners Program Director at Doggie Academy, as well as the author of *BKLN Manners™: Positive Training Solutions for Your Unruly Urban Dog*. Both in print and in person, she focuses on the various manners issues that urban dog owners face, including disruptive barking, leash-walking woes, and exuberant jumping. Kate also helps clients work through their dogs' more serious behavior issues, from reactivity to resource guarding, using force-free methods. She often employs tricks, games, and sports not only to elicit good manners from her doggie students but also to give them healthy outlets for their energy and enjoyable ways to build confidence in the big, noisy city. For instance, scent work is a great way for energetic dogs to blow off steam while cooped up inside; parkour and rally obedience can transform a dog's leash walking; and tricks can give an overly exuberant puppy calm alternatives to jumping on and biting people.

Kate is drawn to senior and special-needs rescues, and you'll see her dogs Batman and Beans demonstrating some of the lower-impact behaviors in this book. Batman is a sassy senior Chihuahua mix who always gives 100 percent when practicing rally, scent work, and parkour. Beans is a sweet, sensitive, one-eyed Chihuahua/Jack Russell Terrier mix who also plays these sports recreationally, but her true passion is barn hunt.

With *Play Your Way to Good Manners*, Sarah and Kate have combined their professional experience to bring you a book that tackles manners training in a new way: entirely through sports, games, and tricks. It's an approach that has worked for Doggie Academy clients, and it can work for you, too!

INTRODUCTION

You've got the day off. No plans, no laundry to do, no e-mails to write. What would you rather do: go to work or spend some time on your favorite hobby?

It's a ridiculous question, right? While a few of us would gladly trot to the office on a sunny Saturday, the vast majority of people would prefer to go out and play tennis, catch up on a favorite TV series, or meet a friend for brunch.

Now, let's think about your dog. You know—that furry roommate for whom every day is a day off. If we gave him the choice of going to work or engaging in play, which do you think he'd choose? Just like us, there are a few dogs who revel in having a job, but most pups are happiest when playing a game or hanging out.

As we know (but your dog may not), life isn't always fun and games. Sometimes we have to work. Even your dog sometimes has to work, meaning that he has to be well mannered: walk politely on leash, come when called, sit-stay when he'd rather not. But why does work have to be boring? For both you and your dog, wouldn't it be nice if work were truly fun and rewarding? If work made you feel like "I *want* to do this" rather than "I *have* to do this"? It wouldn't feel like work anymore, and you would choose to do it even

when you weren't forced to. This is the aim of *Play Your Way to Good Manners*.

Training your dog shouldn't feel like a burden to either you or your dog. In the following pages, you will find all of the techniques you need to teach your dog polite manners indoors and out. These techniques are intended to make the training process not only fun but also applicable to your daily life. That's why we've drawn from numerous dog sports, games, and tricks to create a training plan for all your manners needs.

Why include sports in manners training? Canine sports are growing by leaps and bounds, and with good reason: dogs love them! What trainers and owners have found is that, by practicing a sport, dog and handler learn an abundance of practical skills that can be applied to everyday situations. Dogs who practice agility learn to communicate with their handlers, even at high speeds and from a distance. As you can imagine, this might be useful when you need to get your dog's attention at a distracting place, such as the dog park. Likewise, dogs who compete in rally obedience have leash-walking skills that are the envy of every other owner. Each sport has behavioral benefits. Therefore, in this book, you'll find a number of behaviors that are used in canine sports. Should you decide to pursue a canine sport in the future, you'll be well ahead of the game!

This book also includes numerous games for you and your dog to play. From football to chess, we humans are drawn to games. Our dogs are not so different. They often try to engage each other, and even us, in rounds of fetch, tug, chase, or wrestling. Humans and dogs are special in the animal world for remaining playful throughout adulthood, while most species show comparatively less playfulness as adults.

Patricia McConnell, in her book *The Other End of the Leash*, calls humans and dogs "Peter Pan species" because we hold on to juvenile (in the scientific, rather than derogatory, sense) behavioral traits long after adolescence. So let's utilize this lifelong playfulness not only to interact with our dogs but also to teach them. You'll find games in this book, ranging from recall to scent games. In the broader sense, every behavior in this book is a game; you and your dog are a team of two playing a training game with certain goals, and when your team meets those goals, you both win.

And then there are tricks. Why is teaching a trick like Paw more fun than teaching an obedience-type behavior like Stay? After all, the training sequence is pretty much the same, involving elements such as cues, marking, rewarding, and so on. The difference lies in the handler's attitude. If you are teaching your dog to give you his paw, there's no urgency, no stress, no expectations from your friends and family to complete a perfect Paw right away. But when teaching a "necessary" behavior like Stay, there is the added pressure of meeting your (and others') expectations for having a polite dog.

For instance, we often hear from clients, "My mother-in-law is coming next week, and she's afraid of dogs, so Buster has to learn to stay whenever I ask him to." Oh, boy. The compounding stress of a complex training behavior, a tight deadline, and family dynamics will surely suck all of the joy out of teaching Buster to stay. If a dog learns Paw faster than Stay, it's no wonder. Tricks teach us to loosen up. When we loosen up, we are able to communicate better with our dogs and give positive feedback. As a result, we can make faster progress with more lasting results. The best part is that tricks have a lot of practical benefits, too. For example, while your dog is sitting quietly and giving his paw to everyone at the family gathering, isn't he also by default doing lots of Stays?

SOUND FAMILIAR?

Debra and Marcus, a bubbly Brooklyn couple, brought their three-year-old Havanese, Lola, to the Brooklyn Dog Training Center for a private lesson with Kate. The couple hoped to take Sarah's agility classes with Lola but wanted to do some basic training first. Their other dog, a one-year-old terrier mix named Buttons, tagged along "just to watch." For the first few minutes, Kate let the two dogs explore the training center, with its fascinating smells and funny-looking agility equipment. Lola, their agility hopeful, casually sniffed the floor, half-interested, and eventually settled into a spot next to Debra. Meanwhile, younger brother Buttons was practically bouncing off the walls, running wildly back and forth between Debra and the equipment laid out on the training floor. Debra and Marcus explained that, at home, Lola rarely engaged in destructive or inappropriate behavior, while Buttons destroyed anything with stuffing and incessantly barked at the slightest noise. Neither dog had had any formal training.

"Do you think Buttons is a bit... off?" Marcus's question took Kate aback for a moment. Though they were both looking at the same little dog, they were having completely different interpretations of his character. Granted, Marcus, Debra, and Kate all saw a wild child, a tiny bundle of energy unable to focus for more than a split second. To Buttons's owners, this indicated instability, lack of intelligence, and untrainability. Kate, on the other hand, saw the exact opposite: a dog who loved to explore and engage with his environment but who also had enough of an interest in his humans to occasionally check in with them, despite having had no training. Kate knew Buttons would be easier to train than his older sister Lola, who showed only a mild interest in her surroundings.

Whether for fun or competition, agility training has physical and mental benefits for dogs.

They decided to include both dogs in that day's manners lesson. By the end of the lesson, both Debra and Marcus were left speechless at how Buttons had thrown himself into the training. He was offering Sits to his owners without being asked, and had decided that Come was the most exciting activity in the world. Lola, whom they had assumed was the smarter dog because she was less naughty at home, turned out to be far more challenging to motivate. She obliged Debra with a few Sits before retreating to her napping spot, and she wasn't initially convinced that Come was really worth the effort. Needless to say, when the couple showed up to their first agility class, it was with Buttons, and Lola tagged along "just to watch."

CONTROL YOURSELF!

Why did Debra and Marcus assume that Buttons was "off"? It all comes down to impulse control, of which Buttons had none. In the home, he jumped up on the dining room table, barked frantically at birds, and stole socks by the dozen. On leashed walks, only his back paws ever touched the ground, and he had lost his off-leash privileges long ago after running away one too many times. To put it plainly, he was naughty.

In actuality, Buttons was a dog who was practically screaming, "Someone—train me!" He loved interacting with his human family, enjoyed treats and toys, and had lots of energy to burn. As is so often the case, the dogs who love training are the dogs who *need* training; without it, they destroy your furniture, treat your guests like punching bags, and bark hysterically at the slightest triggers.

Dogs, like humans, aren't born having much impulse control. The dog who snatches a ball from your hand isn't so different from the toddler who steals his playmate's toy. In both cases, they think, "I want that," and they simply react. In the case of dogs, it's our job as owners to teach them that only polite behaviors will get them what they want. Acting on impulses, such as jumping on the person who's holding a ball, is not the way for a dog to get the desired item. Instead, polite behavior, such as sitting, is the only way to get that ball thrown. No Sit, no ball.

Some owners, despite their frustration, see their dogs' naughty behavior as expressions of their personalities. They fear that training these dogs will dampen their spirits. We believe the

HANK'S JOURNEY

After Sarah adopted her Lab mix, Hank, she quickly found that he was the embodiment of a "naughty" dog. When Hank was young, Sarah felt exhausted because she had to keep an active eye on him at all times. It only took a split second for Hank to pee on the bed, destroy couch cushions, or get into some other kind of trouble. The most challenging part was that he had no interest in being with Sarah. If she sat down on the floor to spend time with him, he would promptly make himself comfortable in the farthest corner of the room. It wasn't exactly the most rewarding relationship.

Because Sarah was striking out at home, she started taking agility classes with Hank to give him an outlet for his energy and to do something fun together. The class involved Hank doing an exercise and then Sarah rewarding him with cheese, chicken, or a squeaky toy. This pattern gave Hank an "aha!" moment, and he realized how fantastic Sarah was. Agility taught him not just to value Sarah's participation during class but also how to build a relationship with her in general. Hank started paying attention to her a lot more because she was both the giver of the cues and the distributor of the cheese. By learning to communicate together in a fun way, Hank flourished and has gone on to earn a long list of titles in agility, rally, and more.

More than a decade after attending those first agility classes, Hank still has his challenging moments, but he's become an accomplished competitor, he can be trusted off leash on hikes, and, above all, he is a champion cuddler.

exact opposite: by training your overly exuberant dog in a positive, force-free way, you can channel his spirit toward healthy, polite activities that please both dog and human. Giving your dog the appropriate outlet for his energy through positive-reinforcement training will enrich his life and give him the tools to interact appropriately with the world around him. If you attend an agility trial or other sporting event, you'll find that it's full of turbo-charged dogs. But these dogs have been given a fulfilling way to focus their energy; they've been given a purpose. Without the channel of activities like agility, freestyle, or rally, these dogs would be left with an overabundance of energy and no productive way to apply it.

Your dog doesn't have to reach agility superstardom to be well behaved. This book will bring the sports to you, so your dog can reap the behavioral benefits of sports, games, and trick training without the pressure of competition.

TRAINING SHOULD BE TRICKY

Training is supposed to be fun. You've probably been told that before. In reality, training your dog to walk politely on leash or sit while people pet him can feel anything but fun. When you focus on all of your dog's "problems" and have specific expectations for the outcomes of your training, it can put undue stress on both you and your dog.

Teaching your dog tricks, on the other hand, does not carry the same weight as regular "obedience"-type training. When you teach your dog a trick, the purpose is usually just for personal enjoyment ("I *want* to do this"), not to solve a behavior or manners problem ("I *have* to do this"). As a result, your attitude is far more relaxed. Both you and your dog can enjoy the process, even if it takes weeks to master the trick. Because you're approaching training with an open mind and no particular expectation, there is no need to feel stress. And wouldn't you know it—you and your dog are having fun and learning even faster than you'd expected.

Think of little Buttons, whose willingness to learn wasn't apparent to his family. All he wanted to do was play and run and bounce around, which looked like disobedience to them. But once they channeled his party-all-the-time energy in a productive way, he learned quickly. To him, leash walking and Sit-Stays were games, not drudgery. As long as his family continues to approach training as fun, he will follow along.

This book is not a tricks book, per se. It does include a number of tricks that have practical applications, plus exercises used in dog sports and training games that can teach your dog polite manners. Regardless of which behavior you're practicing from this book, we encourage you to think of it as a trick or a game, in the sense that you and your dog are learning something fun together. No judgment, no expectations. Just enjoy the journey.

As mentioned, training your dog should be a matter of "want to" rather than "have to." As you practice the behaviors in the following chapters, keep this idea in the back of your mind, and make sure that you truly want to be practicing at that time. For your dog, too, the attitude of "want to" is essential. If training feels like a game to your dog, he will jump for joy when you start to practice a new behavior and will feel disappointed when the training session is over. If, however, your dog doesn't want to do the training with you, it will be a struggle to make even the slightest progress, and what you've practiced probably won't stick. When the process feels like work to either of you, it's time to take a break and reevaluate. If necessary, put that behavior on the back burner and try something else, just for fun.

WHY POSITIVE TRAINING WORKS

Think back to the teacher, coach, or mentor who shaped you the most. The one who motivated you and possibly led you to pursue a certain academic or professional path. What qualities did that individual have? A good teacher generally:

- presents material clearly, without either jumping too far ahead or laboring over the same point for too long;
- engages you in the learning process and recognizes your successes, giving you a rush of excitement as you learn new things;
- methodically pushes you to work harder, learn more, and stretch your abilities;
- knows how to pace your learning, including when to stop pushing you; and
- listens to you without judgment.

Positive training means your dog will always be excited to come back to you.

Now think of yourself as the teacher and your dog as the student. Imagine you'd like to teach Scout to fetch, which is a lengthy sequence in which the dog follows a ball as it's thrown, picks it up, brings it back to you, and drops it at your feet. If you do not approach Fetch methodically and clearly, Scout will not be able to follow your instructions. He'll get frustrated and give up. If you punish him for making mistakes, many of which are due to misunderstanding your cues, Scout will lose his motivation to work with you. Who wants to play a game with a partner who is always yelling? Fetch is supposed to be a fun game that you and your dog enjoy together, but when you approach it with a negative attitude or confusing instructions, you and your dog can quickly become adversaries.

In the training process, you and your dog are on the same team, with you as the coach. Just as your favorite coach always had your back, so should you have your dog's. When you train in

this way, you are both willingly working toward a goal together. If either individual becomes frustrated or overwhelmed, it's time for you both to take a breather and consider how to tackle that obstacle together. This kind of positive attitude might sound simple, and, in theory, it is. In practice, however, we are susceptible to getting annoyed when the dog doesn't respond as we'd like, and it's all too easy to put the blame on the "stubborn" dog. So, as you train, always think of yourself as the kind of coach you would want to have. If you can't be that coach at that moment, it's best to take a break.

Why do we keep using words like "teacher," "coach," and "teammate" when referring to your role as handler? Many owners may feel concerned because they want to be seen as the dog's *leader*. "Leader" is a loaded term in dog behavior and training, and worrying about your position as pack leader can put unnecessary pressure on you to act in a way that is confrontational or unkind to your dog. But there's good news! By clearly communicating with your dog and rewarding him when he does what you've asked, you are, by default, acting like a good leader. In other words, lead naturally by your actions. A natural leader does not have to prove her leadership qualities; it is obvious based on the way she presents herself. By following the guidelines in this book, you will show your dog that you are his leader in the training process, based on your ability to clearly communicate what you expect him to do and by acknowledging his accomplishments with rewards. In this way, you will become someone your dog *wants* to follow, rather than someone he *has* to follow.

WHAT GRADE IS YOUR DOG IN?

Did you ever find yourself in a class that was way too advanced for your abilities? Consider this scenario: Philosophy 101 is full, so you choose to enroll in Philosophy 201 instead. You think, *How hard could it be*? But after the first week of classes, you find yourself huddled in a ball, muttering, "I think, therefore I am" over and over. By week two, you're begging the registrar for your tuition fees back and have already recycled your

textbooks. However, had you started with the appropriate introductory-level class, you might have actually enjoyed the material and pursued philosophy at the higher levels.

Let's apply the same logic to dog training. With your dog as the student and you as the benevolent teacher, avoid asking him to perform behaviors that are beyond his abilities at that moment. Set your dog up for success by asking him to do only behaviors that are within his capabilities. This especially pertains to distractions. Normally, dogs can learn polite behaviors inside your home, but your training falls apart outdoors. Why? Because indoor learning presents no significant distractions; it is the equivalent of elementary-school doggie tasks. Paying attention and being polite outdoors are college-level tasks, given the distractions of squirrels hopping around, other dogs and their owners walking by, and delicious garbage lining the street. Would you expect a third-grader to understand college-level schoolwork? Of course not. Nor should you expect your dog to handle outdoor distractions if you haven't prepared him for all of the intermediate steps.

When training your dog, ask yourself, *What grade is my dog in for this behavior*? For some behaviors, he might be in kindergarten; for other behaviors, he may already have his PhD. Here is an example for Stay. Where does your dog fall?

- **Kindergarten:** Sadie can sit for only a few seconds.
- **Elementary school:** Sadie can do Stay in your living room when no one else is there.
- **Middle school:** Sadie can do Stay in your living room when some family members are there.
- **Junior high:** Sadie can do Stay in your backyard or on an empty sidewalk.
- **High school:** Sadie can do Stay in your backyard while the kids are playing, or on a sidewalk with activity in the distance.

- **College:** Sadie can do Stay on a moderately busy street.
- **Grad school:** Sadie can do Stay on a crowded city street, or when calm people come into your house.
- **PhD:** Sadie can do Stay anywhere, even when people come right up to her. She can do Stay when guests, repair workers, or other strangers ring the doorbell and come in.

That's a lot of levels! Sometimes we get so excited about teaching our dog a new behavior or trick that we push him too far too fast. Use this grade-level guide and modify it to your needs so that you can keep your training methodical and fun for your dog.

FOR THE "PROBLEM CHILD"

Many people assume that their dogs are not ready for trick training or canine sports because their dogs have not yet developed good basic manners. This thinking, believe it or not, is backward. In countless cases, dog sports and fun tricks have helped dogs learn manners and stabilize their emotions. Anxious dogs can learn to alleviate their fears by engaging with the world in fun ways. Sports, games, and tricks teach excitable dogs how to focus on a task. Fun activities like those in the following chapters even give bossy dogs a reason to patiently listen to their handlers.

Believe it or not, Sarah's Border Collie, Fever, has never taken a single manners class, nor has she learned the typical cues that most owners find standard, such as Leave It. She never had to! Because of the foundation training that Sarah did with Fever for agility, teaching Leave It and other impulse-control behaviors has not been necessary. Through sports training, Fever has developed impulse control that is not based on being told when to leave something. For instance, if Fever sees an item and is unsure about taking it, she looks to Sarah for guidance. If someone

drops food on the floor, Fever waits for Sarah to tell her whether she can take it. And if, for some reason, she is about to make a bad choice while approaching a half-eaten sandwich on the sidewalk, Sarah can just call Fever's name, and then Fever's little head will whip around to look at Sarah, and Sarah can praise and reward her right past the soggy "street meat." Whenever Fever makes a good choice, it is largely due to the sports training she has done. Fever's attitude about training and about her handler has always been positive, which, by default, has given her a solid foundation of manners.

Training leads to good manners while out and about.

Kate's dog Beans is the polar opposite of Fever in many respects, but she has also benefited from taking a fun approach to training from the get-go. Beans, a sweet and sensitive girl, saw the world as a very scary place. Knowing that Beans would always be a pet dog rather than a competitor of any kind, Kate approached training with less of a focus on results and more on building trust and communication. So, for example, when teaching Side Sit, Kate initially focused much more on Beans' attitude when performing the behavior rather than the straightness of her Sit. Did Beans have fun with that repetition? No? OK, let's change something next time. Maybe she was too close to the wall and feeling confined. Next time, I'll give her more space. By practicing rally and parkour in such a way, Beans has become comfortable in a number of scenarios that originally frightened her. She has even become Kate's "demo dog" for classes at Brooklyn Dog Training Center, showing students how to do certain leash-walking and impulse-control activities.

DOG SPORTS OVERVIEW

The skills you'll learn in this book are drawn from a number of canine sports, each growing in popularity every year. You may have seen or even

Agility is fast-paced fun for both dog and handler.

dabbled in some yourself, while others might be entirely new to you. This section gives you a brief overview of the sports that have influenced the training behaviors in this book. While we can't claim to make your dog a champion in agility

or guarantee him a job in search and rescue, we hope that by introducing you to both basic and advanced exercises used in canine sports, you'll learn practical and fun applications that promote everyday doggie manners. Of course, if you and your dog are drawn to certain activities in this book, we encourage you to look for more tailored, advanced training in that sport. See Chapter 8 for ways to get involved in these sports beyond recreational enjoyment.

AGILITY

Agility is an obstacle-based dog sport focusing on precision and speed. Obstacles can include a variety of jumps (including tire jumps and double and triple jumps), tunnels, weave poles, a dog walk, an A-frame, a teeter-totter, and a pause table. Each obstacle has its own rules for completion, and it is the handler's job to guide the dog around the course in the correct order as quickly and efficiently as possible.

Agility carries numerous behavioral benefits. The sport is an excellent outlet for active dogs because it burns both mental and physical energy. It can also help nervous dogs build confidence by celebrating small successes, such as going through a tunnel for the first time. And it is a fantastic way to bond with your dog. Just as you enjoy seeing your dog accomplish new things, your dog enjoys the rewards and praise you dole out.

Focus on teamwork is imperative in agility because every course is different, and a team gets only one chance to run the course in competition. If your dog gets distracted for just a second, it could mean a dropped bar, off-course obstacle, or other disqualifying event. This focus training has a rollover effect on your relationship with your dog as well.

Agility dogs have improved recalls, attention, and impulse control. In agility, the handler cues the dog where to go and what to do, with the dog off leash and often running at a distance from the handler. Wouldn't it be cool if you and your dog could communicate this way, too? Exercises in the following chapters will teach you numerous behaviors used in agility so that you and your dog can learn to attentively listen to each other, even when distractions are present or your dog is far away from you.

FREESTYLE

Canine freestyle is a general term that includes activities such as heelwork to music as well as "dog dancing." At its core, freestyle is a collection of dog tricks, choreographed to music, that involve the handler's participation to create the sense that the team is dancing. "This is a very personal sport in that you select your music, teach your dog the behaviors to go along with it, work on your own movements, and decide on a costume for you, a collar for your dog, and any props you want to go along with your routine," shares top trainer and competitor Beverly Blanchard, KPA, of Periwinkle Dog Training.

Because freestyle has so much flexibility, nearly everything labeled as a trick in this book can be part of a freestyle routine. In this manner, tricks and sports heavily overlap. Likewise, the basic and advanced heeling techniques in Chapter 4 are essential parts of freestyle. Beverly says, "Canine freestyle gives you the opportunity to learn to move with your partner, feel the rhythm of the music, and let yourself go with the enjoyment of seeing your dog really strut [his] stuff!"

By learning a handful of tricks and practicing your heelwork, you can come up with your own freestyle routine, tailored to your dog's strengths. Beverly continues, "Canine freestyle is equally as good for puppies to teach body awareness and coordination as it is for older dogs to stay limber and vibrant. Dogs learn to spin in circles and walk forward and backward, as well as from side

Beverly Blanchard shows how freestyle lets you get creative and show off your dog's strengths.
Photo by Pat McGowan Photography

to side. They can go up on their back legs and down into bow positions. Tricks such as crawling forward and backward work on building body awareness and strength. Dogs can also learn to lift each foot independently. The list goes on and on. If you can imagine it, it can be done!"

PARKOUR

Yes, you read that right. Dog parkour is a new canine sport, modeled after the human version. The dog version of parkour is intended to give you and your pup a new way of interacting with the everyday objects that surround you on walks or even inside your home. A tree stump is the perfect platform for your dog to hop on with two front paws, two back paws, or all four paws. Your dog can jump over, walk along lengthwise, or possibly crawl under a fallen tree. A fire hydrant is an ideal obstacle to run around in a circle. You'll never see walks in the same way again, and your dog will learn to interact with you in fun ways outdoors, rather than chasing that squirrel or barking at the approaching mailman. Plus, parkour gives your social media photos a ton of flair, as Fever demonstrates in the photo on the next page.

Jude Azaren, founder of All Dogs Parkour, lists the numerous benefits of this sport. "For timid, reactive, or fearful dogs, parkour is a great confidence booster. Knowing [that] your physical support is always there, your dog will be more adventuresome and willing to try new things. In addition, parkour teaches dogs to become more aware of their bodies. Better body awareness helps dogs avoid stressing their joints and muscles. Parkour exercises also promote strength, flexibility, and balance. Parkour builds attention. Dogs learn to focus on the individual parkour tasks, even in distracting environments."

RALLY

In rally obedience (also known as "rally-o" or simply "rally"), a dog-and-handler team navigates a series of tasks in Heel position. A rally course includes ten or more numbered stations, with one sign at each station to instruct the team to perform a certain obedience task before moving on. Signs may ask the dog to do a Sit/Down/Sit sequence, heel in a serpentine pattern, or stay by your left side as you pivot. Unlike traditional obedience, handlers in rally may encourage— and, in some cases, even reward—their dogs throughout the course.

Slower than agility and more structured than freestyle, rally provides an excellent way to bond with your dog by turning obedience into a game. The first levels of rally are performed on leash, so loose leash walking and heeling are critical components of this sport. Dogs must be able to follow their handlers' cues despite the many distractions of the trial environment. Beyond the novice levels, dogs perform the course off leash, and the courses become longer and more challenging. Dogs who regularly trial in rally tend to have high levels of off-leash reliability in a variety of environments.

Since part of rally training is to work together despite distractions, you can and should practice in a variety of real-world environments. Doggie Academy students have been known to train in airports, Grand Central Terminal, and the bustling streets of New York City. Your dog's leash-walking and impulse-control skills can improve a great deal by following the guidelines for rally exercises in the following chapters, particularly in Chapter 4.

SCENT WORK

Scent work (or nosework) is a sport that draws on the dog's most notable ability: his knack for tracking odors. Many canine "jobs" are also based on scent detection, whether it is looking for earthquake victims or for contraband. While some dogs are more driven to find odors than others, all dogs can enjoy and benefit from

games based on scent work because these games provide a great mental workout and let the dog work independently from the handler to problem-solve.

Scent work involves a dog searching for a particular odor within a designated area. When he's found the target odor—hooray!—he wins a reward. It's reminiscent of a scavenger hunt for kids. The placement and type of *hide* (the odor that he's looking for) vary depending on the dog's level. In the beginning, the dog may simply be looking for treats hidden in one or more boxes. It's the dog's job to find the box(es) with the treats, and, when he does, he rewards himself by eating them. As his skill level increases, he starts looking for other odors, such as birch, and in other contexts, such as inside a car. You'll find several scent work–inspired games in Chapter 7 of this book.

OTHER SPORTS

The sports represented in this book are by no means a full list of all canine sports. In fact, it seems like new dog sports are popping up all the time. Here are a few other sports your dog may benefit from.

Barn hunt: This is a sport that encourages your dog to search for a rodent. (Don't worry; the rodent is never harmed.) It is a fantastic outlet for dogs who are innate ratters, because they can finally do the job for which they were bred. In barn hunt, the dog looks for one or more rats, which are safely enclosed in tubes hidden among hay bales. The dog must also run through a tunnel made of the hay bales and jump on an elevated surface during the run. This sport encourages your dog to use his nose and think independently, just as in scent work. While this sport is challenging to replicate at home, you can find barn hunt clinics and trials in many places.

Disc dog: If your energetic dog would like an active fetch-based sport, disc dog is for you. There is a wide variety of games within the disc-dog world, so if your dog isn't a long-distance catcher, you still have many options outside of the typical "toss and fetch." For example, in freestyle, the handler and her dog perform a variety of choreographed catches and tricks with the disc. Sometimes, a dog will run between his handler's legs and then make a catch. In other cases, the handler will throw several short tosses, one right after the other to different locations, and the dog will catch all of them. A dog may even ricochet off his handler's back to make a catch, a maneuver called a *vault*. There are games for distance and accuracy, and even some that incorporate agility equipment. While each disc-dog organization has its own rules, at the heart of them all is the dog's ability to fetch. (See Chapter 3.)

Dock diving is a great way to build a dog's confidence.
Photo by Kevin Johnson of KJ Photography

Dock diving: For athletic, water-loving dogs, it doesn't get any better than this. Dock diving encourages a dog to jump as far as possible into a body of water. While it's not an activity you can do anywhere at any time of year, you may be able to find a dog-sport facility that offers lessons. According to Lindsay Hill, dock diving instructor, competitor, and multiple-time national finalist, "Dock diving is a great sport for building confidence. I use it as an introduction to dog sports, as there are few to no expectations on how the dog needs to perform. Dogs tend to *love* this sport, so once we build confidence, we can also work on specific training issues that normally are not desirable around the house and in other training settings, such as barking or pulling on leash to get on the dock or breaking a Stay to jump for [a] toy. This sport is also a great way to work on your recall; the only way your dog gets to jump for [the] toy again is if [he] decides to come out of the water!"

Flyball: Natural runners and/or fetchers will love this high-octane sport. Flyball is a team sport, set as a relay race with four dogs per team. The first dog on the team runs over four hurdles, grabs a ball, and runs back over the four hurdles. As he finishes his leg, the second dog will start his. Not all dogs are suited for the physical demands of flyball, but athletic dogs can really show off their abilities in this sport.

Treibball: You'll see a lot of herding dogs at treibball events, because the sport essentially involves dogs herding large inflated balls into a specified area. Dogs with an aptitude for herding animals, including humans, take to treibball, but it can be fun for any dog.

SAFETY FIRST

Safety is not only important for the obvious reason of avoiding injury. Just as importantly, your dog needs to trust you completely when you are training. If you ask your dog to do something that causes him pain or leads to an accident, the emotional damage may last much longer than any physical suffering. Putting your dog in a dangerous situation can set your training back and instantly erase the progress you've made. Keep a few points in mind.

- Consider your dog's age, health, stamina, and conformation when doing any of the more active behaviors in this book. If you're not sure if a certain behavior is safe for your dog, refrain from doing it until you can ask your vet.
- When doing any exercises in which all or part of your dog is elevated above ground, be extra careful. The guidelines set by All Dogs Parkour require your dog to be in a sturdy back-clip harness and leash, with you gently holding the leash above him in case he falls. It happens more than you might think! Jude Azaren explains, "Your dog needs to wear the proper type of harness. You must learn how to 'spot' and how to safely support your dog when coming down from elevated surfaces. Doing parkour in an unsafe manner can result in your dog being frightened or injured. Poor handling

FIND US ON SOCIAL MEDIA!

Looking for more doggie info, videos, and tips?

- Find Doggie Academy (@doggieacademy) and Brooklyn Dog Training Center (@brooklyndogtrainingcenter) on Facebook and Instagram (@doggieacademy and @bkdogtrainingcenter).
- We've made training videos to accompany some of the behaviors in this book. You can find them on Doggie Academy's YouTube channel and Facebook page, plus Kate's BKLN Manners™ YouTube channel and Facebook page (@bklnmanners).
- Sarah's dog Fever (@bordercolliefever) and Kate's dog Beans (@beans_cant_even) are on Instagram.

skills can cause a dog to lose confidence in the handler."

- When jumping, keep the jump height low. How do we define "low"? For young dogs, keep jumps no higher than the dog's hocks until his growth plates have closed. (This happens around eighteen months old, but check with your vet.) After that, with your vet's permission, jump height can be as high as 2 inches (5 cm) below the dog's withers (his back at the base of the neck), according to the rules set by American Kennel Club (AKC) agility. When in doubt, keep the jumps low. You're not trying to break any world records here, so keep your dog's health and safety in the forefront. Just because your dog is capable of jumping very high obstacles, it doesn't mean that it's good for him to jump this way over and over again.

- Avoid repeating the same activity again and again if it puts strain on one area or set of muscles. For instance, Meerkat (a trick in which the dog sits back and up on his haunches; see Chapter 5) gives your dog quite a workout in his back and core, so avoid overdoing it in any one session. Similarly, jumping repeatedly can strain muscles. Work at your dog's current ability, which may mean very short training sessions, especially in the beginning, when your dog is moving his body in new ways.

IMPORTANT—HOW TO READ THIS BOOK

This book has a lot of information, but it should be easy to find what you're looking for. The chapters address various components of good manners, such as building impulse control (Chapter 2), teaching Come (Chapter 3), dealing with numerous leash-walking issues (Chapter 4), and so on. Within each chapter, you'll find several basic behaviors or exercises, followed by several more advanced ones. Each behavior is labeled as either *basic* or *advanced* as well as whether it focuses on *manners* or is drawn from a *sport*, *game*, or *trick*. (There may be some overlap; remember that most tricks can also be applied to the sport of freestyle.) If the behavior is labeled as a sport, we have included which sport(s) in the description of the behavior.

LOOK FOR THESE LABELS ACCOMPANYING EACH BEHAVIOR:

| Basic | Advanced | Manners | Sports | Games | Tricks |

Note that, for clarity and consistency, we generally refer to a dog as "he" and a person as "she" throughout the book. We have designated the terms "owner" and "handler" to identify the person living with and training a dog; nevertheless, we realize that these words fall painfully short of describing the dynamic relationship between human and canine family members.

If you find that you are struggling to teach your dog the behaviors in this book, or if your dog is reacting to your training efforts with fearful or aggressive displays, look for a qualified force-free trainer who offers in-person or virtual lessons.

01
FOUNDATION:
EVERYBODY, JUST CHILL

s explained in the introduction, learning how to communicate with your dog is paramount to being able to train him to do even the simplest behavior. But how, exactly, should you communicate with your dog? While doggie-speak is easy to follow once you've gotten the hang of it, it may not come naturally to you at first. This is because humans and dogs, despite our many similarities, communicate in surprisingly different ways. Following the guidelines and practicing the exercises in this chapter will teach you how to communicate with your dog in a way that he understands. And not unlike the thrill of meeting a new friend who just "gets" you, when your dog sees you communicating in a way that is crystal clear to him, he can't help but feel a closer connection to you and a rush of motivation to work with you.

DON'T FORGET TO BREATHE

To a certain extent, dogs mirror their owners' energy. However, there are many factors that go into a dog's personality, so your energy may not fully explain why your dog is a diehard couch potato or perpetually bouncing off the walls.

Nevertheless, your emotional state and your behavior while in his presence can have an impact on how he feels and how he behaves.

During training sessions, stay aware of the ways that your energy can influence him. When you set out to train your dog, take a few deep breaths and make sure that you are in a sufficiently relaxed state of mind. A wound-up teacher can produce wound-up students, while a calm and level-headed teacher can more easily connect with and guide students. Aim to be a good teacher who leads by example, rather than one who expects calm behavior from her dog without being able to achieve it herself.

FIRST, TRAIN THE HUMAN

In order to communicate with your dog clearly, the first step is to be quiet. Don't say anything at all. It sounds simple, but it is in fact very difficult for almost any untrained human. Compared to us, dogs are an incredibly quiet species. When does your dog bark? Usually it's at the doorbell, or when he is demanding that you throw the ball for the hundredth time, or in similarly arousing situations. When simply hanging out, dogs are quiet outside of the occasional groan or huff. Loud vocalizations are generally reserved for highly distressing or exciting situations. So when you are begging Rover to "sit, *sit*, SIT," your tone mimics that of a frantic dog. No wonder your dog doesn't listen! Why would he take orders from someone who appears to be in the midst of a meltdown? Instead, Rover tends to feed off of your excited energy, creating a situation in which everyone is all worked up and nothing can be learned.

SEQUENCE FOR TRAINING

Think of your voice as a training tool. Using the right word at the right time makes training clear and fun for your dog, but using your voice in

"EVERY MOVE YOU MAKE, EVERY STEP YOU TAKE…"

Living with a dog is a bit like living inside that classic Police song "Every Breath You Take." Your dog is learning from you all the time, not just during formal training sessions. Every moment is, for better or for worse, a training session.

That scrap of food you just fed Roscoe from the dining-room table? You've just taken a step toward training him to beg. After a few package deliveries, Peaches has learned that the doorbell predicts a scary intruder; therefore, she's decided to sound her alarm whenever she hears "ding dong." In Kate's house, when someone opens the crisper drawer of the refrigerator, Beans expects to see her favorite snack, kale (no, seriously!); she quickly learned to run to the kitchen every time she hears the rattle of the crisper.

While some of these learning experiences can lead to unwanted behavior, such as begging and barking, there are plenty of things you can do in your daily routine to promote good behavior, too. Roscoe wants a piece of your dinner? Telling him a brief "nope" and turning your back to him will teach him that there's no point in begging. Peaches gets a piece of chicken every time she hears the doorbell? With consistency, it can become her favorite noise. When Kate started giving Beans kale on her dog bed, Beans gave up running to the kitchen and instead runs to her bed when she hears the crisper drawer opening. When you think of everyday situations as trainable moments, you will find that your dog develops generally good manners naturally.

an unsystematic, haphazard way will confuse and frustrate Fido. In this chapter, the exercises require very little to no verbal communication with your dog. This is to get you thinking like a trainer, communicating in terms that your dog can easily comprehend.

Humans tend to focus on the "cue" (formerly called the "command"), meaning that when we say "sit," we actually expect the dog to know what that means. This is counterproductive when working with an individual who doesn't speak your language. Imagine you're in a waiting room, and you notice a non-English-speaking man trying to figure out how to pour a glass of water from the water cooler. You can yell "pull the blue lever!" until your voice gets hoarse, but it won't teach the person anything. On the other hand, if you *show* the person how to pull the lever—*voilà!*—water comes pouring out, and the man has just learned a new "trick" to get what he wanted.

The point here is that, whether communicating with a human or a canine, you should avoid relying on the cue to teach a new behavior. More important is the outcome. In the case of the

Speaking harshly to your dog does nothing to correct undesirable behavior.

In the early stages of training, you can lure the dog into the behavior with only a treat, not a verbal cue.

water cooler, the outcome is that the man got what he wanted when he pulled the blue lever. He is most likely going to do the same behavior—pull the blue lever—the next time he's faced with a water cooler. Likewise, when teaching a new behavior to your dog, focus on having a positive outcome when your dog sits, lies down, or does whatever the target behavior is.

Following is the beginning sequence for most training activities in this book and in general.

1. Without speaking, encourage Baxter to sit (or perform any other desired behavior). Do this by luring with a treat, waiting for him to sit on his own, or other means described in future sections.

2. Baxter sits.

3. Mark it. The moment Baxter's rear end touches the ground, say "yes!" or "good dog" or click with a clicker. While "yes" is preferred over other verbal markers due to its less common usage in nontraining scenarios, the word itself is not so important. Just be sure that you use the same word every time, and you say it at the exact moment that the

dog does the desired behavior. Marking is the way Baxter connects "butt on the floor" with "yay, I win a reward!" Which brings us to...

4. Reward it. In the early stages of learning, rewards encourage the dog to try the behavior again. It was so rewarding the first time, why not sit next time, too? It's important to give the reward while the dog is still sitting so he learns how awesome this position is.

5. Release. Say "OK" or "free" to indicate to Baxter that he's done with that training behavior. Avoid giving a treat at this point because you have already rewarded him for doing the Sit.

SMALL TALK

You'll notice that the behaviors in this chapter involve very little verbal communication on your part. In the context of training, make sure that any noises or words you produce have purpose; extra talking can distract and confuse your dog.

Notice what is missing from this sequence? We do not give a verbal cue, "sit," until the previous sequence is consistently successful. If you say "sit" and Baxter repeatedly jumps up to grab your treat, you've just attached "sit" to jumping. So get the correct behavior first, and then label it. Once your dog consistently understands the sequence—butt on the floor/mark/reward/release—you can add the verbal cue in the very beginning of the sequence.

What if your dog makes a mistake, jumping up for a treat rather than sitting for it? You can mark this, too. We call it a "no reward marker" (or NRM)—using a word like "oops" or "nope" in a gentle tone to mark the moment he lost his chance for a reward. By clearly identifying the right and wrong moments with a specific marker, your dog will be able to figure out what you want much more easily. Less confusion means faster learning and a happier pup.

CUES AND REWARDS

You're ready to add a cue to a behavior once your dog can reliably perform it. Every word you say during training should have meaning, so, from now on, make sure to say the cue only once—and then silently count to ten in your head. All too often, you'll say "Lulu, sit," and before she can even process what you've said, you're barking at her again to "sit, *sit*, SIT!" Part of being a good teacher is to give your student time to figure out the problem. In most cases, if you had said "sit" only once and then waited for five seconds, Lulu would have connected the dots and plopped her rear on the floor.

There are other drawbacks to repeating the cue. By saying "sit" ten times in a row until your dog actually sits, it gives your dog one more reason to tune out the sound of your voice. Lulu can blow you off the first nine times because she knows there will always be another chance. You don't want your dog to consider your voice as simply white noise in the background. You want your voice to have a purpose.

What happens if you follow these instructions perfectly, cuing only once at the beginning of the sequence, but Lulu still doesn't sit? Don't panic! Before you repeat it, ask yourself, *Why didn't she sit?* In most cases, there is too much distraction in the surroundings, making Lulu too excited or stressed to respond. By following the steps in this book, you'll be able to teach your dog to sit (and so much more) not just indoors when the windows are shut, the TV is off, and the kids are asleep. You'll also learn how to build your dog's ability to respond to your cues even when faced

In the beginning, your dog may be too distracted by his surroundings to focus on you.

with various distractions. If Lulu can't respond to your cue, plan to modify the scenario to make it easier for her to listen next time. Perhaps you'll move to a slightly quieter area.

As mentioned earlier, your dog is always learning. Your pup is an expert contextual learner, meaning that if you use a special harness for long hikes in the woods, your dog will quickly learn to connect the harness to hiking. Subsequently, he will go bonkers every time you pull that harness out. Likewise, if you regularly clear your throat before you say "sit," clearing your throat can become part of the cue, in your dog's mind. The one time you don't clear your throat before saying "sit," your dog may legitimately not understand you. Sarah's coach once pointed out that she did a little bounce on her heels before cuing Hank; this bounce had become a necessary part of the cue, telling Hank

Food rewards get most dogs to pay attention.

to "listen up." Many of us use hand or body movements when we train—pointing, folding our arms, standing up straight, and so on—without even realizing it. But your dog *does* realize it, and he will incorporate those elements into the training sequence.

To be a good teacher, you should build an awareness of what all of your cues, intentional or not, are. A cue can be anything that precedes the behavior. Many of these cues revolve around food, giving the impression that your dog will only listen if you have treats. Do you adjust your treat pouch before you cue him to come? Do you put your hand in your pocket as you say "sit"? To your dog, these are clear cues. It doesn't mean that your dog is a furry food vacuum who only responds to you when treats are present; rather, it means that you have taught him that food is part of your cue. Many trainers have some treats in their pockets at all times, not just during training sessions. (The clothes hamper must smell like a buffet to a trainer's dog!) This does not mean that trainers just hand out treats to their dogs willy-nilly. Instead, it allows trainers to switch into training mode on a moment's notice, without complicating the cues by adding the crinkle of their treat bags. So be aware of what your whole body is doing right before or while you cue your dog. If you're not sure, take a video of yourself to see if you shift your weight to the left ever so slightly each time you tell Fido to stay, or if you clutch your treat pouch before asking him to come. Dogs are experts at recognizing patterns; in some ways, your dog knows you better than you know yourself.

And then there are rewards, which can be large or small, tangible or intangible. Especially when teaching a new behavior, rewards will help your dog learn more quickly, happily, and efficiently. Food rewards are a natural choice for most trainers because they:

- are easy to carry;
- can be given without fumbling while the dog is in a certain position (like Down or Meerkat);
- don't excite or distract dogs in the same way that toys or even petting can;
- are inherently motivating to dogs; and
- can be varied depending on the situation, for instance, using dry food while practicing at home, using hot dogs when practicing in public, or giving a "jackpot" of several treats when the dog does something really impressive.

Nevertheless, don't rule out other kinds of rewards. A great reward for Fetch is for you to throw the ball again. For toy-motivated dogs, ask for a Come and reward with a game of Tug. If what your dog really wants is your attention, reward his polite Sit by inviting him on the couch with you. Going even further, there are numerous *life rewards* that can and should be incorporated into your routine. Essentially, a life reward is anything you have access to that your dog wants. Jameson's ready to play Tug? Cool, but he has to sit before you present the toy. You and Fiona are going to the dog run? Awesome! But only if she calmly waits for you to open the dog run gates.

When choosing the appropriate rewards, ask yourself, "What does my dog want in this moment?" Let's say you and Jameson are in the park, and he wants you to throw his ball. First, you ask him to sit, which he does. Good dog! But now what? Should you give him a treat? Some petting? No! The last thing he wants is to be pet. If he could, he'd be screaming, "Just throw the dang ball—now!" So as soon as he sits, mark it with "yes!" and immediately throw him the ball.

Later, imagine you're teaching Jameson to lie down. He's just lowered himself into a perfectly calm Sphinx position. Throwing him a ball as a reward would not only force him to break his Down in order to chase the ball, but, after that, you'd be waiting five minutes for him to relax

enough to try another Down. For behaviors that require stillness or precision, as with many tricks, a more realistic choice would be food rewards.

Let's say that you follow all of the steps perfectly, yet your dog responds in a rude way. Perhaps you asked for a Sit, but he barked in your face instead, as if to say, "Gimme that treat, human!" Rather than punish, you'll simply use your NRM of "nope" and turn away from him, taking your delicious treats with you. While polite behavior earns your pup a reward, rude behavior results in the reward being removed.

Start off your training on the right foot (or paw!).

This is a language your dog understands: that his actions have immediate consequences. The consequence of sitting when asked is getting a tasty piece of cheese, while the consequence of barking or jumping is the tragic loss of cheese. This is a nonconfrontational and safe way to set boundaries for what kind of behavior will and will not work in your household.

As you practice the training topics in this chapter, your goal is to develop impulse control—not your dog's impulse control, but your own. If you are the "sit, *sit*, SIT" kind of trainer who

TREATS: HOW MUCH? WHAT KIND?

When doling out food rewards, trainers are often much more generous than the typical owner. That's because trainers don't see treats as bribery or charity; rather, they see them as reinforcement for a job well done. Just as a student loves to see an "A" on her test, or a salesperson works hard for a commission, your dog is motivated by food rewards to think and work harder. This especially pertains to the early stages of learning, when your dog is trying to figure out what behavior you're asking him to perform.

You don't want your dog's weight or health to be compromised, however. Use extremely small pieces of the treat, just enough so he gets the taste. Your dog won't complain about the size—we promise! Training treats, which are already small, can be divided into even tinier pieces, especially for small dogs. This allows you to reward your dog frequently without stuffing him like a turkey.

The value of the reward should be consistent with the difficulty of what you're asking your dog to do. Performing a Sit in your own home might be worth a few pieces of dry food, whereas performing Sit in the middle of Times Square would definitely be hot-dog-worthy. Experiment with different kinds of treats to see what really gets your dog's motor running, and don't rule out human food, such as pieces of meat or cheese. We should note here that feeding your dog human food will not cause begging unless you feed him from the table! To dogs, food is just food, whether it comes from the grocery store or the pet store.

shouts out cues and flails her arms, the activities in the following pages will show you how to quiet your voice and start to calmly wait for your dog to find the correct solution on his own. Here are the points to keep in mind.

- Before a training session, take a deep breath and imagine yourself as the kind of teacher you would want for yourself.
- Approach training as a game. The focus is to communicate and learn the game together, nothing more.
- Stay quiet. This includes your voice, your body language, and even your mind. Let your dog figure out what he has to do to get his reward, without interference on your part.

FOR THE DOG

The exercises that follow are designed to teach you and your dog impulse control together. Dogs, by nature, are impulsive. If you drop a chicken wing on the floor, Roscoe is unlikely to weigh the ethical pros and cons of eating it. A dog who

jumps, barks, and even playfully nips is not a bad dog. He is just doing what dogs do: acting on impulse. Dogs needs to be explicitly taught patience and politeness. It's possible to teach any dog to leave a dropped chicken wing or to avoid a squirrel he sees hopping along the sidewalk. But before expecting your dog to be able to handle high-level distractions like these, he needs to learn how to focus on you and calm himself in a variety of less-distracting situations.

Part of the recipe is to let your dog think for himself. All too often, we humans assume that dogs aren't able to make polite choices on their own, so we are constantly telling them what to do. *Sit there, be quiet, come over here.* Many dogs, being so attached to their owners and naturally willing to please, simply fall into line and may stop thinking for themselves altogether. While there are many situations in which your dog will need your explicit guidance, there are just as many times when he could choose to be polite on his own.

Most trainers and owners have thankfully moved past the days of teaching Sit by pushing the dog's hind end to the ground. In this way of teaching, the trainer is the one doing all the work while the dog remains passive, so the dog doesn't have to exert any mental effort to learn what "sit" means. Sitting, in that case, is something done *to* him, not something he does *himself*. As such, you've just squandered a perfect opportunity to teach your dog how to problem-solve.

To a lesser extent, teaching a dog to sit only when you give the "sit" cue is a waste. This may sound strange, because you certainly want your dog to sit when you tell him to. Instead, what if your dog learned that sitting is just what he should do when he wants your attention, even without being asked? Now *that* is a polite dog! The way to teach this life skill is outlined later in this chapter. Yes, it might take a little longer to teach in the very beginning. Yes, he will make more mistakes than if you just push his rear end to the ground. But isn't that what real learning is about? When he figures out that sitting is what gets him everything he wants, all on his own, without any prodding or coercion from you, then you've got a dog who develops independent thinking skills that can be used for polite behaviors. Clyde thinks, *In the past, whenever I sat, she gave me what I wanted. Sitting works! I really want permission to come up on the couch, so I'm just going to sit and see if she invites me.* Because Clyde was encouraged to learn the polite behavior on his own, and because the behavior "worked," he's able to apply that to other situations in which he wants something.

CLICK AND TREAT

You have likely seen people training with clickers and have maybe even purchased one yourself. What's the big deal with a clicker, anyway? This

The noise of the clicker serves as a "marker" for desired behavior.

little piece of plastic, while not exactly a silver bullet, can facilitate your training in sometimes magical ways. The purpose of the clicker is to mark the moment your dog performs the behavior you are looking for. So, for instance, if you are teaching your dog to bark on cue, you would click right after he barks. You always follow the click with a treat or other reward. This is the same mark-and-reward sequence as if you said "good boy!" or "yes" at the moment he barks. Whether you're using a verbal marker or a clicker, marking tells the dog, "Yay, you just did the right thing!" The subsequent reward encourages him to do it again and again. So you might be wondering why trainers use an extra tool when we can simply say "yes."

A clicker provides certain advantages that your voice can't quite achieve.

- Every click sounds the same, so your dog receives very clear feedback. In the case of your voice, it can fluctuate in pitch, volume, duration, and so on, providing a less accurate marker. A click is also an easy sound for your dog to pick out in a noisy environment, whereas your voice might get drowned out.
- A clicker has only one meaning—to mark a behavior prior to a reward—so dogs quickly learn that it's a super-cool sound. Voices, on

Clicker training is a popular positive-training method.

the other hand, may carry different meanings and convey a variety of emotions. In many cases, human voices have no relevance to dogs, so some dogs have learned to tune out the voices of their humans. Think of how much you talk in a day, and what tiny percentage of that talking is actually directed toward your dog's training.

- When using a clicker, some people find that they have more precise timing than when marking with their voices. (Consider how many people pause or gasp before exclaiming "good boy" or forget to verbally mark entirely.) A clicker tends to get the human into training mode, too, which leads to more accurate marking and faster learning.
- Some dogs become click addicts. They find the click so motivating that they will do anything to keep the game going.
- For teaching complicated behaviors, a clicker can help you break the behavior down into manageable increments. For instance, rolling over doesn't come naturally to every dog. You can click your dog for making small steps toward the full behavior. For example, first

click and reward for lying down, then for leaning slightly to one side, then for leaning a little more heavily, and so on until he rolls over completely.

A clicker also has some potential disadvantages to consider.

- If you're already juggling a leash and treats, you may struggle to handle a clicker properly. That said, you can buy a clicker that is attached to a bracelet or that slips on your finger like a ring.
- Certain dogs may find the clicking sound startling. To get around this, either try a clicker designed to be extra-quiet or leave the clicker in your pocket to muffle the clicking sound. By reducing the intensity of the clicks and "charging" the clicker fully before training anything new (as explained in the upcoming Charging the Clicker section), most dogs learn to love the sound.
- Adults or kids prone to fidgeting may find it hard to keep their hands off the clicker. By clicking it at any time other than when marking, you're reducing the potency of the clicker and confusing your dog. Good coaches don't confuse their team members.

A click is always followed by a reward, usually food. As such, the clicker is meant for teaching new behaviors for which a treat is given after every correct repetition. There will come a point in your dog's training when he does not need a clicker. It isn't always clear to the typical owner when it's time to stop using the clicker for a certain behavior.

If your dog is an independent thinker, a couch potato, or one who doesn't exactly jump for joy when it's time to train, we highly recommend clicker training as the first step. Before trying any other games, sports, or tricks, get started with Charging the Clicker, Clicker Training: Warm-Up Game, and Free Shaping 101 in this chapter, plus Free-Shaping Games in Chapter 7. These games are meant to get the dog really enthused about working for more clicks, and free shaping gives the learner (your dog) a greater sense of control than typical training does. This can turn a seemingly "stubborn" dog into a pup who is excited about the training process. From there, you can use the clicker to teach a number of the other activities in this book, because your dog will have already learned that clicker training with you is the best thing ever.

Ultimately, it is your choice whether to include a clicker in your training. It can be a highly useful tool, but only if used correctly. While some of the activities in this book are specifically designed to be used with a clicker, most allow you to choose whether to mark with a click or with your voice.

BASIC BEHAVIORS

  ### CHARGING THE CLICKER
Basic • Games

Before starting the clicker games, you have to teach your dog what the clicker is and how it works. To do this, you're going to do what trainers call "charging the clicker." This is a basic classical-conditioning exercise: teaching your

dog that every time he hears a click, it will be followed by a treat. The click (technically called a "conditioned stimulus") generates excitement from your dog (his "conditioned response") because of its association with treats. This kind of classical conditioning happens to us, too. For instance, how do you feel when your phone "dings" to indicate that you've received a text message? When you hear that familiar ding, you likely get a surge of excitement, making everything else irrelevant. You could be in the middle of a job interview or working at the top of a ladder, but when that text message beckons, it's as if you're powerless against checking it. This is because we have been classically conditioned to associate the ding with an enjoyable consequence: a message from mom or a funny meme from a friend. However, if your phone goes haywire and starts dinging without any actual texts coming in, you will eventually lose that rush of excitement. The ding is only significant when it precedes something desirable. Since dogs respond the same way to classical conditioning, trainers love

By "charging" the clicker, the dog quickly learns to associate the click with his reward.

to click and treat to get their dogs enthusiastic about training.

Clicker activities are useful for dogs who:

- get into trouble due to curiosity (in the form of destructiveness)
- are highly active or like to problem-solve
- need more outlets for their energy
- are afraid of getting close to their owners
- would benefit from confidence-building activities
- tend to be bossy or needy
- cannot be physically active due to health, weather, or other reasons
- have short attention spans
- tune out their owners' voices when training
- a host of other situations!

HOW TO DO CHARGING THE CLICKER

1. Bring your dog to a quiet place with a clicker and about two dozen small pieces of a very high-value treat: deli meat, hot dog, cheese, or something similar. Hold the treats behind your back or in your pocket or treat pouch.
2. Let your dog hang out or walk around. Do not ask him to sit or perform any other behavior. This kind of training is only teaching him the association between "click" and "treat," so it does not matter what he's doing.
3. Click once and immediately toss a treat on the ground (or pop it in your dog's mouth). The treat should follow within a split second of the click so he makes the connection.
4. Pause a few seconds, and then click and treat again. Repeat. You can shuffle around the room as you do this activity; you don't need to have your feet planted in one spot. Repeat this until all of the treats are gone.

From There

Practice once or twice a day for a few days. Once your dog gets laser-focused on you when he hears a click, you're ready to vary the response time of your click slightly. For the next few sessions:

- sometimes click and wait a half second to treat
- sometimes click and wait one second to treat
- sometimes click and wait two seconds to treat
- sometimes click and wait three seconds to treat

This will help your dog gain a bit of flexibility for future training, which will help in case you can't whip out a treat at the moment you click. He will learn that, even if it takes a few seconds, a click is always followed by a treat.

CLICKER TRAINING: WARM-UP GAME

Basic • Games

Prerequisite: Charging the Clicker

Think about all the freedom you have in life. If you want to cook pasta tonight, you can easily go to the grocery store, buy the ingredients, and cook your meal exactly as you'd like. Bored and want to be entertained? You can choose whether you'd like to go out or stay in, and what kind of entertainment you're in the mood for. Want to get some fresh air? Just walk outside.

Your dog isn't able to make these choices. You choose the food he eats, the activities he engages in, and the amount and nature of the exercise he gets. Dogs are incredibly smart animals, and it's important to let them feel a sense of autonomy. That doesn't mean giving Fido the keys to your car or free access to the fridge, but you can give your dog more decision-making power through clicker training.

With this kind of game, you will give your dog an object, such as an empty box. You won't force, coax, or lure him to interact with the object, but when he thinks to interact with it on his own, he will get a click and treat. His choices will dictate whether he "wins" a click or not. Once your dog understands how to get more clicks, he can interact with the object in any way he'd like. It's as if he's calling the shots—"I know how to make you click. Watch this!"—which can be a powerful activity for many dogs.

For this game, you're not yet looking for a specific interaction with the object, so any of these behaviors (plus others) will earn him a click and treat:

- looking at the box
- approaching the box
- touching the box with his nose or other body part
- pawing at the box
- putting his head or paw(s) in the box

You don't have to use a cardboard box for this activity. A plastic food-storage container or small storage box serves the same purpose. Occasionally, a dog is afraid of these household items, so it's fine to use any object, like a folded towel, dog toy, or other familiar item. The only other tools you'll need are a clicker and a handful of great treats. Some dogs might go over the moon for their regular kibble, which is fine. But if your dog prefers something tastier, don't hesitate to use a high-value reward to pay your dog sufficiently for his efforts. He's thinking hard, after all.

HOW TO DO CLICKER TRAINING: WARM-UP GAME

1. Bring your dog, clicker, treats, and box into a quiet room. Put the box on the ground.
2. If your dog goes right toward the box to investigate, click and toss the treat near the box. If your dog doesn't show interest in the box, be patient. When he even slightly turns his head toward the box, click for the head turn and toss the treat. Click for all of the interactions, however subtle, he offers.
3. From there, any time your dog interacts with the box in any way, click and toss a treat. Spend only five minutes or less on the game, ending it while your dog is still enthusiastic.
4. Practice this game whenever you have a few minutes to spare. Once your dog is having a lot of fun interacting with the box, you can move on to the advanced behavior, Free Shaping 101.

This game is great practice for you, too. It teaches you to rely on your click rather than your voice as the main source of feedback. While you aren't restricted from giving him verbal praise, make sure that the click comes first and is immediately followed by a treat. You are welcome to cheer after that!

CHECK ME OUT
Basic • Manners

Does your dog forget that you exist when you're walking him on leash or letting him play in the park? Asking him to perform behaviors like Sit or Stay at such times is useless because he's forgotten that you're even there. If he can't even acknowledge your presence, how can he sit on cue? First, you need to remind your dog that you are right there next to him. Only then can you ask him to do more complicated behaviors. Check Me Out teaches your dog that it's incredibly cool for him to check in with you by giving you eye contact, even when there are squirrels hopping by or a half-eaten bagel on the sidewalk in front of you. This simple training game can have a huge impact on the dog-human relationship because it teaches your dog how to communicate with you. Simply by looking at you, your dog has a direct line to reach out to you. And since you understand this way of "speaking," you can respond by either giving your dog what he's asking for or gently declining his request. Sound too good to be true? It's not as hard as you might think, provided you start from a simple level and build your dog's skills gradually and methodically.

The first step of Check Me Out tends to be the most challenging, so start the exercise in a location with few distractions. In the beginning, your dog will be rewarded for even the slightest glance at your face. The criteria are relatively low at first to make sure that your dog is successful. More success early on will motivate him to work harder at the higher levels. If your dog has played the previous clicker training game, we recommend using a clicker to mark his eye contact. Your timing will likely be more accurate (a dog's glance can pass by very quickly), and the clicker will get him even more excited to play Check Me Out.

Step 2: Hank looks at the treat in Sarah's hand. She holds still and does not say anything.

Check Me Out is useful for dogs who:
- jump, bark, or do other undesirable behaviors when they want something
- struggle to focus
- forget that their owners are there during leashed walks, at the dog park, and in similar situations
- are new to their homes and have not yet bonded with their owners
- avoid eye contact with their owners
- have an independent streak

HOW TO DO CHECK ME OUT

1. Sit or stand facing your dog. Have a treat in your outstretched hand. Don't ask your dog to sit, and don't say anything. Maintain eye contact with your dog so he knows you're paying attention, but keep your eyes and body relaxed and inviting.

   TIP: If you're not sure whether your body or eyes look relaxed, practice in front of a mirror first. You don't want to inadvertently appear confrontational to your dog.

2. Wait (and wait and wait) for the dog to look at you. Most dogs look at the treat, jump up to get the treat, bark, whine, and so on. Ignore it all!

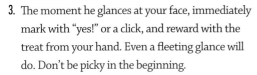

Step 3: Success! Hank looks Sarah right in the eye.

Sarah immediately rewards Hank.

3. The moment he glances at your face, immediately mark with "yes!" or a click, and reward with the treat from your hand. Even a fleeting glance will do. Don't be picky in the beginning.

From There

Practice Check Me Out in a number of increasingly distracting environments.

Elementary school: Practice indoors, rewarding with treats, his food bowl, or a toy he wants to play with.

Middle school: Require your dog to do Check Me Out to have doors opened, to join you on the couch, or to do other indoor activities. You do not need a treat for this because the reward is permission to do something.

High school: Practice outdoors with treats or toys in low-distraction areas.

College and beyond: Practice outdoors with treats, toys, or permission to go somewhere (such

THE TROUBLE WITH FREE-FEEDING

One of the most powerful rewards for good behavior can be your dog's meals. You have to feed him anyway, so why not have him sit while you prepare his food? There are some dogs, however, who have free access to their food day and night. We discourage this practice and highly recommend giving your dog regularly scheduled meals each day, with only a limited time to finish them. But why?

Food is a very effective tool to encourage your dog to practice good behavior, but if he always has access to it, the food loses its value. Dogs who are free-fed are often the most difficult to train with positive reinforcement. A free-fed dog thinks, *Why should I sit for your reward when I can just eat whenever I want, no sitting required?* It's similar to the privileged teen who has unlimited access to her parents' bank account; she never learns the value of money because she always has some of it lying around. Why would she want to work, waking up early and taking orders from a boss, when she doesn't need the money? Similarly, your dog will not be motivated to sit politely for a treat if he has a bowl full of free treats waiting in the kitchen. By controlling his access to resources like food, you increase their value and thereby increase the dog's motivation to work for them.

as at the gate of the dog run) in increasingly distracting areas.

Once your dog views Check Me Out as a fun game, he might look up at you once in a while during your walks, just to check in. If he does, mark and reward him generously. This indicates that he considers *any* time to be training time, which is the foundation of good overall manners. The more you reward and celebrate his good choices, the more good choices he will make in the future.

  ## SAY "PLEASE"
Basic • Manners

Remember when you were a child and there was always one requirement to get what you wanted: saying the magic word, "please"? If you refused to say "please," then too bad—no dessert or permission to play outside for you. Your dog can learn a magic word, too. But because dogs communicate with their bodies rather than with words, their "please" takes place, well, with their butts. We're talking about the almighty Sit, of course! If your dog is sitting, by default he's not jumping, nipping, or thrashing around. A Sit is a naturally polite behavior, and sitting can be the way your dog asks for everything he wants. (That said, if your dog finds a Down more comfortable, as Beans does in the photos, that's also a perfectly polite way of saying "please.")

The goal, with both humans and canines, is to teach an individual to choose to be polite on his own whenever he wants something. You should not have to remind a fourteen-year-old child to say "please" every time he wants a snack, nor should you have to remind your dog to "sit, sit, SIT" every time he wants you to throw his ball. To that end, you will not be explicitly telling your dog to sit. Your dog will have to figure out for himself that, when he sits, he gets the good stuff. When he jumps up, the good stuff goes away. His actions

dictate the result, meaning that he has the power to make good things happen when he sits or make those good things go away when he jumps up.

From this point forward, your dog will have to earn the things he wants by saying "please" with a Sit. No Sit, no reward. Your everyday life is full of training opportunities in which you can ask for polite behavior: feeding meals, playing Fetch or Tug, putting on the leash, opening the door, and so on. If you take advantage of these opportunities, then your dog will learn that training time is all the time, not just during formal training sessions. When training time is all the time, and all good things must be earned with the magic word (well, magic behavior), you have a dog willing to be on his best behavior in general, rather than a dog who will only sit or stay when he sees your treats come out.

Say "Please" is useful for dogs who:

- jump, bark, or do other undesirable behaviors when they want something
- struggle to focus
- barrel past their owners when doors are opened
- are new to their homes and have not yet bonded with their owners
- get frustrated when they don't get what they want
- only seem to notice their owners when they are holding treats

We've provided three activities to practice Say "Please." The first is related to good things that you need to bend down to provide, namely, the food bowl and the leash. The second is related to initiating a game with a toy. The third happens at thresholds, particularly doors and gates.

ACTIVITY 1: HOW TO DO SAY "PLEASE" FOR YOUR FOOD

In this activity, think of your body as an elevator that brings awesome rewards to your dog. The food bowl or food-dispensing toy can easily

Step 2: Beans is offering a polite behavior for Kate, so the "elevator" can start to descend.

Step 3: Notice how Kate places the bowl to the side, not right in front of Beans' face.

Step 5: With the sequence completed, Kate will release Beans...

...and she can eat the treats!

encourage good behavior, because food is inherently motivating. This activity teaches your dog a Sit-Stay (or a Down-Stay) without using any verbal cues. In fact, the only word you will utter is "OK" to release the dog from his Stay. The rest of the communication will all be done through your body language: once the dog is sitting, the elevator (you) slowly brings the food bowl lower and lower. If the dog's rear pops up, the elevator immediately goes back up to the top floor (you stand up straight and start over) until he chooses to sit again.

1. Put a few pieces of your dog's food in his bowl. Stand up straight, bowl in hand, and face your dog. (Kate is kneeling only for the sake of a clear photo here.)

   TIP: If your dog is very close in front of you, hold the bowl out to the side. You want the bowl to be as far away from the dog as possible so that you're not teasing him by lowering it right in front of his face.

2. Wait for your dog to sit (or lie down, as Beans does). You may gently look at him, but don't say anything and keep your body still so that

you don't accidentally give him other cues. If he jumps, cries, or tries to get at the bowl, simply stand still and ignore him.

3. When he sits, the elevator—your body—starts to slowly descend. Remember to hold the bowl as far from your dog's face as possible.

4. It is likely that your dog will stand or jump up when the bowl approaches his nose level. At the moment he breaks the Sit, quickly bring the elevator back up without saying anything. He's just learned that his actions have consequences. Once he's sitting again, the elevator can descend once more. You will likely have to bring the elevator back up several times in the beginning. This is a normal part of the learning process.

5. Once you have placed the bowl on the ground, say "OK" to release him, allowing him to eat the food.

    TIP: If your dog is struggling to hold the Sit, say "OK" when the bowl reaches your hips and then quickly place the bowl on the floor to let him eat the food. With each repetition, reach a little lower—thigh-level, knee-level, calf-level, and so on—before you say "OK." It may take several sessions before you can place the bowl on the ground and then say "OK."

From There

Once your dog has mastered the sequence, wait slightly longer and longer to release with "OK." You can place the bowl on the ground and then stand up straight again before you release. You can then step away from the bowl and release, and so on. You can also apply the elevator technique to other situations.

- If your dog loves to go outside and won't sit still while you clip the leash, do the same activity.
- If your dog loves petting but jumps up when you start to pet him (for instance, when you come home and he's excited), do this activity with your petting as the reward.

For some dogs, playtime with a favorite toy is the ultimate reward.

ACTIVITY 2: HOW TO DO SAY "PLEASE" FOR PLAYTIME

Fetch, Tug, Hide-and-Seek, Chase, and other games are fantastic ways to build the relationship between you and your dog while simultaneously blowing off a little steam. These games are also the perfect times to enforce good manners. Only polite dogs get the reward of playtime with their owners. Rude dogs, however, lose the opportunity to play games. Because play is inherently motivating for your pup, he will quickly learn that it pays to be polite and say "please." The steps that follow are for games involving a toy or ball.

1. Hold the toy or ball in your hand, facing your dog. If he jumps up, barks, or runs around, stay still and quiet. Do not tell him to sit, and do not tell him "no." He needs to figure out for himself that these rude behaviors won't work.

2. When your dog eventually sits for one second, release him with "OK" and immediately start the game by throwing the ball or offering him the toy.

    TIP: Remember that he wants the toy, not food or petting, right now. Avoid delaying the game by petting your dog or giving food rewards.

3. If he starts to jump on you or demand-bark mid-game, the game stops. Immediately turn away from him and ignore him, which sends the message that this behavior actually ends the fun. Once he has sat down politely, you can begin the game again.

4. Repeat Steps 1–3 every time he wants the ball thrown or a new tug game to begin.

From There

As time goes on, ask your dog to sit for a little longer before you mark and reward. After he sits for two seconds, release with "OK," and then prolong it to three seconds, and so on.

ACTIVITY 3: HOW TO DO SAY "PLEASE" AT THE DOOR

Your dog doesn't know it yet, but he has a superpower. He can use the power of his mind to make doors open; all he has to do is say "please" by sitting. Doors, with their knobs conveniently out of paw's reach, are opportunities to teach politeness. By waiting for your dog to sit before you start to open the door, you're ensuring

Good manners at the door is a matter of both politeness and safety.

that your dog has earned the reward of having it opened for him. This rule doesn't apply only to the front door of your home but to any threshold: gates on your property, the entrance/exit to the dog runs, the door to the pet-supply store, and even car doors (assuming your dog is excited to jump into the car).

This is one case where politeness is tied to safety. Door dashing is dangerous, and the last thing you want is for your dog to slip through the front door and into traffic. By enforcing the rule that only sitting gets you to open the door for him, your dog won't have the inclination to door

Jumping up is impolite behavior in dogs of any size.

dash. A bad habit can't develop if you never give your dog the chance to practice it.

Be warned that, on the first day, you will need quite a bit of patience while your dog learns the new rule. Hang in there. Once he learns it, the hard part is over, and the process will go much more quickly from then on.

Expect the first session to take several minutes, so make sure that your dog does not urgently have to go outside to relieve himself.

1. Put your dog's leash on using the elevator technique in Say "Please" for Your Food.

2. With your dog on leash, walk to the front door. When you reach the door, make sure that your body is between the dog and door. Give yourself enough space that you can open the door without bumping into it.

3. Face your dog and gently look at him. Silently ignore any rude behavior, such as jumping, whining, or trying to push past you.

4. When your dog finally sits, unlock the door. The dog will likely jump up as soon as he hears the clicking of the lock. When he pops up, immediately relock the door and wait for him to sit again. Repeat as many times as necessary until he can sit while you unlock the door.

5. Unlock and slowly open the door as long as the dog is sitting. If he stands or jumps up, close the door, wait for him to sit again, and start over. Use your body and leash to block him from actually running through the door; you don't want to slam any doggie toes in the door as it closes.

6. Now, with the door fully open and your dog in a sit, release with "OK" and walk out the door together.

From There
Follow these steps for any door or other threshold, such as permission to:

- enter the kitchen while you're cooking
- be invited to join you on the couch or bed
- come into a room containing a tempting Christmas tree, expensive furniture, or other items of concern

THAT'S ALL
Basic • Manners

When you give your dog a treat, does he beg for more? No matter how many times you play Fetch, will he be jumping and crying for you to throw it just one more time? It's usually not your dog's fault that he's demanding your food, toys, or attention. You need to teach him a clear cue that means "that's all; no more attention for you right now." It's incredibly simple and can have a huge impact on your dog's behavior. The hardest part of That's All is that you have to mean it! Once you say "that's all," you will walk away from the treat bag, the ball, or whatever else your dog is begging for. If you say "that's all" and occasionally give in, it will become both confusing and frustrating to your dog. Sticking to your guns every single time is actually much kinder to your pup.

That's All is useful for dogs who:

- jump, bark, or do other undesirable behaviors when they want something
- pester their owners for food, play, or attention, even when their owners have stopped giving it
- get frustrated when they don't get what they want

HOW TO DO THAT'S ALL

1. Give your dog a treat. Pause until he's done chewing and then give him a second treat. Now he's excited!
2. Once the second treat is down the hatch, say "that's all" and give a visual cue. It could be shaking your head back and forth, folding your arms, shrugging, or anything else that comes naturally.
3. Immediately turn or walk away from your dog. Ignore any attempts he makes to get your attention back.
4. Once he has given up on the treats, you can give him attention again.

From There

You can use That's All for anything your dog might demand, such as:

- petting
- Fetch or Tug
- training sessions

ADVANCED BEHAVIORS

Once both you and your dog have developed impulse control through the basic behaviors in this chapter, you can expand these skills in a variety of directions. As before, less is more when it comes to verbal communication with your dog. These activities are designed to teach your dog how to stretch his independent-thinking skills even further, maintain a calm position for a longer period of time, and control his impulses in the presence of more intense distractions. In all cases, not reacting impulsively is what will win your dog his reward. The more situations in which you can practice this principle, the more it will become part of his regular way of interacting with the world.

CLICKER TRAINING: FREE SHAPING 101
Advanced • Games

Prerequisite: Clicker Training: Warm-Up Game

In the warm-up game, you clicked and treated every time your dog interacted with a box. Now, this new game tightens the criteria and introduces a style of training called "free shaping," in which you click and treat for increasingly closer steps toward a specific end goal. With free shaping, you will have a training goal in mind. For instance, your goal might be to have your dog put his paw inside a box. You won't touch either the box or your dog, nor will you give him any explicit instructions. Rather, you'll step back with your clicker and a handful of amazing treats, letting your dog figure out the game on his own. He will learn, based on when he gets the clicks, what the goal is. First, you'll click for even the slightest interaction with the box, meaning that your dog either looks at it or takes a step toward it. Eventually, he will touch it with a paw and then put his paw inside the box.

To start, select an item with which your dog will interact. Next, choose a goal: one simple interaction that your dog can do with the object. For dogs who like using their noses, the goal can be a nose-touch on the object. Some dogs like to paw at things, so putting a paw on the object would be fitting. For other dogs, such as Fever in the photos, jumping inside the box is the ultimate source of fun. The following steps correspond to Fever's free-shaping activity, but you can have a totally different behavior in mind.

HOW TO DO FREE SHAPING 101

1. Put a box in a quiet location and wait for your dog to notice it. He glances at the box. You click and promptly toss or give a treat. Repeat this several times until your dog is repeatedly looking at the box to get a click. (It should be several glances per minute, not one glance every few minutes.)

2. Raise one criterion to get you a tiny step closer to your end goal. When your dog glances at the box as before, do not click. Wait and see what else he will offer. When he makes any movement that gets him closer to the box, click and treat. It could simply be a step toward the box. Click for repeated movements at this level.

TIP: Some dogs will raise the criteria on their own very quickly. Other dogs need a number of clicks at one level before being ready to raise the criteria. Work at your dog's pace.

3. Continue shaping the behavior in tiny increments toward the end goal. In this case, the dog would put one paw on the box, and then inside the box. Another paw goes in, and, eventually, all four paws are in the box.

4. Once your dog has reached his goal over several repetitions, you can put the behavior on cue. For the example here, you can say "hop in!" and then let him jump into the box for a click and treat.

From There

Play this game with a number of interactions with various objects. You can teach nose and paw targets this way, and you can even teach your dog to fetch an item, push an item, and so on. Some of these games will be discussed in Chapter 7.

Step 3: Fever has gotten two paws in the box. She's halfway there!

Step 4: Now that Fever has gotten all four paws in the box several times, Sarah can put the behavior on cue.

PATIENCE PAYS OFF
Advanced • Manners

Prerequisite: Any basic behavior, such as Sit, Down, or Hand Target

Used in: Agility

When you drop a piece of food on the floor, what does your dog do? Wait patiently and ask for your permission to eat it? Of course not! He probably launches himself onto the food the second it hits the ground, snatching it before you even know what's happened. Patience has to be taught.

This activity puts your dog in proximity of a reward, be it a treat, a toy, or a "life reward," such as access to the couch. However, he can't just have it; he'll have to earn it by performing a simple polite behavior first. Only by listening to you will he get permission to have his reward. In other words, listening to you is his ticket to treats, toys, freedom, and all of the other good things in life.

Patience Pays Off is a foundation skill used in agility, in which high-octane dogs often have to start the course in a Sit-, Down-, or Stand-Stay until they are released by their handlers to the first obstacle. Without practicing impulse control, these dogs wouldn't be able to hold still under such intense pressure and excitement.

Patience Pays Off is useful for dogs who:
- generally lack impulse control, especially around food or toys
- jump, bark, or do other undesirable behaviors when they want something
- get frustrated when they don't get what they want

HOW TO DO PATIENCE PAYS OFF

1. Have your dog on a 4- to 6-foot (1.2- to 1.8-m) leash and a harness that will not cause pain if he lunges or pulls.
2. Toss a toy or treat about 5 feet (1.5 m) away. The distance depends on your dog: the item should be far enough away that it's tempting for your dog but not so tempting that he can't tear his attention away from it.
3. Your dog will likely pull toward the object. Hold steady so he cannot reach it.
4. Ask your dog to perform a simple behavior he's already learned. Sit, Down, or Hand Target are good options.
5. It's likely that your dog will be too focused on the goodie to listen. If he does not perform the behavior immediately, wait patiently and avoid repeating the cue. Count to ten in your head, which gives your dog the opportunity to problem-solve all by himself. If you have

Step 3: Not so fast, Batman!

Step 6: Batman is giving Kate a polite Sit with eye contact, so she will release him to get his treat.

clearly lost his focus at that point, walk him out of the area and start over. Next time you approach that tempting goodie on the ground, stop him several feet farther away.

6. Once again, ask for a polite behavior. When he does the Sit (or other behavior), mark it and release him with "go get it!" in a cheerful tone. Now he has earned his reward.

From There

This is a game you can play in numerous contexts. You can increase the difficulty in several ways.

High school: Vary the location of the reward. Slowly bring the toy or treat closer to your dog.

College: Use rewards that are increasingly tempting, gradually moving up to a favorite toy or a piece of "real" food. (If your dog can't focus on your cue, it means that your reward is too tempting.)

Grad school and beyond: As your dog learns more tricks in the following chapters, ask for increasingly higher-level behaviors.

 **TUG FOR POLITE PLAY**
Advanced • Games

Many dogs, especially puppies and adolescents, aren't terribly skilled at regulating their level of excitement. This is why a friendly wrestle at the dog park can sometimes tip into a fight, or why a fun game of Fetch can lead to your dog biting at your hand. This doesn't mean you have to avoid playing with your dog; rather, it is up to you to teach him how to play politely with you.

Tug (a name we prefer over "Tug of War") has gotten a bad rap. While it's true that there are a few dogs who should not play the game, Tug is actually a great activity to play with most dogs. In fact, when taught properly, a game of Tug can teach your dog to manage his impulses and regulate his level of arousal. Using the guidelines that follow, playing Tug can even prevent the kind of impulsivity and aggression that it is claimed to cause.

Tug is useful for dogs who:
- jump on you or bark at you to initiate play
- get increasingly excited during play
- tug too hard
- lack impulse control around toys
- have yet to learn Drop It
- need an outlet for their energy
- need some human bonding time

HOW TO DO TUG FOR POLITE PLAY

1. Choose a long toy, like a rope toy, that is only mildly interesting to your dog. Show your dog the toy but don't let him grab it yet.

2. Wait for your dog to sit as in Say "Please" for Playtime.
   TIP: If he does not sit, turn away and try again in a few seconds.

3. Present the toy. If the dog jumps up or charges for it, use your NRM of "oops" and remove the toy before he can grab it.
   TIP: Remember the NRM (no reward marker)? It marks the moment your dog made a mistake. Revisit the Cues and Rewards section earlier in this chapter if you need a refresher.

4. Start over. Once he can sit while you present the toy, happily say "take it" to give him permission to start playing.
   TIP: If he's now reluctant to take it, move the toy back and forth on the ground, mimicking the movements of a small animal.

5. At the first indication that your dog's arousal level is climbing, calmly say "shhhh" and stand like a relaxed statue for a few moments. If you are kneeling, let the toy droop to the ground. Though you're still holding the toy, your body is indicating that you are just relaxing there.

6. Wait for your dog to relax his body, even briefly. After a moment of calm, cheerfully say "OK" and gently start playing again. If he has spit out the toy, tell him to "take it" as before.

7. Repeat this as needed during play sessions with low-value toys.

From There

High school: Once your dog is able to respond to "shhhh," you can introduce a slightly higher-value toy. In all cases, your dog's arousal level will determine when you're ready to graduate to higher-value toys.

College: Add Drop It during Play (Chapter 4) to your play sessions, too.

Grad school and beyond: You can use "shhhh" in other contexts, too.

- Jump around, cheer, and get your dog a little excited for a few seconds before saying "shhhh" as you relax your body and quiet your voice.
- Play a surprise game of Chase Me (Chapter 3). If your dog start jumping on you, say "shhhh" and take a short break before doing another rep.

Step 3: Sorry, Fever. Jumping won't get you that toy.

Step 4: Much better! Sarah will give Fever the toy now that she's sitting.

Tug is a great game as long as your dog can control his excitement.

Step 5: Sarah relaxes the toy and her whole body, so Fever can calm herself for a moment.

02
MAKE SITS, DOWNS, AND STAYS FUN

In most cases, when an owner says, "My dog has bad manners," trainers interpret it to mean, "My dog lacks impulse control." Dogs who jump on people, beg at the table, counter-surf, or door dash all exhibit the same inability to control their impulses. The solution to such seemingly diverse problems? Often, it starts with simple Sits, Downs, and Stays to build a dog's ability to stay put. A sitting or lying dog, by default, isn't decorating your neighbor's jacket with muddy footprints or stealing the cheese plate when your in-laws come over. Sits and Downs are inherently polite, so you want your dog to love doing these behaviors. The more rewarding Sit is, the more willingly he'll do it, and the better behaved he'll be in general.

This chapter will give your dog a solid foundation of impulse-control behaviors, starting with basic Sits. From there, you can move up to advanced tricks and sports techniques to hone your dog's impulse-control skills indoors and out. Remember, these activities are intended to be fun, so avoid attaching deadlines or unrealistic expectations to your training. Practice these not just at home but also out on the street, and you might find your neighbors ooohing, ahhhing, and whispering to themselves, "I wish my dog could do *that!*"

BASIC BEHAVIORS

  SIT
Basic • Manners

Used in: Rally, agility, freestyle

Sit is usually the first thing we teach our dogs, and with good reason: sitting is inherently polite. After all, a sitting dog can't dart into traffic or jump on your countertops. But before asking your dog to sit politely during a dinner party or other distracting event, make sure that he can handle basic Sits. Sit looks deceptively easy to a human, but in fact it can be extremely difficult for your dog to sit when there are distractions present. Reread the What Grade Is Your Dog In? section in the Introduction to ensure that you're not pushing your dog past his ability level.

Good manners are all about impulse control.

FOUR-FOR-FOUR

As you've probably noticed, we can't get enough of comparing you, the handler, to a good teacher or coach. And if you've ever seen one of those inspirational movies that take place in the classroom or the locker room, you've seen that a good leader knows when and how much to push her students. With training your own dog, however, it can be a challenge to know when to push him to a higher level. After all, you are learning this material for the first time, too.

If you're not sure when to push your dog—for instance, when to move up from a five-second Stay to an eight-second Stay—use Kate's four-for-four rule. If your pup can do a five-second Stay correctly four times in a row, then he's probably ready to move up to the eight-second Stay. However, if he struggles to do the five-second Stay, repeatedly only getting one or two correct Stays before making a mistake, five seconds might be too hard for him. When a dog continues to struggle achieving four-for-four over several tries, it's best to drop down to an easier level. For instance, go back to three-second Stays until you get four-for-four, and then move back up to five seconds. This is a way to ensure that you're not pushing your dog beyond his abilities.

That said, if you communicate well with your dog and instinctively know when he's ready to increase the difficulty of a new behavior, go with your gut. There are some quick canine learners who will get bored if they aren't challenged and will totally lose their concentration by the fourth rep. For them, two good reps of a five-second Stay might suffice. On the flip side, many dogs need more than just four reps to grasp a certain level of a behavior. They might need to get four-for-four over the course of several training sessions before they're ready to move up. To complicate things more, some dogs are quick to learn certain behaviors but need a lot more time and repetition to learn others.

In many of the behaviors from Chapter 2 on, we recommend the four-for-four principle. You can take this literally or simply interpret it to mean "practice until your dog comfortably understands the current level of difficulty."

You'll find that Sit is used in numerous dog sports as well as in tricks, such as Meerkat. In rally, a dog must sit every time he halts (unless indicated otherwise). In agility, a dog may sit at the start line or at the table, on which he pauses for five seconds. And in freestyle, handlers can incorporate Sit into a variety of routines.

If you've done the Say "Please" exercises in the previous chapter, your dog may already be a sitting champ. In that case, it's time to put the Sit on cue so that your pup is able to control himself when asked.

Sit is useful for:

- all dogs physically capable of sitting

HOW TO DO SIT

1. Have a stinky treat in one hand, with your palm facing up. Position your hand an inch (2.5 cm) or less above your dog's nose so he can touch the back of your hand with his nose.

2. Very slowly and slightly, move your hand up and away from you so the dog's nose reaches a little upward and backward to follow the scent. If your dog's nose becomes detached from your hand, you're moving too fast or too dramatically. Imagine you're scooping water into your hand in slow motion; that's what the gesture looks like.

3. As your dog's nose follows the scent, he will rock back into a Sit. Mark with "yes" or a click

Step 1: Beans is starting to follow Kate's lure. Note her hand position.

Step 3: Beans is rocking back into a Sit. Once her rear is fully on the floor, Kate will mark and reward.

Step 6: The finished product with an empty-handed cue.

the moment his rear hits the floor, and then reward him while he's sitting. Get four-for-four Sits.

TIP: If your dog is reluctant to sit, and you're certain it's not due to pain, then you can shape the behavior. This means you will mark and reward the dog for simply tilting his head back. Get four-for-four. Next, ask him to tilt a little more before marking and rewarding. Continue asking him to go just a bit farther

each time until he goes all the way into the Sit. When he finally sits, give a jackpot of several treats in a row.

TIP: If his rear pops up while you're feeding him the treat, take the reward away and start over. *Bummer*, he thinks, *I just lost my reward when I stood up*. He will quickly learn that holding the Sit position gets him rewards, while popping up gets him nothing.

4. Say your verbal cue, "sit," right before you start the lure. Remember that, when giving a cue, say it only once. Get four-for-four with the "sit" cue.

5. Now, no more luring. Remove the treat from your scooping hand, making your hand a cue, not a lure. Same as before, say "sit" once and guide with your hand, which is now empty.

Don't skimp on rewards yet, though. Reward from your pocket, treat pouch, or other hand, which you were holding behind your back. Get four-for-four.

6. Gradually move your cue hand away from the dog. After each successful repetition, lift your hand (and your whole body, if you were leaning or crouching) an inch or two (2 to 5 cm) higher so your dog's nose doesn't need to touch your hand anymore. Ultimately, you can cue your dog to sit while you're standing tall or even when at a distance.

From There

Practice Sit in various indoor and then outdoor locations. Remember what grade your dog is currently in, and be sure to increase distractions only in small increments. When you ask for Sit in a new location or scenario, you may have to go back to the beginning and lure him for the first few repetitions. That's fine. A sample progression might look like this:

Elementary school: Sit inside your home when there are no distractions.

Middle school: Sit inside your home when there are mild or moderate distractions, such as family members in the room. (A delivery person ringing the doorbell is not a mild distraction!)

Junior high: Sit outside in a quiet spot, like a backyard or empty side street.

High school: Sit outside with mild distractions present, like a crowded street or a yard with activity in the vicinity.

College: Sit while a person walks past you on the sidewalk.

Grad school: Sit while a person on the street comes over and says hi to your dog.

Once you have reached a certain level, you can slowly start to wean your dog off the treats at the easier levels, trading the treats for gentle praise or other life rewards. For instance, if your dog is getting the hang of high-school-level Sits, you can start fading out food rewards for some of the elementary- and middle-school-level Sits. Avoid going cold turkey and stopping all treats immediately, because any sudden change in the sequence can confuse your dog.

WHEN "SIT" MEANS "DOWN"

When you ask Max for a Sit, does he automatically go into a Down position instead? While both sitting and lying down are desirable behaviors, your dog may get the two confused. There are usually two reasons for this.

First is a lack of clarity on the handler's part. You say, "Max, sit." Max slumps into a Down. *Eh, close enough*, you think, and you reward him. With repetition, this teaches Max that the word "sit" actually means "lie down." Avoid this confusion by being a stickler: in every case, "sit" means to sit, and "down" means to lie down.

There is another possible reason why your dog automatically lies down when you say "sit." It happens when you teach your dog this sequence: "Bella, sit. Bella, down. Good girl! Here's your treat." Bella, being clever, has learned that the sequence is Sit/Down/treat. And it's the Down part that gets the goodie, so why bother with Sit? Prevent this by avoiding predictable patterns. Sometimes say "sit" and then "paw" or "spin," or any other behavior, to keep her guessing. In addition, the timing of your rewards can be accelerated to prevent Bella from collapsing into a Down. As soon as she sits, quickly mark, reward, and release with "OK." Practice several repetitions in a row at this quick pace to break the cycle.

DOWN
Basic • Manners

Used in: Rally, agility, freestyle

Down, meaning to lie down, is a useful starting point for numerous tricks, many of which can be incorporated into a freestyle routine. It is also used in certain canine sports, particularly rally, in which a dog might be asked to lie down while his owner moves around him. Even United States Dog Agility Association (USDAA) agility utilizes a five-second Down-Stay on the pause table.

In addition to sports applications, Down has plenty of benefits for daily life. It is a naturally relaxing position for many dogs, and it can have a calming effect. (As you may have noticed, many dogs are not experts in calming themselves.) You might even find that your dog can maintain a Down (as in a Down-Stay) better than a Sit. That is because his body is more fixed on the floor, requiring a greater effort to jump up than if he were sitting.

Down is useful for dogs who:

- lack impulse control
- are bouncy or excitable
- can't relax themselves
- have difficulty sitting due to conformation or pain
- will be learning a variety of Down-based tricks

HOW TO DO DOWN

1. Face your dog. Start from a Sit but don't actually say "sit." Either lure your dog into a sitting position or just wait for him to sit on his own. Don't reward him yet.

   TIP: If you always say "sit" before "down," you risk teaching your dog a pattern in which he automatically goes into a Down even if you've asked for only a Sit.

2. Hold your hand flat, palm down, with a stinky treat pinched between your thumb and the fingers above. This will become a lure. Slowly draw an imaginary vertical line with your hand, starting from his nose and moving straight down, "from nose to toes."

   TIP: If your dog's nose becomes detached from the lure, it means that you're moving your hand too fast.

3. Pause once your hand reaches the floor between his paws. Some dogs will crouch all the way into a Down as they nibble the treat. Good dog! Proceed to Step 5.

4. If your dog isn't lying down yet, turn your motion into an uppercase "L": after drawing the imaginary line from nose to toes, slowly drag the lure out along the floor, away from dog's body and toward you.

   TIP: Some dogs simply don't lie down by stretching forward. Here are some things to try.

   - Experiment with the direction of your "L." Drag the lure on the floor toward your dog, or even to the side.
   - Shape the behavior. Reward him first for just reaching his head down, and then for dropping his shoulder a bit, and then for each baby step toward actually lying down. This could take several sessions, so be patient and reward even the tiniest improvements.

- Try a different surface. If you were having no luck on a hardwood floor, try Down on a rug. Conversely, if Fido isn't feelin' the rug, maybe a slick surface will help him slump into a Down.

5. Once both his rear end and front elbows are on the ground, mark and reward on the floor between his front paws. Rewarding on the floor will keep him firmly in the Down position for a few seconds. Once he's eaten the treat, release with "OK." Get four-for-four.

6. Add the verbal cue "down" right *before* you lure. Get four-for-four.

Step 1: Sarah doesn't cue Hank to sit. Just by facing him, he chooses to sit.

Step 2: As Sarah starts to lure, her hand is palm-down with the treat pinched between her thumb and fingers.

She lures straight down to the floor between Hank's paws.

Step 3: Hank drops into a Down. If he hadn't, Sarah would have slowly dragged the lure on the floor toward her.

Step 8: Sarah can stand straight when she cues the Down.

Make Sits, Downs, and Stays Fun

7. Take the treat out of your hand, making it a cue, not a lure. From now on, you'll reward from your pocket, treat pouch, or other hand hidden behind your back. Repeat the previous sequence above with an empty cue hand, getting four-for-four.

8. Fade the dramatic visual cue of reaching all the way to the floor. With each repetition, stop your cue hand a few inches short of the previous rep.

   TIP: Most dogs do not need four-for-four at this point. Still, if your dog doesn't respond at a certain point, he might be confused. Return to the previous step (reaching your hand a little lower) and get four-for-four.

From There

As with Sit, your dog can learn a rock-solid Down indoors and outdoors, but you'll have to increase the level of difficulty gradually and methodically. Here are some possible scenarios.

High school: Practice Down indoors during mild distractions, such as family members casually walking around in the room.

College: Practice Down outside on your walk during mild distractions, such as while you stop to chat with a neighbor.

Grad school: Practice Down during moderate or intense distractions, such as during a dinner party or on a bustling street corner.

  STAY
Basic • Sports

Prerequisite: Sit or Down
Used in: Rally, agility, freestyle, parkour

Stay is an essential impulse-control behavior as well as the springboard for many cool tricks and sports maneuvers. Stay means "sit (or lie down or stand) in that spot and don't get up until I release you." It is frequently used in rally, where Stay takes many forms. You might have your dog in a Sit-Stay while you walk in a circle around

him, have him stay while you walk away and then call him to a Heel position, or use Stay for other applications discussed later in this chapter. In freestyle routines, a dog may be cued to stay still while the handler performs. In parkour, dogs are required to do a short Stay while balancing two or four paws on an object.

In agility, it is very helpful if the dog can stay in front of the first obstacle while the handler positions herself ahead of the dog. This allows the handler to get into an advantageous spot before releasing the dog to begin the run. Since the dog is almost always faster than the human, a handler who starts ahead of her dog can cue the subsequent obstacles more quickly. Later in the agility course, when the dog stays on the pause table for a count of five, the handler can use that time to again get ahead of her dog. Without a reliable Stay, the dog and handler have to start running from the same position at the same time, making it more difficult to cue obstacles in time.

You can decide how strict you want your dog's Stays to be. For pet dogs, a less-than-gentlemanly

WHEN COOKIES DON'T CUT IT

You may find that treats don't always motivate your dog to do behaviors such as Stay. In fact, if you have a high-drive dog, giving him permission to do his favorite activity is the biggest reward you can offer. For a dog who loves agility, herding, disc, fetch, or any other "job," the reward for a good Stay is permission to do his favorite activity. Think of it this way: if you were a runner standing in place in the moments before a marathon starts, would a cookie be rewarding? No way! What you really want is the starting pistol to fire, giving you permission to start running.

If this describes your dog, you should reverse the reward and release. For example, when Sarah sets up Fever in front of the first obstacle of an agility course, she asks Fever to stay. Were Sarah to reward this Stay with a piece of steak, Fever would snub it. What Fever really wants in that moment is to start the course. Permission to run is the only reward that her doggie heart desires. Fever, therefore, has learned to stay without the need for treats. When she properly stays at the starting line, Sarah will then release her and cue her to the first obstacle. The release is the reward in itself. (This differs from traditional sequences, where the reward is delivered during the Stay, and then the handler releases.) If Fever breaks her Stay, Sarah calmly goes back to the starting line to reset her. This delays the fun of doing agility and teaches Fever to take her Stays seriously. Therefore, if your dog has a sport or job that he craves, use that activity as the reward for teaching Stay.

sitting or lying position (such as leaning to the side with one hind leg lazily sticking out) is perfectly fine, provided you don't plan to do actual sports trials or competitions in the future, as their criteria are stricter. The moment he stands up, though—*whoops!*—he's just lost his chance for a reward.

Stay has numerous practical applications. It's great for waiting at street corners, while you're chatting with a neighbor during your walk, when you're opening your door to get your pizza delivery, or even when you've dropped a glass on the floor and don't want your pup to walk on the broken shards.

Stay is useful for dogs who:

- lack general impulse control
- struggle to sit still
- are uncomfortable being separated from their humans (i.e., "Velcro dogs")
- jump on guests
- door dash

- can't control themselves in the vicinity of food

There are three main components of Stay, which trainers call the *three Ds*. They are:

- **Duration:** How long is your dog in the Stay position? Start with very short Stays and methodically increase the duration.
- **Distance:** How far away can you walk from your dog while he's in the Stay? At first, you might not even be able turn your back on him, but, with practice, you will be able to walk into another room while he's staying put.
- **Distraction:** Can your dog do Stay on a crowded street? When you answer the door? There are numerous distractions that you and your dog will have to systematically practice before he becomes truly proficient in real-life Stays.

Once you and your dog have sufficiently tackled all three Ds separately, you can ask for Stays that include more than one D. You'll see how to do that in the From There section that follows.

You'll notice that the Stays here do not involve any kind of recall (Come) at the end. This allows you to reward the dog while he is in the Stay position, which makes him think, *Hey, this staying put thing is pretty cool.*

HOW TO DO STAY WITH DURATION

The focus here is to increase the amount of time that your dog can hold still in a Sit or Down. While practicing duration, keep the distance between you and the dog short, and keep the distractions low.

1. Ask your dog for a Sit or Down, whichever is more comfortable for him. You can calmly praise but don't give a treat yet.
2. Say "stay" and give a "traffic cop" hand signal, with your palm held out as if to say "stop," and then drop your hand.
3. Pause for two seconds. Casually look away from your dog during this time, but avoid walking away (as this adds another D, distance).

    TIP: If your dog is bouncy or easily distracted, you may be able to pause for only half a second, which is fine. However, if your dog is a statue, go ahead and start with five seconds. Choose a realistic starting point at which your dog can be successful, and avoid "testing" him.

4. When your eyes return to your dog two seconds later, assuming he is still in the Stay position, mark and reward. Make sure he maintains the Sit or Down while he eats the treat.

    TIP: If your dog popped up while you were looking away, give an NRM of "oops" and start over. Next time, decrease to a manageable duration and get four-for-four at the shorter duration.

5. Say "OK" to release. Don't give a treat after the release. You want the most rewarding part to be the Stay itself, not being released from the Stay.

6. After each successful Stay, you can increase the duration by one to five seconds, depending on your dog's bounciness. If your dog falters at any point, go back to the previous duration (at which he was successful) and get four-for-four before increasing. This will ensure your that dog really understands what you're asking.

HOW TO DO STAY WITH DISTANCE

When practicing distance, remember to keep the duration and distraction levels as low as possible. Think of yourself as a boomerang that turns and walks away from your dog but immediately swoops back to mark and reward. Keep moving at a natural pace, whether it is away from or toward your dog.

Remember that most dogs are hardwired to follow their humans (yes, we all know, even into the bathroom). Asking your dog to stay while you walk away may be very challenging for your pup, especially in the beginning. Teaching Stay with Distance is much more of a marathon than a sprint.

1. Ask your dog to sit or lie down. Say "stay," give the "traffic cop" hand signal, and then drop the hand.
2. Turn your head and torso away from your dog. Don't step away yet, because your dog will likely get up to follow you.
3. Immediately turn back to your dog. (Resist the temptation to add duration while you're turned away.) Assuming he's still in the Stay position, mark and reward while he remains in the Sit or Down. Release with "OK."

    TIP: If he broke the Stay, it means he's not ready for that level of distance. For the next repetition, make your movement even less dramatic, for example, just a head turn. Get four-for-four before proceeding.

4. For the next repetition, repeat the sequence but, this time, turn your whole body 180

Step 1: Kate briefly gives Beans the "traffic cop" hand signal.

Step 2 (and beyond): Work your way up to taking this many steps away from your dog. Notice how Kate has turned her body away from Beans.

Step 3: Kate returns, marking and rewarding while Beans is still in the Stay. Then, she will release her.

degrees. Immediately turn back to mark, reward, and release.

5. Next, turn your body 180 degrees and just barely lean forward, as if you're going to walk off. Immediately turn back to mark, reward, and release. If your dog breaks his Stay, go back to Step 4 and get four-for-four.

6. Take a full step away and boomerang back to your dog. Mark and reward when you reach your dog (but not before) and then release. If that goes well, next time take two steps away and back. Next, take three steps, and so on.

TIP: Any time your dog breaks his Stay, rewind to the previous distance, get four-for-four, and then proceed.

HOW TO DO STAY WITH DISTRACTION

There's no shortage of things out there to distract your dog: doorbells, squirrels, food on the floor or sidewalk, and other dogs barking in the distance, to name a few. Asking your dog to do Stay in the presence of these distractions is no small task; it requires a great deal of impulse control on your dog's part. As with the previous Stays, you'll start with mildly distracting items and incrementally work your way up to higher-level ones. The example we provide will prepare your dog to stay when there is a knock at the door, but you can use any number of other distractions, provided you can introduce them from a very low level. Remember to keep the duration and distance relatively short when focusing on distractions.

1. Ask your dog to stay as before, and briefly introduce a very low-level distraction. We like to start with gently tapping on the wall two or three times with our fingertips.

2. Assuming he has maintained the Stay, mark, reward, and release.

TIP: If your dog was not able to stay during the tapping, decrease the volume and make sure that you weren't inadvertently adding too much duration or distance into the mix. Get four-for-four before proceeding.

3. On the next repetition, make the tapping slightly louder. Avoid increasing the duration of the tapping or other aspects; focus only on volume. Assuming your dog has stayed put, mark, reward, and release.

4. Continue increasing the volume of the tapping until it becomes a gentle knock and then a vigorous knock.

5. Practice Steps 1–4 with a variety of distractions, such as dropping a toy or food, opening a door, (you) sitting on the floor and getting back up, and any other distraction that you can gradually increase.

From There

Once you've reliably taught your dog all three Ds separately, you're ready to combine them. Here are some examples:

High school: The dog stays while you walk a few steps away and bend down to pick something up. (See Stop and Stay 911 later in this chapter for more on this.)

College: The dog stays while you walk a few steps away, pause, and drop a treat or toy.

Grad school: The dog stays while the doorbell rings, you answer the door, and you get your package from a delivery person.

Keep in mind that every dog is unique, so what constitutes a "high school" or "college" Stay will be different for each dog. There is the occasional dog who doesn't bat an eyelash when the doorbell rings (oh, to be his lucky owner!), so doorbell Stays might be only high-school level for him. But when he sees you open the oven door to remove your piping-hot holiday cookies, he practically jumps inside. His most challenging Stays will likely take place in the kitchen, and this will be a great excuse for you to bake more cookies.

ADVANCED BEHAVIORS

 ## SIDE SIT
Advanced • Sports

Prerequisite: Sit
Used in: Rally, freestyle

Normally, when you cue your dog to sit, he'll position himself right in front of you. In your dog's mind, this face-to-face position is a necessary component of the Sit. Therefore, if you ask him to sit in a different spot relative to your body, your dog will probably think you've completely forgotten what "sit" means. When teaching the Side Sit, expect to start from scratch so that your dog can become familiar with these new parameters of Sit.

A Side Sit involves you and the dog standing next to one another, facing the same direction, with the dog at your hip. When you plan on moving forward with your dog, as in a Heel, a Side Sit is a much more logical starting point than a traditional Sit. (Walking forward is pretty awkward when your dog is sitting in front of you, facing you.) Side Sit is ideal for waiting at crosswalks, at a farmers' market while you pay for your veggies, in line at the bank, or while talking to friends on the sidewalk.

Rally obedience courses use Side Sits frequently. In fact, every time the dog stops, unless indicated otherwise, he must go into a Side Sit. Why not implement this in your own walks around the neighborhood? A pet dog who learns to sit at street corners or while you stop to tie your shoe is under greater control than a dog who wanders back and forth. It's not only practical but also safe.

Side Sit is useful for dogs who:
- need to improve leash walking skills
- lack impulse control, especially while on walks
- are easily distracted
- go out in public with their owners or live in urban areas

HOW TO DO SIDE SIT

1. The dog is on your left side as you start walking together. Be prepared with a stinky treat in your left hand. Hold the leash in your right hand and keep it short enough that he can't wander too far from your side.

2. Stop walking and use the treat to lure your dog into a Sit. You want the dog's head to tilt slightly up and back, just as in a face-to-face Sit. Here, because the dog is next to you, your left hand will move backward and upward just a hair so his nose can follow it as he rocks back into a Sit. Don't say "sit" yet.

   TIP: If your dog's Sit is crooked, try these modifications:
   - Use a wall as a barrier to the left so he can't swing his body around.
   - Ensure that your leash is short enough to prevent him from lagging behind or darting forward.

- If he tries to circle in front of you, extend your left leg to block his path.
- When you lure the Sit, make sure that your hand is next to your left hip; if you accidentally clutch the treat near your chest or stomach, your dog will end up in front of you.

3. Once he's in the sitting position, give him a few treats in a row from your left hand to encourage him to stay in that position for several seconds. After he's finished the last treat, release him with "OK" and start to walk forward. Get four-for-four.

4. Follow the same sequence as before but add the verbal cue "sit" right *before* you lure with your hand. The sequence will be: say "sit"/lure into Sit position/mark/reward/release. Get four-for-four.

5. Now, no more luring. Your left hand is empty, so the motion is now a cue, not a lure. Still

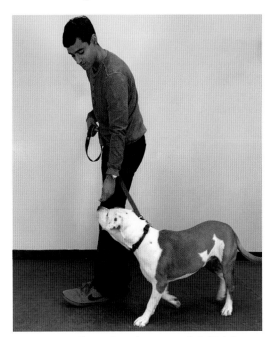

Step 1: Navin walks Bandit with a treat ready in his left hand. (Fun fact: Bandit is completely blind, but it doesn't slow him down at all!)

Step 2: As they stop, Navin lures Bandit into the Side Sit. Note his hand position.

RALLY TO THE RESCUE

Sierra, a four-year-old Cardigan Welsh Corgi, is more than just a pretty face. She's also got a growing list of accolades. With the help of her human partner, Stephanie, Sierra has already earned her CGC (Canine Good Citizen), CGCA (Advanced Canine Good Citizen), Advanced Trick, and Rally Novice titles. The pair also does coursing ability tests and herding classes. While that is a lengthy list of honors, Sierra started out just like any other dog, working on basic manners and slowly building her skills until she was ready to compete.

Rally obedience has had a lot of practical benefits for this fun, friendly dog. Being low to the ground, Sierra encounters many delicious smells on sidewalks and in the rally ring. Stephanie explains, "Rally has really helped Sierra with her focus. As much as I like to think I am the most interesting thing in her world, in reality I'm competing against very interesting and smelly distractions. Teaching Sierra the value of sticking close to my left side and keeping eye contact really has helped us in the ring and when we're walking in new, interesting places."

Stephanie and Sierra use Side Sit and Heel on a daily basis in their apartment building, on the sidewalks, and even in subway and train stations. "We live in a dog-friendly building, but not all of the residents are dog-friendly. I've had a couple of people mention their fear of dogs to me in passing but compliment us on how well behaved she is. Sierra can get into 'rally' mode anywhere we go, and I've had other dog owners come up to us and ask how we get her to walk so well on leash. Once a man even asked me if she was my service dog!"

reward, but with a "surprise" treat from your pocket or treat pouch.

TIP: Avoid rewarding from your right hand, as it tempts your dog to stand up and meet you halfway as you reach the treat around your body.

From There

This is how you can gradually fade the treats for Side Sit, depending on your dog's progress. Completely fading out treats is often a process taking weeks, not days.

High school: For "easy" Side Sits on familiar, quiet streets, you can swap the treats for enthusiastic praise and the permission to cross the street. (No Sit, no crossing.) You can also start to ask for Side Sits in more distracting situations. When working on any behavior at a new, more challenging, level, reward for every correct response. For example, when asking for a Side Sit on that same street corner just as school has gotten out and kids are running like wild animals in all directions, the treat reward will help keep your dog focused.

College and beyond: Continue fading the food rewards in more challenging scenarios, such as noisy streets, pet-supply stores, or crowded farmers' markets. Your dog will tell you—by breaking the Sit—if he's being asked to do something too hard.

SIT/DOWN/SIT
Advanced • Sports

Prerequisites: Side Sit, Down
Used in: Rally

Want to spice up your Sits? This version of "puppy pushups" is also a rally exercise. In the show ring, it involves the handler and dog walking to the sign, where the dog does a Side Sit, then lowers into a Side Down, and then goes back to the Side Sit before walking off again. It's a great exercise for periods when you're asking your dog to remain in one spot for more than a few seconds, such as when waiting at a crosswalk or for an elevator. Sit/Down/Sit has added value because it forces your dog to listen to your cues carefully rather than just guess what you might want.

Keep in mind that some dogs, due to age or health, are not good candidates for Sit/Down/Sit. If your dog is resistant to this training exercise, look for physical causes.

Sit/Down/Sit is useful for dogs who:

- are confused by the difference between "sit" and "down" cues
- are physically active
- get easily bored or antsy
- would benefit from some basic strength building

HOW TO DO SIT/DOWN/SIT, PART 1

If your dog isn't familiar with a Side Down, follow these steps.

1. Ask for a Side Sit. A reward is not necessary here.
2. Pause and ask for a Down. If your dog has never lain down from the side, use a treat to lure him "from nose to toes," just as when you first taught a face-to-face Down.
3. Mark and reward your dog while he's in the Down position and then release with "OK." Get four-for-four with a food lure.

Part 1, Step 1: Lizzie starts with Phineas in a Side Sit.

Part 1, Step 2: She cues the Down. Luring is also fine.

Make Sits, Downs, and Stays Fun

Part 1, Step 3: She will mark and reward from her left hand.

4. Get rid of the lure, using an empty hand to cue Down. After you mark, reward from your pocket or treat pouch, using your left hand to reward. (If you treat from the right hand, you'll be reaching uncomfortably far.) Get four-for-four.
5. Gradually make your visual cue less dramatic so you do not have to reach all the way to the ground.

HOW TO DO SIT/DOWN/SIT, PART 2

Once your dog can comfortably do a Down to your left side, follow these steps.

1. Start from the Down position. Don't reward the Down.
2. Ask for a Sit. Your dog may be hesitant at first, so, if necessary, help him by placing a food lure at his nose and *slowly* leading his head (and body) up into a Sit.
3. Mark and reward in the Sit position. Get four-for-four by luring.
4. Use an empty hand to cue the Sit. Mark and

reward from a pocket or pouch, using your left hand.

5. Put it all together. Ask for Sit/Down/Sit. Reward your dog at different times within the sequence. Sometimes reward a Down, sometimes a Sit. This motivates your dog to listen carefully and wait for cues instead of simply predicting a behavior chain once you say Sit.

From There

Increase the difficulty by practicing in many different environments. Here are some examples.

High school: Practice during your walks, when there are no major distractions nearby.

College and beyond: Practice when there are moderate distractions nearby, such as crosswalks—but don't stop there. Incorporate this and other rally behaviors into an impressive Heel sequence! (See Chapter 4.)

Part 2, Step 2: Lizzie lures him into a Side Sit. Note the treat in her hand.

Part 2, Step 3: She will reward him at the completion of the Side Sit.

  ## SIT/WALK AROUND AND DOWN/WALK AROUND
Advanced • Sports

Prerequisite: Side Sit or Side Down
Used in: Rally, freestyle

This exercise builds up your dog's ability to stay while you walk in a circle around him. It's used primarily in rally but can be easily adapted to a freestyle routine. It's not easy for a dog to remain in a Sit (or a Down) while his handler is moving, especially when this person walks behind him. Many dogs rely on eye contact from the handler when training, but this form of Stay teaches the dog that he needs to remain in the position even when the person is out of his line of vision. Teaching your dog to stay when you move around is a very practical skill, for instance, when you need your dog to stay while you briefly leave the room, when you'd like your dog stationary on the sidewalk while you search through your bag or answer your phone, when you drop a plate of food and need your dog to keep still while you clean it up, and so on.

You can practice this exercise in either a Sit or Down.

Sit/Walk Around and Down/Walk Around are useful for dogs who:

- rely on your eye contact to remain in a Stay
- lack general impulse control
- are easily distracted
- are "Velcro dogs"

HOW TO DO SIT/WALK AROUND AND DOWN/WALK AROUND

1. Ask for a Side Sit (or Side Down) with the dog in Heel position to your left.
2. Say "stay" and flash the traffic-cop hand signal.
3. Walk around your dog in a counterclockwise circle. As you walk, let him gnaw on a treat from your left hand.

   TIP: If your dog is short, and you have difficulty reaching down to feed him as you circle, consider a treat that squeezes out of a tube. This gives you several extra inches. Your pet-supply store may carry a squeezable edible filling in a container that resembles a toothpaste tube or a large lip balm container. (You can also make your own.) Let him lick the food as you walk in a circle.
4. Once your feet are back in the original Heel position to your dog's right, pause as you let him finish the treat. Release with "OK."
5. Next time, repeat the sequence but introduce the treat one step later: say "stay" and take one step around your dog before feeding him the treat during the rest of the steps.
6. With each successful repetition, introduce the treat later and later until you can get all the way around him and then reward.

   TIP: If your dog can't hold still, go back to the last level at which he was successful and get four-for-four before increasing the difficulty.

Step 2: Kate cues the Stay (while Beans seems to be giving a cue of her own).

Steps 3-6: Kate walks counterclockwise around Beans. (To see how to feed while walking, check out Call Front Return to Heel on page 128.)

Beans may keep her "good" eye on Kate, but she shouldn't break the Down.

Step 4: Because Beans was able to stay as Kate circled her, she gets her reward at the end, before being released.

From There

High school: Practice each D separately. For instance:

- Duration: Circle your dog more than once.
- Distance: When safely off leash or on a long line, vary how wide the circle is.
- Distraction: Practice at intersections while the walk sign is red.

College and beyond: Combine the three Ds, ensuring that you continue to gradually raise the level of difficulty.

  STOP AND STAY 911
Advanced • Manners

Prerequisite: Stay

Used in: Freestyle

You might see variations of Stop and Stay in freestyle routines; for instance, during a pause in the music, the dog and handler hold a cute pose. Stop and Stay also has numerous practical applications, particularly in an emergency. You've just dropped your sandwich on the floor—don't panic! Tell your dog to stop and stay right where he is while you clean up the mess. Outdoors, it can be a lifesaver, too. Imagine that your dog has escaped from his harness and is running toward the road; you can tell him to stop and stay. Or even when leashed, after your dog does his business, you crouch down to pick it up, but he starts walking away. Rather than let him drag you down the street, tell him to stop and stay.

This sequence is more advanced than it may appear. All of the aforementioned cases involve two elements: the Stop and the Stay. The Stop asks the dog to halt his motion. The Stay here is an advanced version that builds upon the basic-level Stays from earlier in this chapter. Here, the handler crouches down (for example, to pick up an item) at a distance from the dog, a situation that requires a significant amount of impulse control.

Stop and Stay 911 is useful for dogs who:

- lack impulse control, especially around items dropped on the floor
- have not yet mastered Leave It or recalls
- go off leash in parks or on hikes
- are curious or lack concern for their own safety

HOW TO DO STOP AND STAY 911: PART 1

First, teach your dog how to stop on cue. You will be gently tossing a treat, so use your dominant hand for this activity. Choose a treat that your dog can easily see.

1. Your dog starts by your side, in no particular position. Toss a treat a few feet in front of you. While your dog is pursuing the treat, wedge a new treat between any two of your fingers.
2. As your dog walks back to you, say "stop!" and quickly reach your palm above your head, as if doing a high five with a very tall person.
3. When your hand reaches the high-five position, immediately toss the treat so it falls behind your dog. (Steps 2 and 3 are part of the same motion.)
4. Set up the next repetition as your dog goes to find the tossed treat.
5. Practice until you get four-for-four reps in which your dog is actually stopping his motion briefly as you say "stop" and reach up.
6. With each successful rep, pause a little longer before tossing the treat when your hand is in the air. The sequence is: say "stop"/high five/pause/mark and reward by tossing the treat.

    TIP: If your dog struggles at any point, go to an easier level (in this case, a shorter pause) and get four-for-four before proceeding.

HOW TO DO STOP AND STAY 911: PART 2

Now that your dog will stop on cue, we'll add the Stay.

1. Ask your dog to stay as in the Basic Behaviors section of this chapter. In this case, your dog may remain standing.

Stop, Step 2: Kate has a treat between her fingers. Batman, intrigued, has stopped.

Stop, Step 3: A moment later, Kate tosses the treat behind Batman.

2. Take a few steps away and bend your legs. Return to your dog to mark, reward, and release.

   TIP: If he was unable to stay still when you crouched, bend your legs a little less next time and get four-for-four before proceeding.

3. With each repetition, increase one criterion slightly. You can adjust:

   ■ **Distraction:** bend down a little lower,
   ■ **Distance:** move farther from the dog,
   ■ **Duration:** increase how long you remain in the crouched position.

4. Once your dog can handle you bending down to touch the floor, repeat the sequence but gently drop an item before you bend down. You can start with a boring item, like a coaster, and work your way up to really enticing items, like treats and toys.

From There

When your dog can do both Stop and Stay reliably, it's time to combine them.

High school: Face your dog and ask for a Stop. Then, ask for a Stay as outlined above.

College: Gradually increase the distance between you and your dog before you cue Stop.

Grad school and beyond: Practice in distracting areas, such as a park.

With time, your dog may be able to respond using only the Stop cue. Feel free to drop the Stay cue if you no longer need it.

Stay, Step 4: Kate bends down and drops a treat.

She returns to Batman to mark, reward, and release.

PEEKABOO
Advanced • Sports

Prerequisite: Sit

Used in: Agility, freestyle

This technique is used by many agility competitors to get their dogs in a specific spot at the start line. Peekaboo also makes a cute addition to a freestyle routine. It teaches your dog to approach you from behind and sit directly underneath you, between your legs. In addition to being an adorable trick, this position has practical benefits. It builds trust between you and your dog, as your dog has to get into a potentially vulnerable position, sitting between your feet and under your torso. This style of Sit reinforces how awesome it is to be close to you. Start training this indoors or in an enclosed outdoor area where you can work off leash.

Peekaboo is useful for dogs who:
- lack impulse control around your body (e.g., jumping on you)
- need help gaining confidence around your body

HOW TO DO PEEKABOO

1. Stand with your legs spread apart. Throw a treat a few feet directly behind you. Your dog will chase the treat.

2. Bend your torso down so you can see your dog from between your legs. Once the dog has eaten the treat, call him back to you while holding a treat between your legs. Your hand will look as if you are pointing between your legs, with a treat between your thumb and pointer finger. (Don't look over your shoulder or twist your torso to one side. You want to connect with your dog only through the gap between your legs.)

3. When he reaches your hand, he gets the treat. Get four-for-four.

   TIP: Some dogs are afraid to go between your legs. Start by spreading your legs and

Step 3. Fever comes through for a treat. Note Sarah's hand and body position, as described in Step 2.

Step 4: From here, she asks for a Sit.

tossing treats here and there around your feet. Once your dog is comfortable eating those treats, shape him getting closer and closer to you. When you eventually extend your hand with the treat, he doesn't have to come through your legs at first. Gradually reward closer and closer to the point between your legs.

4. Repeat the sequence but, when he reaches your hand, cue him to sit. Reward while he's in the Sit position. Get four-for-four.

5. This time, repeat the same sequence, but omit the Sit cue. Simply wait for your dog to offer the Sit on his own. Get four-for-four.

6. Next, add a new verbal cue. You will say "peekaboo" (or the cue of your choice) before calling your dog and completing the sequence. Get four-for-four.

7. Now only use "peekaboo" (or the cue of your choice) without calling your dog. Get four-for-four.

8. Eliminate the treat between your legs and now use an empty-handed pointing gesture. Reward from your pocket, treat pouch, or other hand.

From There

High school: Rather than throwing a treat behind you, wait for your dog to walk a short distance away from you and surprise him with "peekaboo." Practice this in a quiet location.

College: Take it on the road (or, rather, the sidewalk). This can be practiced on leash and, when safe, off leash. Start with a relatively quiet outdoor spot. When you try it in this new location, start from Step 7, using the treat lure. This will set him up for success.

Grad school and beyond: Practice in the vicinity of distractions, starting with very mild ones. This teaches your dog that, even when there is another dog across the street, he can have more fun interacting with you.

CHILL
Advanced • Tricks

Prerequisite: Down

Chill is the more innocuous name for "play dead," where the dog lies flat on his side as if sleeping. While this falls under the "trick" category, teaching a dog to lie on his side is actually an excellent way to encourage him to relax himself. Dogs aren't always the best at self-calming. This means that, once a dog gets worked up after seeing a squirrel, hearing the doorbell, or noticing you refilling the treat jar, he keeps bouncing off the walls for several minutes. But you can help your dog calm down by asking him to engage in a calm behavior. Chill puts your dog in a relaxing position on his side, which in turn leads to relaxed feelings.

Chill is useful for dogs who:

- don't think to chill on their own
- have trouble relaxing after getting wound up
- need help remaining still during grooming, nail trims, or vet visits

This behavior uses a combination of luring and shaping. It's unlikely that your dog will flop

USE CHILL FOR GROOMING AND MORE

Does your dog dislike nail trims, ear drops, or grooming? Teach him to chill while you perform these necessary functions. Follow the steps for Chill and then very gradually introduce the ear drops or other tool. The first several sessions will probably involve asking for Chill while just showing your dog the ear drops. After that, increase it to a Chill while gently touching the bottle to his ear, and so on. Make sure to give lots of amazing treats when asking your dog to stay still for something so invasive.

all the way onto his side the first try, so you will shape the behavior, meaning you'll reward for closer and closer approximations of the desired behavior. You can work with four-for-four, but as with other behaviors, some dogs catch on quickly and can proceed faster. Other dogs might need more than four good reps to feel comfortable at each level.

HOW TO DO CHILL

1. Ask your dog for a Down.
2. With a treat, slowly lure your dog's head toward one of his shoulders.

   TIP: If your dog is already leaning on one hip, take advantage of his position. For instance, if the dog is lying with his left hip to the floor, turn his head toward his right shoulder.
3. When your dog's nose gets close to his shoulder, mark and reward with his head still turned.
4. Once Steps 1–3 are smooth, repeat the lure but wait for your dog to turn his head a bit more or shift his weight on his hip. Mark and reward while he is in the desired position.
5. Once your dog willingly shifts the weight in his hips, continue your lure around to the dog's withers. Mark and reward as he turns his head and shifts his weight to the side even more.
6. Now wait to mark and reward until he has fully rolled onto his side.

   TIP: Remember to keep your own energy in check. When asking your dog to perform a calm behavior, make sure that your voice and body language are soft and reassuring.
7. Once you can reliably lure the dog to lie on his side, begin to place the reward on the floor in front of the dog. This will encourage him to keep his head low to the floor.
8. After four-for-four, when the dog is in the desired position, calmly reward on the floor

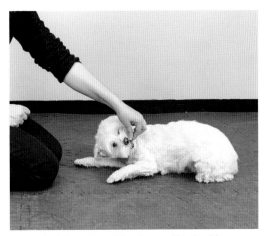

Step 2: Lizzie lures Trevor's head toward his shoulder.

Step 5: Trevor is now shifting his weight to one side.

Step 6: Trevor is in the Chill position and rewarded there.

with one tiny treat, then a pause, then another tiny treat, pause, treat.

9. Eventually your dog will realize that it is easier to eat with his head down than while holding it up. When your dog puts his head all the way down on the floor on his own, jackpot! Mark the behavior and calmly give him five or six tiny treats on the floor in front of his nose, rapid-fire.

10. Once you can get the full behavior, give the verbal cue "chill" right before you start luring the dog. Get four-for-four.

11. Fade the lure. You can have a treat in your luring hand, but your dog never actually gets it. Treat from your other hand, as if it's a surprise. Get four-for-four. Next, get four-for-four by cuing with an empty hand, rewarding from your other hand. Finally, you can fade out how dramatic your hand gesture is, little by little.

From There

High school: Practice at home when your dog needs to take a break for a moment. For instance, alternate a short game of Fetch and then Chill. You can also ask your dog to chill when you have company over and he is underfoot.

College and beyond: Use Chill when trimming nails, giving your dog ear drops, getting a vet exam, and so on. (See sidebar on page 72.) Because these might be highly stressful activities, reward your dog throughout the experience as frequently as needed to keep him in the desired position.

  ## ROLL OVER
Advanced • Tricks

Prerequisite: Chill

Once your dog can do Chill, he is already halfway to rolling over. Some dogs take to this trick naturally, even preferring it to a regular Down. Other dogs need a slower introduction

to rolling over, especially when gravity starts to assist them in flipping from one side to the other. For these dogs, be sure to work at their pace and avoid the temptation to push them (literally) too fast. There are some dogs, due to conformation, health, or other reasons, that are not comfortable rolling over. This is fine. For this or any other behavior, if it causes your dog any pain or extraordinary stress, skip it and spend your time on the behaviors he truly enjoys.

Roll Over is useful for dogs who:

- need a polite way to interact with guests or children
- are active

HOW TO DO ROLL OVER

1. Start from a Down position.
2. Follow the directions for Chill, up to Step 5, so your dog's weight is shifting onto one hip.
3. Continue your lure around the dog's withers and down to the floor, as if your lure is circling his head. You will likely need to shape this in several steps, luring just a hair farther each time. Ultimately, he will roll over to follow the lure.
4. When your dog rolls all the way over, mark and place the treat on the floor in front of his face. Rewarding here will encourage him to complete a full rollover instead of stopping in the middle. Get four-for-four or practice until it's smooth.
5. Add the verbal cue "roll over" right *before* you start to lure.

From There

High school: Do the same sequence but with an empty hand. Treat from your other hand or your pocket. For the first few repetitions, give a few extra treats to teach your dog how much cooler it is now that you have an empty cue hand.

College: Fade the visual cue. Over time, gradually make the circling gesture less dramatic.

Step 2: Sarah uses the lure to encourage Hank to shift his weight.

Step 3: She continues luring in a circular direction around his head...

...and around he goes!

Grad school and beyond: Encourage friends and family to practice this trick. This is a big crowd-pleaser, especially with kids, so teach your dog that "roll over" means the same thing no matter who is saying it.

  SPLAT
Advanced • Tricks

Prerequisites: Down and Chin Rest

Splat is a trick that requires a fair amount of impulse control from your dog. He will be lying Sphinx-style as in a typical Down, but with his chin resting on the ground. Therefore, your dog should be familiar with Chin Rest in Chapter 5 before starting Splat.

Splat is useful for dogs who:

- don't easily relax on their own
- have trouble calming down after getting wound up
- lack general impulse control

HOW TO DO SPLAT

1. Ask for a Down. You can praise, but do not give a treat yet.
2. Practice several repetitions of Chin Rest, with your hand inching slightly lower each time, until your knuckles can rest on the floor.
3. Give the Chin Rest cue, placing your hand on the floor between your dog's front paws.
4. When your dog rests his head in your hand, mark and reward by placing or holding the treat on your cue hand so he eats it from the Chin Rest position. Release with "OK." Get four-for-four.
5. Add the verbal cue "splat" (not "chin" anymore) before placing your hand on the floor. Mark and reward as before. Get four-for-four.
6. Give the Splat cue, mark, and hold the treat on your hand as before. Don't let him eat the treat yet (though he can nibble at it). Gently

slide your hand out from under his chin and place the treat reward on the floor. The goal is to reward the dog at ground level, right in front of his nose.

TIP: You might have to shape this by sliding your hand out slightly farther each time until you rely only on your verbal cue.

From There

You can make Splat more challenging by increasing one of the three Ds: duration, distance, and distraction.

High school: When your dog is in the Splat position, pause for one second before releasing with "OK." After four-for-four, increase to two seconds, and so on.

College: Cue Splat from a few inches away from the dog. Get four-for-four and then increase the distance between you by a few more inches.

Grad school and beyond: Ask for Splat in slightly distracting or exciting environments. For instance, alternate short periods of play or activity with a quick Splat.

Step 2: Start from a Chin Rest. Sarah will drop her hand a little lower with each successful rep.

Step 4: Sarah places the reward on her forearm so that Fever can eat it while she's in the desired position.

Step 6: Sarah has changed the cue and removed her hand, rewarding on the floor.

Voila! Sarah has a (temporarily) relaxed Border Collie.

03
RELIABLE RECALLS

What is your biggest fear as a dog owner? If you're like most of us, you shudder at the thought of your dog slipping from his harness and running off, getting smaller and smaller until he's completely out of sight. Prevent this from happening by teaching your dog a solid recall from day one. Even the most docile dog can get loose while taking a walk, or sneak through your front door, or jump over your backyard fence. You need to know that he'll come back to you even when he's excited or distressed.

When your dog has distanced himself from you, as in the off-leash dog park or after slipping from his harness, your first response is probably to call "come!" At that point, your dog has a choice: to comply with your cue or to ignore you. The farther away he is from you, the harder it will be for him to choose you over the other exciting things in the environment. Furthermore, if he is aroused or stressed, responding to your cue may be quite a challenge for him. Before you find yourself in this kind of emergency, make sure you've taught your dog that coming to you is *always* the best choice. Yes, even at the dog park! Coming when called should be second nature to your dog.

Recall is a necessary skill in many dog sports. Most sports—rally, agility, freestyle, disc dog, barn hunt, some scent work exercises, and others—are done off leash and require reliability amid distractions. Imagine the importance of a solid recall when your dog is in the ring or in the field, surrounded by new sounds, sights, smells, and temptations. Therefore, even the basic recall games in this chapter have practical applications to a number of sports.

Whether you plan to pursue sports or simply want to take your dog to the park, the goal is to make recall a fun, rewarding activity. Dogs run toward owners they trust, not owners they fear. Therefore, there are two rules to follow when teaching your dog recall.

1. Start simple, with basic recall exercises. At first, recall should appear to be a game that your dog can easily "win." And when he wins, he wins big by getting an extremely high-value reward. Gradually introduce more distance and distractions in your recall exercises in such small increments that your dog doesn't even notice you've upped the level. By doing this, your dog will learn to choose you regardless of the distance or distraction.

2. Whenever your dog comes to you, make sure you welcome him with a positive attitude and a fantastic reward. This holds true even if he took his time coming to you or made a detour to sniff a shrub before reaching you. No matter how frustrated you are, do not punish him for a lackluster recall. Rather, celebrate that he came back to you, even if it wasn't how you would have liked, and promise yourself to practice it more in the future. A poor recall could indicate that your dog had negative consequences when he obeyed the Come cue in the past. Perhaps you scolded him for coming too slowly, and he is now

afraid of getting close to you. Or, after he came when you called him in the park, you immediately clipped his leash on and dragged him away from the fun. Dogs will quickly figure out if Come works in their favor or not. By always celebrating when your dog comes to you and rewarding for a job well done, you're ensuring that when your dog is off leash or in a dangerous situation, he'll choose you over the other options.

BASIC BEHAVIORS

These basic recall activities focus on having fun and building the communication and bond with your dog. Dogs, playful even as adults, respond much more quickly and enthusiastically when their owners approach training as a game rather than an obligation.

Depending on your dog's age, personality, and ability to focus, you might want to start training recall indoors. A young puppy or newly adopted adult dog is often overwhelmed by outdoor distractions, which makes training a challenge. By starting these recall games in your living room or hallway, you can teach him the principles (and rewards) of recall. It will be much easier, then, to transition these skills to outdoor environments.

CATCH UP WITH ME
Basic • Games

Used in: Rally, freestyle

This game is so simple that it doesn't even have a cue. Catch Up with Me is an effective warm-up to formal recall exercises because it teaches your dog that, even when there are distractions present, the best spot is the one by your side. By teaching recall as a game, you're working on an emotional level to win your pup's heart and earn his trust. Your dog can choose whether to come to you or to ignore you, and this game makes

his decision much easier. Catch Up with Me also lays the foundation for other behaviors. For instance, the Heel techniques used so frequently in rally and freestyle are dependent upon your dog being comfortable at your side. In fact, Catch Up with Me is an informal version of the Recall-to-Heel exercise used in rally. This game can also facilitate Fetch, as your dog will dart away from you to pursue something rewarding, but he'll be motivated to return to you right away.

Your dog should be either off leash (if safe) or on a long line, in a place where you can wander around without major distractions. Have two levels of rewards, for example, some of his dry food and a few pieces of hot dog. He will have to run away to find the dry food, but when he returns to you, he will get the hot dog. This teaches him that the most rewarding place to be is next to you.

Catch Up with Me is useful for dogs who:
- go to the dog park, go hiking, or visit other off-leash areas
- are reluctant to come up close to their owners
- like to play
- have a history of not coming when called

HOW TO DO CATCH UP WITH ME

1. Have two levels of treats hidden in your pocket. Stroll with your dog. If he is on a long line, do not forcefully keep him close; you want him to feel as if he's off leash.

2. Toss a low-value treat a few feet behind you. Your dog will turn back to get it. You keep casually walking ahead.

3. When your dog returns to your side, mark and reward with the high-value treat. Give him the treat next to your body so your dog has to come right up to you to eat it. *This is the place to be*, he thinks as he's right next to you.

   TIP: Want to prime your pup for Heel? Hold the high-value treat against your left leg so that your dog's head is in line with your pants seam. After giving him the treat at your side, pause and then give him another, and then pause and give another. Walk slowly as you do this. Now you're heeling!

4. Repeat several times as you walk. You will find that your dog is willing to run behind you for

Step 2: Kate throws a piece of kibble for Beans to find.

Step 3: "Hey, Beans, you're back!"

"Here's a piece of chicken!"

his low-value treat but has much more pep in his step as he runs back to you for the high-value treat.

5. End the game while your dog is still having fun. You want to leave him hungry for more.

From There

Increase the challenge by methodically increasing the distance and the distractions.

High school: In some cases, increase the distance. Use a long line to practice in low-distraction areas. Other times, practice in moderately distracting areas but keep the distance between you and your dog short.

College and beyond: Combine distance and distraction. Play the game in increasingly distracting areas, using a long line if the area is not enclosed. At the highest level, play Catch Up with Me when there are loud noises, delicious barbecue smells, or other animals nearby. Remember, a game isn't fun if the player always loses. In other words, avoid pushing your dog beyond his abilities. Only increase the difficulty if

he has successfully won the previous level of the game several times.

 **CHASE ME**
Basic • Games

This training game lays a solid foundation for recall and introduces the Come cue. Similar to Catch Up with Me, Chase Me teaches your dog how awesome it is to run toward you. It's a simple game that can be played off leash indoors or on leash outdoors. Start the game in an area with minimal distractions: inside your home, in your yard, on a very quiet sidewalk, or in a peaceful corner of a park.

Chase Me utilizes your dog's natural inclination to chase you. In the beginning, it will look more like playtime than a true recall, but that's exactly the point. You're training your dog on an emotional level so that he *loves* the word "come." To make this game even better, your dog will get a fantastic reward at the completion of the recall. The reward can be a tasty treat or a

RULES FOR CHASING

Does this scenario sound familiar? Baxter picks up your slipper. You gasp, "No, Baxter!" and promptly run toward him to rescue your slipper. Baxter, in turn, thinks, *Hooray! Game time!* and runs off with your kidnapped slipper, loving every second of this "can't-catch-me" game. Having learned that stealing your belongings leads to the most fun ever, he begins picking up items of higher and higher value to get a reaction from you. But what happens when he picks up your bottle of ibuprofen? Or when he finds a ball in the off-leash park and then gallops into the road?

Chase Me should always be a one-way street. While you should encourage your dog to chase you, never chase your dog. If your dog learns how fun it is to run away from you, it not only sets back your training but also puts your dog's safety at risk.

The next time your dog picks up your slipper, blow his mind and play Chase Me instead. Yes, actually run away from your dog! Because he's in game mode, he will likely chase you. Run toward an appropriate dog toy or the treat jar and then promptly "trade" the toy or treat for the slipper. If, however, he doesn't chase you, then ignore him entirely. His antics will not get a rise out of you. In this case, remove all inappropriate items from his reach and practice Chase Me with toy or food rewards in the house consistently to teach him the "right" game.

toy that you can then play with together (as in a Tug or Fetch game). We don't recommend using petting to reward this or other recall activities because an excited dog rarely wants to be petted.

Another purpose of Chase Me is to teach your dog to come right up to you. Some dogs play the keep-away game: when their owners say "come," they will run up to them but stay just out of reach. *Ha ha, you can't catch me*, they seem to say as they dart away from their owners' hands. Recall is useless if you can't actually catch your dog, so Chase Me will teach your dog that, in order to get his reward, he has to come all the way up to you and tolerate his collar or harness being momentarily and gently grabbed. By pairing the collar grab with a reward, he will learn that being caught is actually pretty great.

Chase Me is useful for dogs who:

- go to the dog park, go hiking, or visit other off-leash areas
- are reluctant to come up close to you
- like to play
- have a history of not coming when called
- have selective hearing or need to hear a cue many times before responding

HOW TO DO CHASE ME

If you practice this on leash, ensure that your dog is wearing equipment that will not cause any pain if he reaches the end of the leash. Have a really tasty treat in your pocket.

1. Stand next to your dog.
2. Get his attention by saying his name and then enthusiastically say "come!" once.
3. Start to run, playfully encouraging your dog to follow you.

    TIP: Your body language speaks volumes to your dog. Crouch a little as you run, clap, or use encouraging words like "yeah, let's go!" Avoid facing your dog, as face-to-face positioning can tell him to stop or stay away from you.

Step 3: Go, Beans, go! Kate's body language invites Beans to chase her at top speed.

Step 5: Kate rewards very close to her leg. If your dog is wearing a collar or harness, gently grab it with your other hand.

4. Run forward about ten steps. It doesn't matter if your dog runs a little ahead of you.
5. Stop running. Grab your reward and hold it against your leg at your dog's eye level. As your dog takes the reward, momentarily grab his collar or harness gently, and then let go.

If your dog is overly enthusiastic about his recalls, perhaps biting or jumping on you, you can practice a calmer version of this game.

1. Start with a Sit, and then say "come."
2. Run (or walk) only three or four steps to prevent your dog from getting too excited.

3. Finally, end on another Sit. When your dog is in the final Sit, he can have his reward and a gentle collar grab.

From There

When you step up the difficulty of Chase Me, you will be increasing either the distance between you and the dog, or the distractions present. Whenever you advance to a new level, be sure to reward the recall every time; however, you can throw in easy recalls once in a while, for which you give only verbal praise.

High school: Add distance. Stand several feet away when you ask the dog to come and then turn around, run away, and reward as before.

College: Add distraction. Practice in areas with more activity, such as a park with kids playing nearby. Start with very short recalls in the vicinity of the distraction.

Grad school and beyond: Combine distance and distraction. Remember to treat every time your dog performs a difficult recall.

  ## HIDE AND SEEK
Basic • Games

Prerequisite: Chase Me

We don't know who has more fun with this game, the dog or the human. Hide and Seek invokes such a playful attitude with us that it will naturally appeal to your pup. Be sure to start this game in an environment where your dog is comfortable and not distracted, such as your home or backyard. Because your dog is looking for you and not a treat, toy, or other scent, Hide and Seek is great way to remind your dog how "valuable" you are to him.

Hide and Seek is useful for dogs who:

- need to see their owners as a source of fun
- don't keep an eye on their owners' whereabouts
- like to play
- are motivated by their owners' attention
- have a history of not coming when called

HOW TO DO HIDE AND SEEK

1. With your dog occupied on a different activity, partially hide yourself behind a wall, piece of furniture, or something similar. Have a toy or treat reward with you.
2. Cheerfully say "come" and use repeated audible encouragement, such as cheering or clapping, so he can locate you.
3. When your dog finds you, immediately reward him by playing a game or giving him the treat.

From There

You can increase the difficulty in several ways, but increase only one criterion at a time.

High school: Gradually make your hiding places less obvious so your dog has to search a little harder. Remember to keep it fun rather than stressful.

College: Practice in more distracting areas, like a park. Bring a long line, which a helper can hold, for safety.

Grad school and beyond: Add more hidden people. Your dog can find you, and then another family member, and then another.

Get the whole family involved in Hide and Seek.

 **RESTRAINED RECALL**
Basic • Sports

Used in: Flyball, dock diving

This is a basic recall strategy intended to get your dog motivated to come to you. It's particularly useful for dogs with an *I'll come when I'm ready* attitude. Restrained Recall involves you calling your dog, but, for a moment, he's gently held back by a helper and therefore unable to reach you. This builds your dog's drive to get

Restrained Recall requires the assistance of a helper to hold your dog.

to you so that, when he is released, he comes bounding to you and feels an immense sense of relief. This gets him thinking, *Phew, I thought I would never get to you.* As with Hide and Seek, this game makes you more valuable to your dog.

If you've ever watched flyball or dock diving, you'll see the handler holding the dog back until

it's time for the dog's run. His energy is like a soda can being shaken, ready to burst. Just as when you crack open that can, when the handler releases the dog, watch out! That pup takes off full speed ahead, laser-focused on his target. Restrained Recall creates the same kind of energy, but, in this case, the target is you.

For this game, make sure your dog is wearing equipment that won't hurt or otherwise punish him for pulling. A soft back-clip harness is best. In this case, you actually *want* him to pull. If practicing in a public or unfenced area, keep your dog on a leash or long line for safety.

Restrained Recall is useful for dogs who:

- need to see you as a source of fun
- like playing with their owners
- take their time coming to their owners
- have a history of not coming when called

HOW TO DO RESTRAINED RECALL

1. A helper will hold your dog's collar or leash.
2. Get your dog riled up in whatever way he enjoys. A little roughhousing is fine here for most dogs.
3. Suddenly, run about 20 feet (6 m) away. (For easily distracted dogs, a shorter distance is better.) Your dog will likely try to run after you, but your helper will restrain him.
4. When you get 20 feet (6 m) away, turn to your dog and excitedly say "Fido, come!" Your handler will release your dog. Continue cheering and using inviting body language as he runs to you.

    TIP: If your dog veers off in a different direction, run away excitedly as in Chase Me. Your helper can also use the long line to keep him from running too far off course.
5. When your dog reaches you, celebrate! Give him a treat with one hand as you gently grab his collar in the other hand. This gets him comfortable with being grabbed.

From There

This is a useful game to play once in a while. You can gradually increase the distance between you and your dog as well as the level of distraction in the vicinity. Here are some examples of higher-level activities.

High school: Do recall past an alluring garbage can. Keep the distance short.

College: Do recall from 30 feet (9 m) away. Keep distractions low at first.

Grad school and beyond: Do recalls involving real-life elements of distance *and* distraction.

  ## HAND TARGET
Basic • Sports

Used in: Freestyle, parkour

This incredibly simple behavior has nearly limitless applications. Hand Target, in which the dog touches his nose to your outstretched hand, is a basis for recall exercises, tricks, and even polite leash walking past distractions. By teaching your dog to touch your hand, you are able to effortlessly (and without dragging) move him into whatever position you want: at your side, in front of you, and so on. Therefore, Hand Target is often used to teach behaviors for freestyle routines, in which dogs may weave between their handlers' legs, move from side to side, and perform numerous tricks. It can also serve that purpose—getting your dog in a certain position—for parkour.

Hand Target is useful for dogs who:

- have selective hearing with the Come cue
- engage in undesirable behaviors indoors: barking out the window, door dashing, jumping on forbidden pieces of furniture, needing to be redirected away from areas of concern
- need to be redirected away from nasty items on walks, such as garbage
- jump on people in public or inside their homes
- get focused on something up ahead and need to be reeled in

WATCH AND LEARN

To see this sequence in action, visit Kate's videos on bklnmanners.com. You'll find a basic Hand Target as well as a reliable Recall video that uses targeting.

- put on the brakes during walks and need a way to get moving forward

HOW TO DO HAND TARGET

1. Hold your index and middle finger barely 1 inch (2.5 cm) in front of your dog's nose, at nose level. Wait for your dog to touch your hand with his nose. He can touch anywhere on your hand.

   TIP: You can rub a treat on your fingertips to make them stinky for the first training session.

2. The moment he touches your hand, mark and reward with a treat from your other hand or pocket. Get four-for-four at about 1 inch (2.5 cm) away. If his touches are more like chomps, it's OK at this point.

   TIP: If your dog hesitates to touch your hand, just hold still and look at your hand. Your dog is likely to follow your eyes and figure it out. If he hasn't touched within ten seconds or so, remove your hand and start over from an even shorter distance.

   TIP: If your dog still won't touch your hand, go straight to Step 5. Some dogs struggle with stationary touches but can do them in motion.

3. Then, add the cue "touch" before showing your visual cue. So, the sequence is: say "touch"/show outstretched fingers from 1 inch (2.5 cm) away/dog touches/mark and reward. Get another four-for-four.

4. Start gradually adding distance, an inch or two (2 to 5 cm) per repetition. Put your hand

HOW TO USE A TARGET STICK

Got a stumpy dog? Or a bad back? All of that reaching down for Hand Targets can put a strain on your muscles. Rather than train in pain, you can teach your dog to touch a target stick instead. A target stick is a thin stick with a ball at the end of it; you can buy one or easily make one yourself. Simply teach your dog to touch the ball at the end of the target stick, and you will get the same result as a Hand Target without the strain. Here's how.

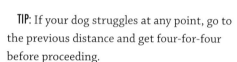

1. Rub a treat onto the ball of the target stick so that it smells appealing. Offer the stick about 1 inch (2.5 cm) in front of your dog's nose.
2. When your dog reaches out to investigate it, he'll bonk it with his nose. Mark and reward.
3. Remove the stick and offer it again at nose level until you get four-for-four.
4. Follow the steps for traditional Hand Targets to add distance.

2 inches (5 cm) from his nose, then 4 inches (10 cm), then 5 inches (12 cm). Make sure that your "touch" hand isn't higher than the dog's nose level.

TIP: Keep your hand still. Avoid "helping" your dog by pushing your fingers into his nose.

TIP: If your dog struggles at any point, go to the previous distance and get four-for-four before proceeding.

5. Once your dog is consistently doing Hand Targets from 1 foot (30 cm) away, start taking a few steps away to encourage him to run toward you to "touch." Now it's becoming a recall!

Step 1: Kate holds her two fingers very close to Beans, at the dog's eye level.

Step 2: The moment Beans touches Kate's hand, Kate will mark and reward.

From There

Slowly build the levels of distance and distraction. Here are some suggestions.

High school: When there are no distractions, practice longer-distance touches at home, in your yard, or in a quiet corner of a park.

College: Practice on leash when there are distractions in the vicinity, keeping the distance relatively short.

Grad school and beyond: Combine elements of distance and distraction, asking for long-distance touches while distractions are present.

During the learning process, rewards should match the level of difficulty. Once your dog has gotten to high-school-level targets, you can start to fade out the treats for elementary-school-level responses. Occasionally, reward these easy touches with a lot of praise rather than with food or a toy. On the flip side, when asking your dog to touch in a new or difficult environment, increase your rewards to something extra-tasty or cool. Be a supportive teacher!

  BETWEEN
Basic • Sports

Used in: Parkour, agility

For Between, you'll teach your dog to do a short recall between two objects, such as two shrubs or street signs. Since this simple parkour exercise focuses on distraction, the distance of a Between-style recall remains short and can even be done on a regular leash.

While the description here pertains directly to parkour, you've likely seen a more involved version of it in agility: weave poles. It's quite impressive to watch a seasoned agility competitor navigating weave poles at lightning speed, weaving back and forth between a series of 6 or 12 sequential poles spaced 24 inches (60 cm) apart.

Between is useful for dogs who:
- are uncomfortable around novel objects or tight spaces
- are easily distracted by the environment
- live in an area where long-distance recalls are hard to practice

If your dog is unsure around new objects or tight spaces, start this exercise with two movable objects, such as stools, boxes, or cones. Make the space between them so wide that your dog won't even notice. Then, when he appears comfortable at that level, bring the two objects a few inches closer, narrowing the gap.

HOW TO DO BETWEEN

1. Find two unassuming objects that you can space 3 or more feet (90 cm) apart. Think of them as goalposts with a relatively wide area between them for your dog to make a goal. Set your dog up directly behind the goalposts and ask for a Sit or another stationary behavior.

   TIP: Position your dog as close to the goalposts as possible so that the easiest path forward is right between them. If he is too far back, he may go around the objects (and not make a goal).

2. Position yourself right in front of the goalposts. Say "come" or encourage him to pass through the goal. Mark and reward when he's reached you. Get four-for-four.

3. If he appears totally comfortable with the previous steps, tighten the gap between the goalposts by a few inches. Get four-for-four and then tighten the gap another few inches.

4. Once your dog is reliably doing Between, you can change the cue to "through" instead of "come."

From There

Practice with a variety of objects in the real world. When introducing new objects, set your dog up

Step 1: Batman not-so-patiently waits while Kate sets herself up on the other side of the goal posts.

Step 2: When Kate says "come," Batman strolls through.

for success by spreading them wide apart at first, if possible, and closing the gap gradually. The difficulty will vary depending on the dog, but here is a sample progression.

High school: Practice Between with objects that are spaced tightly together.

College: Add distraction by practicing in bustling areas.

Grad school and beyond: Add distance by having the dog start from farther back. (Use a long line if needed.)

 **UNDER**
Basic • Sports

Used in: Parkour

Some dogs are natural crawlers, relishing the chance to squeeze under objects. This parkour exercise, which teaches your dog how to duck or crawl under an object, is tailor-made for such curious canines but can even be taught to tentative dogs. If your dog is unsure of obstacles or has physical limitations, start practicing this activity with tall objects so he doesn't have to duck at all. Similar to Between, this exercise keeps you only a short distance from your dog but builds his ability to come to you even in highly distracting environments.

Under is useful for dogs who:
- need to build confidence in the environment
- get bored with typical training routines
- have unreliable recalls around distractions
- live in areas where long-distance recalls are hard to practice

HOW TO DO UNDER

For this activity, you'll need to find or create an obstacle that has plenty of clearance over the dog's head to start but can gradually be brought lower. A broomstick laid and secured over two chairs or stools will suffice. Whatever you choose, make sure it is stable and won't injure or frighten your dog. Set it up so that the broomstick is several inches *over* the dog's head, so he won't have to duck at first.

1. Position the dog facing the obstacle and ask for a Sit or other stationary behavior. Get him as close to the broomstick as possible.
2. Position yourself on the other side of the obstacle and say "come" enthusiastically. Mark and reward after he goes under the broomstick to reach you. Get four-for-four.

   TIP: If your dog goes around the broomstick, you should still welcome him (because he did come, after all), but no treat. Position yourself and the dog closer to the broomstick next time, or use a barrier on the sides of the obstacle, so that the path under the broomstick is the best choice.

Play Your Way to Good Manners

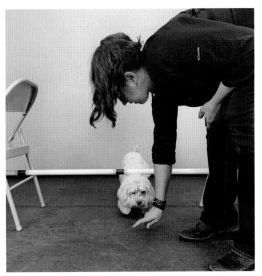

Step 1: Schoffie is in a Sit several feet behind the bar. (In the beginning, your dog should be right behind the bar.)

Step 2: Sarah asks Schoffie to do a recall under the bar.

3. Gradually lower the height of the broomstick until it is as low as the top of your dog's head. Get four-for-four at each clearance height.

4. Once your dog can reliably do Under, you can change the cue from "come" to "under."

From There

Choose your obstacles carefully to ensure that you don't ask your dog to duck under something that is unstable or too challenging for him.

High school: Practice with obstacles that are roughly the height of the dog's withers (the ridge between his shoulder blades) so that it requires a small amount of ducking.

College: Using the high-school obstacles, position your dog with more space between him and the object so that the recall is a little longer and takes more concentration. Meanwhile, practice on even lower obstacles, but keep the distance short.

Grad school and beyond: Practice on obstacles that are low, and position your dog with some extra space between him and the obstacle, so that he has to *choose* to go under, even if it is not the most convenient path to reach you.

ADVANCED BEHAVIORS

The activities in this section build on basic recall skills. Some are games that will make your dog love coming to you even more than before. Others are higher-level exercises used in sports training.

  RECALL PAST A DISTRACTION
Advanced • Sports

Prerequisite: Patience Pays Off

Used in: Rally, freestyle, agility, parkour

This version of recall has practical applications in several dog sports. As with Patience Pays Off, you are teaching your dog to listen to you even when there are temptations and distractions nearby. Imagine performing in the agility, rally, or freestyle ring, where a dog may be asked to do a form of recall while a crowd is watching and dogs are barking nearby. In such cases, the dog and handler need to have trained around a variety of distractions before stepping into the venue.

For your practice here, the distraction will be a tempting object in the vicinity of the dog, such as a toy or a treat on the floor. Should your dog try to approach the item, he will receive nothing. On

The agility course holds many distractions that a dog must ignore.

the other hand, if he listens to you and passes by that item, then he gets to play with the toy or eat the treat as a reward. It helps to have a training partner for this activity, but a one-person-only variation is also explained.

As with all training, avoid getting angry at your dog if he gives into the temptation. You want to give him the choice either to act impulsively and get nothing or to listen to you and get his reward. Let your dog be responsible for his learning process without unnecessary punishments.

Recall Past a Distraction is useful for dogs who:

- have short attention spans
- go to dog parks or other distracting places off leash
- are toy motivated

HOW TO DO RECALL PAST A DISTRACTION

The setup involves you, your dog, a helper, and an item to serve as a low-level "temptation." If you think a toy or treat will be too hard for your dog to resist, start with a boring household object.

1. Place the item on the floor between you and your dog. Your helper will stand next to this temptation, ready to prevent your dog from snatching the goodie.

2. Ask your dog to come, so he will have to run past the temptation on his way. You can make this easier at first by:
   - keeping the distance short,
   - placing the item off to the side, and/or
   - using a very low-value item.

3. If your dog goes for the temptation en route, your partner will gently block it with her body or pick it up. Continue calling your dog until he gets to you. Reward when he reaches you, even if the recall wasn't as smooth as you would have liked.

4. When your dog reaches you without trying to grab the temptation, cheer and reward generously! Then immediately say "get it," sending him to check out the item. Engage him in play with the toy or let him eat the treats. (If it's a household object, just let him investigate it.)

IF YOU'RE TRAINING ALONE

1. Use a very low-value item or a sealed treat toy that allows you to hide treats in a closed (e.g., Velcro) pouch. Place the item on the floor between you and your dog.

   TIP: You can get your dog into the desired spot by asking for a Stay or placing a few pieces of his food in that spot.

2. Ask your dog to come, so he will have to run past the temptation on his way.

3. If your dog goes for the temptation en route, remove it (provided your dog does not resource-guard). He just lost his chance to get that goodie. Reset and try again.

4. Your dog will soon realize that there is no benefit in racing toward the item. When you say "come," and he comes to you directly, reward him by exclaiming "get it" and running over to the toy to give him the treats inside.

From There

You can increase the difficulty by increasing both the level of distraction and the distance.

High school: Increase the distraction. This involves using higher- and higher-value temptations.

College: Increase the distance. Your dog will have to run farther to reach you.

Grad school and beyond: Once you have raised both distance and distraction separately, you can add them together, for example, by doing a long-distance recall past a really delicious treat.

  GO AROUND
Advanced • Sports

Used in: Parkour, agility

This fun exercise teaches your dog to run in a circle around an object, making it perfect for parkour. It is also used in agility to teach tight turns around jumps. Whether in an urban or rural environment, it should be easy to find an object to circle: a tree, a fire hydrant, a chair, or your friend. You won't circle the object with your dog but rather send him off to run around it and then return to you. The shape ends up being more of a teardrop pattern than a true circle. This is a practical behavior because it teaches your dog to run away from you (very briefly at first) and then come back. Therefore, it reinforces the underlying concept of recall without using the word "come."

Go Around is useful for dogs who:

- lose their focus when their handlers are at a distance
- have become desensitized to the word "come"
- have extra energy to burn (although, in this exercise, the handlers do not have to move much at all)
- don't have large areas to practice recall

This technique was introduced to Kate by parkour instructor Kristine Hammar. If practicing this on leash, choose an object that is shorter than your dog's withers so the leash won't get caught.

HOW TO DO GO AROUND

1. Approach the object head-on with your dog walking next to you. As you get to the object, you will "split" it, meaning that you and your dog will pass the object on opposite sides, with the object between you. Continue walking in a straight line past it.

2. After passing it, mark and reward. Get four-for-four.

3. This time, as you start to split the object as before, you'll stop your motion right next to the object. Your dog, expecting the treat, will walk a little past the object and then turn toward you, which will cause him to curve around the object somewhat. When he reaches you, mark and reward. Get four-for-four.

4. Very gradually add distance. Stop your motion a few inches before reaching the object so your

Step 4: Kate has stopped her motion before she reaches the bowling pin, cuing Go Around with her right hand and foot.

Beans makes the full teardrop-shaped circle, and returns to Kate for her reward.

dog will have to make a full U-turn around the object to reach you. Mark and reward when he reaches you. Get four-for-four.

   TIP: As you stop your motion, point your hand and foot toward the direction in which you want your dog to start the circle. Note Kate's body language in the photo, with right hand and foot pointing at about one o'clock, so Beans knows to circle counterclockwise.

5. Continue stopping earlier and earlier. Once you can stop about 1 foot (30 cm) in front of the object and cue your dog to circle it, add the verbal cue "circle."

6. Repeat the same sequence, starting with Step 1, but going clockwise. Use your other hand and foot to "point" to the object.

From There

High school: Gradually continue adding distance so that you are sending your dog off to "circle" from a few feet away and then celebrating when he returns. Additionally, you can add variety by circling different kinds of objects.

When approaching a new object for the first time, set your dog up for success by starting from Step 1.

   College and beyond: Practice this during times of mild to moderate distractions. Remember to keep the distance between you and the object short when practicing around new or intense distractions.

  FETCH (INCLUDING DROP IT)
Advanced • Games

Prerequisite: Chase Me
Used in: Rally, flyball, dock diving, disc dog
   Ah, Fetch. Elements of this fun game pop up in several sports. Rally includes a relatively sedate retrieve, while flyball has dogs doing a lightning-fast Fetch over a series of hurdles. Disc dog involves catching a frisbee in various athletic ways, and dock diving has dogs catch a dangling toy before splashing into the water.

   Fetch is one of the first games that owners want their dogs to learn. And while some dogs

ROUND AND ROUND

Once your dog knows how to do Go Around, you can double the fun by turning it into a Figure Eight! In essence, a Figure Eight is just a Go Around with an object to your right and one to your left. You will stand at the center point, where the two loops connect. This exercise is related to the agility version of a Front Cross.

How to Do Figure Eight

1. Both you and your dog will stand between two cones or other objects. Your dog is on your left side.
2. Face the cone to your right and cue your dog to run clockwise around it.
3. When your dog completes the circle, you can reward from your right hand. You want your dog on your right side to start Step 4.
4. Immediately turn 180 degrees to face the cone to your left. Cue your dog to run counterclockwise around it.
5. Reward your dog when he returns to you, in the center of the Figure Eight.

pick it up quickly and naturally, for many dogs, Fetch is a behavior that involves several layers of learning and no small amount of impulse control. After all, it contains elements of both recall and Drop It. For many playful dogs, the ball-chasing part comes easily, but, after that, it's the dog who trains the human to fetch the ball. If your pup hasn't grasped why it's rewarding to return to you with the ball, follow these steps to turn the tables.

Fetch is useful for dogs who:

- love toys
- steal items and run off
- need more outlets for running (without you having to run as well)
- need to learn the benefit of dropping items

HOW TO DO FETCH

1. Start Fetch in a controlled indoor area or in a confined, quiet outdoor space.
2. Have a ball (or toy) that your dog really loves. Get your dog super-excited about it by waving it around.
3. Throw the ball or toy a few feet away.
4. Once your dog picks it up, invitingly run away

from him, as in Chase Me. Clap your hands and use your voice to encourage him to follow.

TIP: If your dog tries to entice you to chase him, resist! When he runs away, game over. Say "oh well" and walk away. The only way the game can continue is if he chases you, not the other way around.

5. When your dog runs toward you with the ball and drops it near you, immediately pick up the ball and throw it again. His reward for bringing it back is continuation of the game.

TIP: Avoid using treats, petting, or other rewards for this game, as it takes the focus away from the ball. Also avoid telling your dog to "sit" or "wait" before throwing the ball. All of these things will only interrupt the flow and confuse your dog.

If your dog will chase the ball but won't bring it back to you, try the following steps. It's critical to first teach your dog that returning to you with the ball results in more fun. Don't focus on him dropping it yet; just reinforce the recall. If you grab the ball before he's ready to let it go, you risk teaching him the opposite of what you want: that you are a rude toy-stealer whom he should avoid.

1. Get your dog excited about the ball (or toy) and then throw it a very short distance.

2. As long as your dog is interacting with the ball, praise him and encourage him to come back to you.

   TIP: The moment he starts to ignore the ball, stop the praise.

3. If he comes back to you with the ball, verbally praise him and happily bounce around with him, letting him know what a smart dog he is for bringing his toy to you. You may even play a little game of Tug (if using a long toy), but do not ask for a Drop It yet. Your dog might stop coming back to you if he thinks you'll take his treasured toy away.

4. Eventually, and it might take a while, your dog will drop the ball on his own. At that point, pick it up and tease him with it. Make him chase it while you hold it in your hand, and then throw it a very short distance again.

5. Once your dog will willingly drop the ball for short-distance Fetches, throw it a little farther.

6. You can name the ball-dropping with the verbal cue "drop it." Say "drop it" right before you know your dog will spit out the ball.

7. Always stop the game before your dog loses interest. For example, if you know you can keep him interested for five tosses, stop the game after the fourth toss. This will build his drive for the game and leave him wanting more.

   TIP: Put the ball away after the game, which will make the item special. This also builds drive.

   TIP: You can also have two similar balls. When your dog brings the first one back but refuses to drop it, you can tempt him with the second ball. As soon as he drops ball number one, you throw ball number two.

Step 1: Navin gets Ella excited about the toy...

...and throws it a very short distance. He then encourages Ella to return.

Step 3: He praises Ella for bringing the toy back, and they play a bit.

TEACHING FETCH TEACHES FOCUS

Behold! You're witnessing the rare sight of Ella at rest. Most of the time, this girl is on the go. Ella, a two-year-old mystery mutt, is as sweet as pie but has a particularly short attention span. This has made training a challenge for her dedicated owner, Navin. Much like gifted but unruly students who flounder in school, Ella struggled to learn manners in the traditional way. And, like those students, Ella has ultimately thrived by finding her niche: sports. As Navin explains, "Sports are the entry point she needed for training to make sense and be purposeful for her."

When it comes to challenging behaviors, you could say Ella was well-rounded. Prone to both excitement and fear, she had a penchant for leash pulling and was also easily startled by objects in the environment. Add that to her difficulty focusing, lack of impulse control, and playful mouthiness, and you can imagine what a walk down the street was like for Navin (who also owns a completely chill, completely blind Pit Bull mix, Bandit).

Ella's sports of choice are disc dog and agility, and both have helped immensely with her general manners and emotional well-being. Disc dog has reduced her mouthiness by teaching her the value of fetching and then dropping items. This has even had practical benefits; Ella's sock-stealing tendencies have morphed into a polite game of Go Get Your... (as in Chapter 6), so she can now help with picking up laundry rather than destroying it.

In agility, practicing a Stay at the start line has helped her with self-control in the presence of excitement. Agility has also helped build her confidence around new and strange objects. Navin says, "Instead of assuming that objects are only scary, she seems to have learned that sometimes unfamiliar things end up being a source of great fun!" Thanks to the clear communication and strong bond that Ella and Navin have developed, she is much more enthusiastic and responsive to his training efforts in general.

From There

As with other kinds of recall, you will increase the difficulty by extending the distance and adding distraction.

High school: When you play Fetch, throw the ball a little farther each time. Also, if you have been running away from your dog to encourage him to return to you, start fading out how far you run. The goal is to be standing still while the dog returns to you.

College and beyond: Play Fetch in the presence of distractions,

such as at the park. Be mindful of any other dogs around you, as a flying ball can trigger a dog's resource guarding tendencies, leading to potential fights.

RECALL TO PEEKABOO
Advanced • Sports

Prerequisite: Peekaboo
Used in: Freestyle

As the name implies, this exercise combines recall and Peekaboo. It starts with your dog behind you. You will call him to you, and, rather than come to your side, he will pop his head between your legs for a Peekaboo. Cute! You can imagine how this would complement a freestyle routine.

Recall to Peekaboo is useful for dogs who:

- play "can't catch me" or dislike being grabbed by their collars
- enjoy being challenged
- are suspicious of or bored by straightforward recalls

HOW TO DO RECALL TO PEEKABOO

1. Sprinkle a few treats in a cluster on the ground. While he is eating the treats, turn your back on him and walk one small step away.
2. Say the cue "peekaboo" and reward.
3. With each successful repetition, increase the distance between you and your dog by a few inches.

   TIP: If your dog struggles to do Peekaboo, it may mean that you've increased the distance too quickly. Shorten the distance for him to reach you.

From There

High school: Continue increasing the distance of the recall.

College and beyond: Practice in the presence of increasing distractions.

GO TEAM
Advanced • Tricks

Prerequisite: High Ten

Go Team is essentially a High Ten (as in Chapter 5) with the dog standing on his hind

CAPTURE THE BEHAVIOR

Is your dog a jumper—the kind who greets everyone by leaping on them? You can put your dog's natural enthusiasm to good use. Capturing is a technique in which you let the dog perform a behavior on his own —Sit, Down, Spin, or Go Team—and mark and reward while he is doing it. Capturing the behavior you want (in this case, jumping on you) is a great way to put that behavior on cue. This means that your dog can channel his jumpy energy appropriately by performing Go Team when asked, which, in turn, can reduce or even eliminate unwanted jumping. Follow these steps.

1. Approach your dog in a way that encourages him to jump on you.
2. When he jumps up, take one step back and offer your flat palms as in High Ten.
3. Your dog's paws should now land roughly on your palms instead of your torso.
4. Mark and reward your dog after making contact. He might be confused because he's suddenly being rewarded for a behavior that was previously forbidden.
5. Continue Steps 1–4 every time your dog attempts to jump on you until his paws are landing squarely on your hands.
6. As soon as he's about to jump, add the cue "go team" before bringing up your hands.

legs. It is innately rewarding for dogs who love to jump, giving them an appropriate outlet for their bouncy energy. How is this a recall activity, you ask? This trick is so fun that your dog will willingly run to you to perform it. He doesn't even see it as a recall exercise (and you probably didn't at first, either), which is why it works so well. Make sure to cheer and clap when he performs Go Team so he will always have a fantastic emotional connection to this trick.

Sometimes simple tricks can turn into useful life skills. Sarah's dog Fever loves to do Go Team because it's active and always ends in cheering and attention, all of which are highly reinforcing for Fever. One afternoon, Fever had a play session with her dog friend, Mojo. When it was time to go home, Sarah needed to get her back, but she knew that little could peel Fever away from her friend. Sarah decided to cue Go Team, and Fever immediately ran to her and put her paws on Sarah's hands. Recall complete!

Go Team is useful for dogs who:

- are active
- are suspicious of or bored by straightforward recalls
- respond well to hand signals

Fever shows her team spirit with Go Team!

HOW TO DO GO TEAM

1. Warm up with High Ten. Get four-for-four.
2. Ask for High Ten with one small change: offer the palm of your hands a bit higher than before so your dog has to stand on his hind legs to reach them with his front paws. Mark and reward. Get four-for-four.

   TIP: If your dog is hesitant to go up on his hind legs, encourage him to jump up by holding a treat or toy high over his head and reward him with it when he goes up on his hind legs. After four good repetitions, go back to Step 2.

3. Change the verbal cue. Say "go team" and then offer the palm of your hands as before.

From There

To turn this into a recall exercise, add distance to your trick.

High school: Increase the distance gradually, starting with your dog just a few inches away. If your dog is at a distance, make sure to get his attention first by calling his name, and then say "go team" and show your hands.

College and beyond: Practice when your dog is excited or mildly distracted. If you find he's more enthusiastic about responding to this than a typical recall, then you've got a winner. Go team!

04
GET THE MOST OUT OF LEASHED WALKS

Polite on-leash behavior is essential for enjoyable walks.

eash walking is probably the biggest challenge among our Doggie Academy clients—and it's no surprise. There are a million inappropriate things your dog can do on the walk: pick up sidewalk snacks, chase squirrels, refuse to walk home from the dog park, drag you from tree to tree, and so on. There is really only one correct thing the dog can do, in your mind: walk calmly next to you on a loose leash. The underlying problem is usually that, compared to all of the exciting distractions out there, you're just not that interesting to your dog. It's not necessarily your fault; how can you compete with an approaching Labradoodle or a discarded hamburger?

In fact, you *can* compete with these distractions. The primary goal of this chapter is to teach your dog that the best part of walking on leash is getting to interact with *you*, not with all of the other things out there. The more engaging you are toward your dog, the more he will look to you for guidance while on walks. This chapter

also addresses other issues related to walking, for instance, how to walk in a way that efficiently burns mental and physical energy, so you're walking smarter, not longer. You'll also learn techniques for reactive dogs, meaning dogs who tend to have an outburst or a negative reaction when confronted with a certain trigger, such as an unfamiliar dog approaching or a skateboard whizzing by.

Before we get started, make a decision about whom your dog will be allowed to greet while on leash. If your dog is not a polite leash-walker, it's critical not to let him greet anyone or anything that will push him "above threshold," meaning that he will get so excited or agitated that he starts jumping, pulling, barking, or growling. If your dog exhibits any of these behaviors, it is essential to keep him away from those triggers, at least until you have a training protocol in place. If your dog pulls or barks at, say, another dog, he is clearly not responsible enough to handle this interaction. "Saying hi" to that dog will only exacerbate the problem. Therefore, he should not be put in a situation where he will get the reward (or stress) of meeting another dog. Imagine if it were a teenager who was not yet responsible enough to drive. Every time she got behind the wheel, the car ended up in a ditch. Would you continue giving her the keys? We hope not. So, don't give your dog the keys, so to speak, unless you know he can behave appropriately, even in the presence of a trigger.

EQUIPMENT: YOUR FRIEND OR YOUR FOE?

Let's face it: sometimes life with a dog is hard. Here in Brooklyn, simply walking your dog down the street involves dodging chicken bones, changing routes abruptly to avoid the street-sweeping trucks, and weaving through gridlocked cars blocking intersections. If the outside environment won't cut you any slack, at least you can make your life easier by choosing suitable leash-walking equipment. Here are considerations for the most common collars and harnesses.

A **flat collar**, the traditional nylon or leather strap fitted around your dog's neck, is appropriate for dogs who don't lunge or pull. If your dog is a puller or a lunger, avoid these collars, as they can put pressure on your dog's trachea and esophagus. This may lead to serious potential health problems down the road. A **martingale** is a variation of a flat collar that tightens slightly as the dog pulls. It is beneficial for dogs with small heads, as they run the risk of slipping out of a traditional collar. In most cases, neither flat collars nor martingales will teach a dog to stop pulling, no matter how badly he chokes against the pressure of the leash.

The number of different **back-clip harnesses** can make your head spin. They all have one thing in common: a clip for the leash at the top, along the dog's spine. These harnesses are typically a safer alternative to flat collars. Dogs are less likely to slip out of a well-fitted harness or suffer damage from pulling. That said, a back-clip harness does nothing to prevent your dog from pulling, as any dog can easily transform into a sled dog by leaning into the harness with all of his weight. As a result, back-clip harnesses are not the best choice for pullers. Small dogs, however, do well in this

A traditional flat collar is fine for a dog who does not pull on the leash.

the leash doesn't get tangled under their little legs. Back-clip harnesses are also good for dogs who put on the brakes frequently, as they can't easily slip out.

If your dog is a puller, consider a **front-clip harness**, of which there are many choices. This type of harness has the leash attachment in the front, near the breastbone. As a result, whenever your dog starts to tug on the leash, the harness will gently pull his body back toward you,

It's hard for a dog to slip out of a back-clip harness.

reducing the intensity of his forward motion. The extent to which the harness mitigates pulling depends on the harness, the fit, and the strength of your dog. Some front-clip harnesses also have a clip on the back, for more options.

If your dog is a puller *and* a street-snacker, or if you've tried a front-clip harness with no luck, a **head collar** might be what you need. Fitted like a horse's halter, a head collar stops the dog's forward motion like a front-clip harness does. In this case, the leash attaches to the head collar under the dog's chin so, when he pulls ahead, his head turns toward you, stopping his forward motion. Because you have control of the dog's head, your dog is less likely to be stealing snacks from the sidewalk, too.

On the downside, while head collars do not inflict pain, some dogs find them uncomfortable and don't acclimate to them overnight. This means that you should thoroughly teach your dog how this equipment works indoors first, before walking your dog outside in it. Because you have control of your dog's head and neck, be extremely sensitive to his safety; don't ever yank the leash or let him lunge ahead, and do not engage in training activities involving speed or distance. A head collar is not appropriate for every dog, but if your pooch has not responded to other kinds of force-free equipment or eats street garbage, it could be the right choice.

Leashes also come in a variety of choices, some safer and more effective than others. For most activities, a standard 4-foot (1.2-m) (for tall dogs) or 6-foot (1.8-m) (for short dogs) leather or nylon leash is all you need. This no-frills type of leash gives your dog sufficient slack when he's reasonably close to you, and it tightens when he's reached the end. Within this category are leashes with traffic handles (an additional loop) for short-leash moments, leashes that light up, and so on.

Retractable leashes, on the other hand, are at best a nuisance and at worst a danger when walking down the sidewalk. Teaching loose leash walking becomes a challenge if the leash is never loose. Your dog can also get into all kinds of trouble if he's 20 feet (6 m) away from you and you have no quick way of reeling him in. When practicing the exercises in this book, use a 4- or 6-foot (1.2- or 1.8-m) leash.

A regular nylon leash in a length appropriate for your dog's size is good for most activities.

ATTENTION BEHAVIORS: BASIC

These exercises are all intended to get your dog's focus on you. There is no point asking Samson for a Sit or a Heel if he is completely absorbed in a passing squirrel. First, you need to teach him how to peel his attention away from that squirrel and focus on you instead. Once you can get your dog to acknowledge your existence on walks, you can get started on any number of the fun sports, games, and tricks in the following sections.

  ### WALK WITH ATTENTION
Basic • Sports

Prerequisite: Check Me Out
Used in: Rally, freestyle

Usually the biggest obstacle to polite leash walking is teaching your dog that you're on the walk, too. Walk with Attention is similar to Check Me Out, as it rewards the dog for choosing to make eye contact with you. By looking up at you occasionally, your dog will automatically be walking on a loose leash because he won't be so immersed in the other sights and smells of the outdoors. With practice, your dog will develop a default behavior of frequently checking in with you; this is incompatible with sidewalk snacking, pulling, or squirrel chasing. Once you have your dog's attention, you can teach him any number of more advanced techniques on walks.

Practicing Walk with Attention will set your dog up to grasp the more advanced walking techniques used in rally and freestyle. On a rally course, dog and handler walk next to each other from one sign to the next. The dog needs to have his full attention on the handler throughout the course, which is important because, starting at the intermediate level, dogs perform the course off leash. Freestyle routines also incorporate a lot of loose leash walking (also without the leash). In fact, there is a form of freestyle called heelwork to

SEE IT IN ACTION
To see Walk with Attention in action, check out Kate's leash-walking videos at *bklnmanners.com*.

music, the routines of which are built upon a foundation of Walk with Attention.

Walk with Attention is useful for dogs who:
- need to walk with their owners, on leash or off
- get distracted by things in the environment
- have strong reactions (either positive or negative) to other animals, people, cars, bikes, and so on
- don't think to check in with their owners frequently
- are sidewalk snackers

Before you start Walk with Attention, it's important to hold the leash in a way that facilitates your training. This is a stationary activity, so keep your feet planted in one spot.

HOW TO HOLD THE LEASH WHEN TRAINING

1. Choose which side your dog will be on. If you walk on sidewalks with a lot of foot traffic, consider starting with your dog on the right so your body can act as a barrier between him and other passing distractions.

   TIP: You might be thinking, But I heard the dog should be on my left side! We recommend teaching a dog to walk on both sides of you, as done in freestyle and agility. See the Heel sidebar later in this chapter.

2. Have treats in your hand, pocket, or treat pouch on the same side as the dog.

3. Hold the bulk of the leash, with a little slack, in the hand opposite the dog. If your dog is on your right, hold the leash in your left hand. You can also use your right hand to direct the leash when needed, but once you are teaching Walk with Attention, it won't

be necessary. Holding the leash in the far hand feels unnatural at first, so start this exercise indoors.

4. Give your dog a few "freebie" treats from the hand that is closest to him. This is critical because it teaches your dog that goodies come when he is glued to your side. Avoid treating from your far hand; as you sweep your hand across your body to treat, your dog will gladly meet you halfway, ending up in front of you. That's both dangerous (especially for small dogs) and counterproductive.

HOW TO DO WALK WITH ATTENTION

1. Start the activity standing still, without walking yet. Have your dog on leash at your side. (Here, we will choose the right side.) Have a handful of treats in your right hand or pocket, and the leash in your left hand.

2. Talk gently to your dog, saying whatever comes to mind. A cheerful tone is more important than the words. You don't want to use one specific cue, because then he will only think to look at you when you've cued him. So avoid repeating the same word (like his name); choose a new word or sound each time.

3. The second he looks up at you, mark and reward by giving him a treat from your right hand. Give the treat right next to your leg so he learns that this position is the place to be.

4. Repeat this until he is consistently offering eye contact. Any time he looks up at you, mark and reward from your right hand. He is starting to learn how unbelievably awesome it is to check in with you.

5. Now, choose a quiet place indoors or outside to start walking with your dog on your right. Talk cheerfully to your dog or make a variety of chirping or clucking noises. Any time your dog looks up at you, mark and reward from your right hand. Reward every look he gives

When Beans looks up at Kate, she will mark and reward. Note how Kate's leash is in her left hand, leaving her right hand free to reward.

you, even the ones when you're not talking to him. (These are the best ones! He is learning to check in on his own.) Remember to reward very close to your leg.

TIP: If your dog doesn't look at you outside at all, start by practicing indoors.

6. Practice in short intervals, about twenty to thirty seconds at a time. Take a break to sniff, stroll, or jog, and then practice again. If your dog looks to you when he's "on break," reward the heck out of him. Good choice!

TIP: Practice this on the left side, too.

From There

Once your dog starts to learn the game in a quiet environment, he might be checking in with you all the time, which means that you can graduate to higher levels of distraction. As your dog moves up to high school, you can gradually fade out the treats for elementary-school-level check-ins, rewarding mainly with praise. Remember to always reward when practicing in a new or particularly distracting environment, in relation to his current level.

High school: Practice Walk with Attention outside around mild distractions. Reward every look with a treat. Meanwhile, reward mostly with praise (and occasionally a treat) for eye contact in areas with zero distraction.

College: Practice in more crowded areas where you will have to walk past pedestrians, other dogs, cyclists, and so on. Body block, using your body as a barrier between your dog and the distractions, if needed. Reward every look with a treat. Meanwhile, reward mostly with praise (and occasionally a treat) for eye contact in areas with zero or mild distraction.

Grad school and beyond: Take a field trip to a bustling train station, farmers' market, or street fair, or go for a walk in the woods, surrounded by chipmunks, birds, and other little critters. Reward as needed.

 WHERE'D YOU GO?
Basic • Games

Used in: Agility, rally

This is in the "game" category because, like many games, its purpose is to keep the players on their toes. For many dogs, their walks become monotonous: the same boring streets with the usual dogs, the same shrubs to pee on, and so on. By practicing Where'd You Go? with your dog, your movements become unpredictable, so your dog will learn to pay attention to where you're going. This activity turns your surroundings into an obstacle course, so you'll have to stay on your toes, too!

In agility, the dog needs to be in tune to where his handler is and what she is cuing. At the same time, he must be aware of his own speed and direction. It's a balance known as *handler focus* versus *obstacle focus*. A dog that focuses

only on his handler may run off course or injure himself, while one that is too absorbed in his own movements may miss the handler's cue.

Where'd You Go? is useful for dogs who:
- walk with their handlers on leash
- forget that their handlers are walking with them
- get distracted by things in the environment
- get caught around street signs or other obstacles

HOW TO DO WHERE'D YOU GO? GAME 1

1. With your dog on leash, start walking quickly. Keep the leash loose. Be aware of your hand position; you don't want to unintentionally create leash tension.

Where'd You Go? encourages your dog to pay attention to you on walks no matter what happens.

2. If your dog darts ahead of you, immediately change direction to surprise him. Do this right before the leash tightens so that your dog will cause the leash tension if he does not change direction with you. (For very active dogs, you might be doing this repeatedly. Try not to get dizzy!)

3. When he changes direction with you, it is OK but not necessary to reward with food. The loose leash is a reward in itself. This

exercise teaches the dog that if he's not paying attention to where you are, he'll be left wondering, *Where'd you go?*

HOW TO DO WHERE'D YOU GO? GAME 2

1. When you see an obstacle—such as a street sign, fire hydrant, or tree—move around it unexpectedly. If your dog moves around it with you, praise him! If he doesn't, allow the leash to get stuck around the obstacle and let your dog figure out how to get unstuck. You want your dog to backtrack around the obstacle (which is not easy for him), so don't give him enough leash to move forward and entangle himself more.

   TIP: As he backs up, take up the slack on the leash so that he can't go forward again. This process might take time for your dog to figure out, and that's fine.

2. Once your dog is unstuck, go right back into walking quickly to find your next obstacle.

3. Surprise your dog in this way frequently and randomly. He will realize he needs to pay attention to your every move to avoid getting stuck.

From There

Play this game a few times on each walk, choosing different obstacles each time. The goal is to be spontaneous.

ATTENTION BEHAVIORS: ADVANCED

  HEEL
Advanced • Sports

Prerequisite: Side Sit

Used in: Rally, freestyle

Heel is a more formal version of Walk with Attention. Your dog is close to your body at your left side. Like Walk with Attention, Heel is the basis for a number of rally and freestyle exercises. It also has a number of practical applications: walking through intersections, safely getting past distractions (such as food on the sidewalk, other dogs, and skateboards), walking in bustling public areas, going to the pet-supply store, and so on. In essence, Heel is perfect for any time you need to keep closer tabs on your dog and ensure that he is safely by your side. We don't recommend heeling for your entire walk, as it allows your dog little freedom while requiring his full attention on you. Plan to use Walk with Attention for the majority of your leashed (or even unleashed) walking time, using Heel as needed here and there.

Heel is useful for dogs who:

- take walks in crowded areas
- are sidewalk snackers
- are reactive to other animals, people, or moving objects
- are easily distracted
- need to build their focus on their handlers
- plan to do rally or freestyle

HEELING: IT'S NOT JUST FOR LEFTIES ANYMORE

In rally, dogs are taught to heel on the left side of their handlers. This is the traditional style of heeling and is still how many dogs are trained. But why?

It goes back to the old days, when soldiers and hunters carried weapons while walking with their dogs. Since most of us are right-handed, a sword or gun can be held more easily in the right hand. For practicality, then, dogs were kept on the left. But since most of us don't carry swords on our morning dog walks (or so we hope), do we really need to walk Fido on the left?

No way! You can choose on which side you'd like your dog to heel. Better yet, teach Heel on both sides. Dogs who practice freestyle and agility learn to heel on both sides, depending on the handler's needs at each moment. For the typical pet dog, especially a city dog resigned to narrow, crowded sidewalks, it's good to know he can line up with you on either the right or left, whichever is safest at that moment. Kate's dogs, Batman and Beans, generally heel to the right, as this keeps their tiny bodies to the outside of foot traffic. Should some tasty sidewalk snacks appear on the right side, however, Kate will ask them for a Front Cross and then a Heel on her left.

Though the leash-walking exercises in Chapter 4 instruct you to teach Heel on your left, you are welcome to teach a right-side Heel instead. Just make sure you switch all of the "lefts" in the instructions to "rights," and vice versa.

There are many ways to teach Heel. This style of Heel teaches your dog to walk with his ear roughly in line with your hip. Be extra aware of your body's movements as you teach Heel, because your body language may offer many unintentional (but useful) cues to your dog. Do you always step off with your left foot? Do you lean forward a bit when you start walking? Do you lean back when you stop? What are your shoulders doing? All of these details can provide useful information to your dog down the road, when you teach him to heel more quickly, more slowly, as you turn to the right or the left, and so on.

This method of Heel also prepares you for the rally-inspired exercises that follow. As such, the following steps for Heel have your dog on the left, but you can choose a right-side Heel if you prefer.

HOW TO DO HEEL

Consider starting this activity indoors without the leash so that you and your dog get the feel of Heel without distractions.

1. The dog is on your left side. Your leash (if you use one) will be in your right hand, as with Walk with Attention. In your left hand, hold a few treats in a loosely closed hand near your belly button. Your treats should be readily accessible, but avoid luring your dog.

2. Start from a Side Sit and then take two steps forward. (If your dog doesn't follow, use your voice to encourage him.)

   TIP: Take off with the left foot each time you start Heel. The more consistent your body language, the clearer the sequence is to your dog.

3. As you finish your second step, if your dog is still at your side, mark and reward while he is in the Heel position. The desired position is with the dog at your side, facing the same direction as you, with his ear at about the seam of your pants.

   TIP: If your dog surges out in front of you, stop moving and calmly lure your dog back

Sarah rewards Hank when his ear is roughly at her hip.

into Heel position, as in Finish Left. Do not reward, though.

  TIP: If your dog can't walk alongside you for two steps, start with a single step.

4. Get at least four-for-four correct sequences. (More than four repetitions might be necessary to get the feel of Heel.)

  TIP: Make sure that the leash is loose whenever your dog is in Heel position. If your leash tightens because your dog is moving away from you in any direction, continue practicing with just one or two steps for as long as needed.

5. Repeat the sequence but, this time, take three steps before marking and rewarding. Get at least four-for-four.

6. Once your dog is clearly following you for these few steps, you're ready to add the verbal cue "heel" before you step off. So the sequence is: Side Sit/say "heel"/walk for three human steps/mark and reward in the Heel position.

7. Get rid of the treats in your hand but continue to reward from a pocket or treat pouch on your left side. Practice the same sequence as in Step 6 but with an empty hand. Get four-for-four.

  TIP: Continue rewarding from your left hand, as it reinforces the appropriate position from the dog. Rewarding from your right hand will encourage the dog to try to cross in front of you.

8. If your dog is short, have you been bending down to teach Heel? If so, with each repetition, bring your body up a few inches until you're in a natural walking posture.

9. After each successful Heel, add one more step to the next rep. At this point, you don't need to get four-for-four at every distance; nevertheless, if your dog struggles to stay focused at, say, ten steps, reduce your Heels to seven or eight steps and get four-for-four.

From There

There are two components of a solid Heel: the distance you cover and the distractions present. Here is one way to break it down.

  High school: Focus on adding distance in low-distraction areas. A good goal is roughly the distance needed to cross a street.

  College and beyond: Practice short Heels in areas with increasing distractions. As your dog's ability to heel strengthens, combine distance and distraction.

  You may also wish to drop the Side Sit. In the beginning, the Side Sit is helpful because it gives you time to collect yourself before stepping off. Once your dog is heeling smoothly, it's fine to cue the Heel from a stand or a walk.

SEE IT IN ACTION!

Check out Doggie Academy's YouTube channel and Facebook page (@doggieacademy) to see demonstrations of some of the training behaviors in this book.

FINISH RIGHT AND FINISH LEFT
Advanced • Sports

Prerequisite: Side Sit
Used in: Rally, freestyle

This rally-inspired move gets your dog into a Heel position to your left side, and it does so with a little flair. Imagine that your dog is walking in front of you, and you'd like him to line up by your side on cue. Finish Right and Finish Left give you two options for how to achieve this. With Finish Right, your dog starts off in front of you, facing you. You ask him to move to your right side, and then he circles behind you until he ends up on your left in Heel position. Finish Left has the dog approach you from the left side and then flip himself around so he's facing the same direction as you. Both allow you to easily set your dog up for a Side Sit or Heel from there. This behavior is a rally staple, and you can find variations of it in freestyle routines.

Finish Right and Finish Left are useful for dogs who:

- tend to walk in front of their owners
- pull or lunge toward things
- are working on Heel or Side Sit
- need to build their focus on their owners

HOW TO DO FINISH RIGHT

1. Start with your dog facing you. Have a treat in each hand.
2. With your right hand, lure your dog around your right side and behind you. Let him eat the treat behind your back.

    TIP: If your dog is reluctant to go behind you, treat him more frequently. For instance, give him a treat when he reaches your right side and then again when he is behind you.

3. Your left hand picks up where the right hand stopped. Reach your left hand behind you and lure your dog into Heel position at

Step 1: Benah and Kodi start by facing each other.

Step 2: Benah lures behind her with her right hand.

your left side. At the completion of this 270-degree turn, mark and reward. Practice until it's smooth.

    TIP: Too much reaching? Got a short dog? Consider a series of nose touches with a target stick instead. (See the sidebar in Chapter 3.)

4. Fade the lure. First, remove the treat from your right hand, so you are sweeping your right hand behind you but not treating. Only reward at the completion of the behavior

Step 3: With her left hand, Benah lures the rest of the way to a Heel position.

Kodi can have the treat in Heel position.

from your left hand. Once that's smooth, do the whole sequence empty-handed and then reward from your pocket or treat pouch, using your left hand.

5. As your dog gets proficient at this, you can fade how dramatic your visual cue is and add a verbal cue such as "around" or "finish" right *before* you point.

HOW TO DO FINISH LEFT

1. Start with the dog facing you. Have a few treats in your left hand.

2. Lure your dog toward your left side. As you "pull" him to your left, continue drawing your hand behind you, passing your hips. If your dog is medium- or large-sized, step back with your left foot, too, so you can reach farther back. Treat here, while reaching back, if needed.

   TIP: If you plan to do proper rally, you'll eventually have to fade out your foot movement. The handler's feet should not move as the dog does Finish Left.

3. Now, lure your dog into a U-turn toward you so he ends up facing forward. If you had stepped back with your left foot in Step 2, bring your foot back to its original position.

4. Once you're both lined up, with your dog next to your left hip and facing the same direction as you, mark and reward from your left hand. Practice until it's smooth.

5. Get rid of the lure; your hand movement now becomes a visual cue. Add a verbal cue such as "line up" right *before* you point.

Step 1: Benah and Kodi start by facing each other.

Step 2: Benah steps back with her left foot as she lures Kodi behind her.

Step 3: Kodi makes a U-turn toward her.

From There

You can add complexity by combining this behavior with other behaviors, as well as by adding distractions.

High school: After your dog has completed the Finish, ask for either a Heel or Side Sit. Keep in mind that your dog will be working hard to perform more than one behavior, so reward accordingly.

Step 4: Benah brings her left foot back to its original position, and Kodi gets his reward.

College and beyond: Practice these sequences in the presence of mild distractions. For instance, if you see some street garbage up ahead, do Finish Right or Finish Left to get your dog into Heel position and then heel past the garbage.

  BACKWARD HEEL
Advanced • Sports

Prerequisite: Heel
Used in: Freestyle, rally

In freestyle routines, sometimes you will see the handler and dog heeling... backward! This behavior also makes an appearance in rally. Walking backward on cue is a bit awkward for many dogs at first, so you'll reward even the slightest step back in the beginning.

Backward Heel is useful for dogs who:

- tend to hurry
- pull or lunge toward things
- need to learn that they have hind legs, too
- need to build their focus on their handlers

HOW TO DO BACKWARD HEEL

1. Start by standing with your dog in Heel position on your left. You are on the dog's right side, and a wall or fence should be on his left. Your body and the wall will act as barriers to keep him backing up straight.

2. Hold a treat a bit over his head, as if you are pulling it from his nose toward his ears. Shift your weight back as you do this.

   TIP: If he sits down, simply take a step forward to get him back into standing position.

3. As soon as he takes a small step backward to follow the treat—even if he moves just one paw a little—mark and reward with that treat.

4. Gradually shape the behavior. At first, reward any shift or step backward. Next, wait for a slightly bigger step before marking and rewarding. Continue like this until your dog is offering multiple steps backward (which means that you will be walking backward, too).

5. Add the verbal cue "back" and then present the treat over his head. Get four-for-four at this level.

6. Start fading the lure and develop a hand signal instead. Put the food in between your thumb and forefinger. After saying "back," open and close your fingers as though waving your dog backward. Get four-for-four.

7. Repeat Step 6, but with an empty hand. It is now a cue, not a lure. Reward from your pocket or pouch, using your left hand.

From There

High school: Gradually fade the presence of the wall by giving your dog more and more space on his left side. While fading the wall, take only a few steps back so your dog remains straight.

College and beyond: Practice Heel Backward at different paces: normal, slow, and fast.

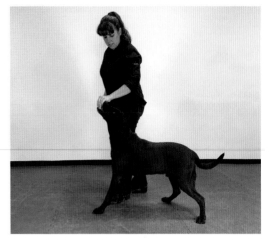

Step 3: Sarah marks and rewards Hank as he shifts his weight back. Notice how her lure is slightly above and behind his mouth. Practicing this against a wall will keep your dog straight (but makes for unclear photos!).

Step 6: Your cue can be a wave backward, with your fist opening...

...and closing.

 **MAKING TURNS**
Advanced • Sports

Prerequisite: Heel

Used in: Rally, freestyle

In rally and freestyle, turns make up a significant portion of the course or routine. Turns include right turns, left turns, about turns (180 degrees), 270-degree turns, and 360-degree turns. Is your head spinning just thinking about it? These turns can be integrated into your walks as well. Imagine how monotonous it is for your dog to walk in a boring old straight line down the sidewalk on every walk. It's no wonder he starts to drift off and look for his own fun. By surprising your dog with the occasional turn, you will keep him from getting bored, which consequently keeps him from getting distracted. Practicing these turns also encourages your dog to stay within loose leash range. If he's too far ahead or behind, he's not able to turn with you, so he has an incentive to stay close to your side.

Following are the steps to do a number of different turns. You can mix and match them on your walks to keep things interesting. In proper rally, the turns are not pivots; your motion continues as you turn. However, the turns should be tight enough for handler and dog to fit roughly inside a hula hoop. Recreationally, you can choose how tightly you want to turn.

Making Turns is useful for dogs who:

- are bored by simpler walking exercises
- have to walk the same route every day
- get stressed on walks and need diversions
- tend to hurry
- pull or lunge toward things
- are sidewalk snackers
- need to build their focus on their handlers

HOW TO DO 90-DEGREE RIGHT TURN

The dog needs more speed than you do for a right turn, and he has to cover more ground than

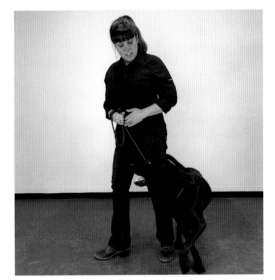

Sarah's feet and shoulders show Hank it's time for a right turn.

you do to complete the turn. Therefore, you'll simultaneously slow your own pace through the turn while encouraging your dog to increase his speed.

1. Have your dog in a Heel, moving straight ahead.

2. A moment before you turn, you can give your dog a verbal heads-up by saying "this way" or encouraging him to pick up the pace.

3. Plant your left foot and swing your right foot 90 degrees to turn. This creates a smoother turn and prevents you from accidentally kicking your dog as you turn. As long as your shoulders move in the same direction as your right foot, your dog should know to follow your body.

4. If your dog has stayed in the Heel position through the turn, mark and reward right next to your hip as he completes the 90 degrees.

TIP: If your dog does not turn with you, use a food lure to encourage him. Right before you start to turn, put a treat in front of his nose and spin his head along with your body. Reward after the turn is complete.

HOW TO DO 90-DEGREE LEFT TURN

For this turn, you will cover more ground, so the dog will have to slow down and bring his back end in.

1. Have your dog in a Heel, moving straight ahead.
2. A moment before you turn, you can give your dog a verbal heads-up by saying "this way."
3. Start your turn by stepping into it with your left foot. Be careful not to kick your dog as your left leg swings around the turn.
4. As you turn, pull back your left shoulder and arm, which tells your dog that you are turning toward him.

   TIP: If your dog leaves your side while turning, use a lure to turn his head to the left while applying gentle leash pressure to hold him close. This will encourage him to turn his back end more while remaining at your side, leading to a tighter, cleaner turn.

Sarah's body language, especially her left shoulder, tells Hank a left turn is coming.

5. As long as your dog has remained in the Heel position through the turn, mark and reward right next to your hip as he completes the 90 degrees.

HOW TO DO 180-DEGREE RIGHT TURN

This turn is a continuation of 90-Degree Right Turn. You will make a clockwise U-turn, ending up walking in the opposite direction. This is a good way to get your dog away from a sticky situation by turning around.

1. Follow the steps for 90-Degree Right Turn, continuing your motion until you have made a 180-degree U-turn. Stay aware of your feet so you don't trip your dog.
2. As long as your dog has stayed in the Heel position through the turn, mark and reward right next to your hip as he completes the 180 degrees.

HOW TO DO 180-DEGREE LEFT TURN

Building upon the 90-Degree Left Turn, you will make a counterclockwise U-turn and end up facing the opposite way. You will be walking faster on the outside as your dog slows or even stops moving through the turn.

1. Follow the steps for 90-Degree Left Turn, continuing your motion until you have made a 180-degree U-turn. Hold your position as you circle to your left. Stay aware of your feet so you don't trip your dog.
2. As long as your dog has remained in the Heel position through the turn, mark and reward right next to your hip as he completes the 180 degrees.

HOW TO DO 270-DEGREE RIGHT TURN

While this is a turn to the right, you actually end up to the left of your original position. Imagine a compass. You start from the south and walk northward, then curve clockwise to the northeast, east, southeast, south, southwest, and exit the curve when walking westward.

1. Follow the steps for 90-Degree Right Turn, continuing your motion until you have made a 270-degree turn. Stay aware of your feet.
2. As long as your dog has remained in the Heel position through the turn, mark and reward right next to your hip as he completes the 270 degrees.

270-Degree Right Turn   270-Degree Left Turn

HOW TO DO 270-DEGREE LEFT TURN

This is the opposite of the 270-Degree Right Turn. You will turn counterclockwise, to the left, until you end up walking toward the right side. If it were a compass, you would start at south, heading northward, and then curve northwest, west, southwest, south, southeast, and finally exit heading eastbound.

1. Follow the steps for 90-Degree Left Turn, continuing your motion until you have made a 270-degree turn. Stay aware of your feet so you don't trip your dog.
2. As long as your dog has remained in the Heel position through the turn, mark and reward right next to your hip as he completes the 270 degrees.

HOW TO DO 360-DEGREE RIGHT TURN

If you haven't spun yourself out yet, it's time to try 360-Degree Right Turn, making an entire

clockwise circle. Your entrance and exit point of the circle will be the same.

1. Follow the steps for 90-Degree Right Turn, continuing your motion until you have made a full circle. Stay aware of your feet.
2. As long as your dog has remained in the Heel position through the turn, mark and reward right next to your hip as he completes the 360 degrees.

HOW TO DO 360-DEGREE LEFT TURN

This is a full counterclockwise circle.

1. Follow the steps for 90-Degree Left Turn, continuing your motion until you have made a full circle. Stay aware of your feet so you don't trip your dog.
2. As long as your dog has remained in the Heel position through the turn, mark and reward right next to your hip as he completes the 360 degrees.

From There

High school and beyond: Practice these turns when there are distractions present. Start with mild distractions and work up to bigger ones.

 **TWO FEET ON**
Advanced • Sports

Prerequisite: Stay
Used in: Parkour, freestyle

This is the first of many dog parkour exercises that can transform how you and your dog walk together. Unlike other exercises that directly address walking and heeling, parkour works more organically; it teaches your dog that you're not a barrier to his fun outside, but instead that you hold the keys to the most enjoyable activities. Two Feet On can also make an appearance in freestyle if props are involved; imagine a dog putting his front paws on a platform, chair, upside-down bucket, or other object.

As the name implies, your dog will learn to put his two front paws on an object. Start with a low, inviting item, like a large folded towel. From there, you can apply this skill to horizontal objects like tree stumps, ledges, or stairs, and then vertical objects such as fire hydrants, walls, or tree trunks.

Two Feet On is useful for dogs who:

- need help focusing on their owners rather than on distractions in the environment
- need help building confidence in the outside world
- always have extra energy to burn
- get bored on walks

If the obstacle is higher than your dog's elbow, official parkour rules require you to support him by holding the leash above him with gentle pressure to ensure that he doesn't slip or fall. Use a back-clip harness and leash that can support your dog's weight; that means no Velcro fasteners and no equipment that puts pressure on his neck.

HOW TO DO TWO FEET ON

1. Find a low, stable object that your dog can comfortably get his two front paws on. (A towel, book, or tree stump will work well.)
2. Lure or encourage your dog to put his two front paws on the object. You may point to the object or pat it with your hand, but do not drag him or manually place his paws on the object against his will.
3. Mark and reward with several treats in a row while his paws are on the object, to show him how cool this activity is, and then release with "OK." Get four-for-four.
4. Add the verbal cue "paws" right before encouraging him onto the object. Get four-for-four.
5. Add duration on the object, little by little. Once he's on it, add a one-second Stay. Mark, reward, and release.

Step 5: Batman stays with his front paws on the object. Kate supports him with a back-clip harness and leash.

From There

High school: Once your dog can comfortably put his paws on several different low objects, ask your dog to hold his position for slightly longer and longer. A good goal is three to five seconds. (If you plan to practice parkour officially, switch your reward sequence so that you release and then reward, as dogs can't be rewarded while on an obstacle.)

College: As your dog's confidence grows, ask for Two Feet On with slightly higher, less stable, or less spacious objects. Always use your leash to spot and support your dog.

Grad school and beyond: Practice Two Feet On with vertical objects, like a wall. Depending on his comfort level, ask for a three- to five-second Stay.

 **FOUR FEET ON**
Advanced • Sports

Prerequisite: Stay
Used in: Parkour, agility, freestyle

This is quite similar to the previous exercise and carries all of the same behavioral benefits. (It also has the same safety precautions.) The only difference is that your dog will put all four paws on an object and remain stable for three to five seconds. But Four Feet On is not just a common parkour behavior; it's also used in agility, where the dog must stay on a pause table for five seconds. Freestyle could even incorporate Four Feet On if the routine uses any kind of platform as a prop.

HOW TO DO FOUR FEET ON

1. Find a low, unassuming object with a platform on which your dog can comfortably get all four paws. Start with an object much larger than your dog's dimensions.
2. Lure or encourage the dog to put all four paws on the object. You can tap on the object or encourage him with your voice; just don't drag him or place him on it against his will.
3. It's OK if he sits once he's on the object. While he's still on the object, mark and reward with several treats in a row, to show him how

Step 5: Batman is adding duration to his Stay. Kate continues to gently support him until all four paws are back on the ground.

cool this activity is, and then release. Get four-for-four.

HELP! MY DOG IS AFRAID OF THE OBSTACLE

Parkour is a great way to build confidence in dogs who are cautious around new things. In some cases, though, the dog is afraid to approach or interact with the object. It could be a platform you'd like him to put his paws on, a fence you'd like him to crawl under, or any number of other "scary" objects. How should you proceed?

First, avoid coercing or tricking your dog into approaching the object in any way. This means no picking up the dog and putting him on or near it. You should also avoid luring your dog all the way onto or under the object. Luring can be an effective strategy in teaching new behaviors, but, if fear is involved, it can backfire. When you lure a fearful dog to do something he wouldn't otherwise do, he may be following the treat because he can't resist it, but it does not mean that he is relaxed and willing. Once on the obstacle, he may feel even more afraid and, furthermore, may lose faith in you as his trusted teacher.

What you *should* do is let your dog interact with the obstacle at his own pace. Do the free-shaping activities in Chapter 1 with the object. These games allow the dog to get as close as he feels comfortable, without coercion or expectations. Because he can choose how intimately he wants to interact with the obstacle, he will ultimately view that object and any related training with a more confident attitude.

4. Add a verbal cue, like "step up," right before luring or encouraging him onto the object. Get four-for-four.

5. Add duration on the object, little by little. Once he's on the obstacle, add a one-second Stay. Mark, reward, and release.

From There

High school: Practice on increasingly smaller objects, with platforms ultimately smaller than your dog's body length so he has to balance more carefully. Keep the height of the obstacle and duration of the Stay very short at first.

College and beyond: Combine challenges, one small increment at a time, such as decreased size of the obstacle, increased height of the obstacle, and increased duration of the Stay (up to five seconds). (If you plan to practice parkour

officially, switch your reward sequence so that you release and then reward, as dogs can't be rewarded while on an obstacle.) Always keep safety in mind when adding height or reducing the size of the platform.

AVOIDING CONFRONTATIONS: BASIC

Perhaps something sets your dog off. Common triggers include other dogs, squirrels, skateboards, small children, and trucks, to name a few. Rather than let your dog bark, growl, or lunge at a trigger, you can teach him that it's OK to avoid it. Bigger dogs are threatening? Not if you simply walk the other way. Skateboards are fun to chase? Well actually, it's even more fun to turn away from the skateboard. This recipe can be applied to

CONFIDENCE BOOST FOR BEANS

Like countless other dogs, Beans has learned to come out of her shell with the help of sports. After Beans was rescued in a hoarding raid, Kate and her husband brought this middle-aged, one-eyed Chihuahua/Jack Russell mix to her new life in Brooklyn. It quickly became apparent that Beans was terrified of nearly all man-made things, from furniture to flooring to even her food dish. Kate sought out activities to help Beans feel more comfortable with the world around her, but it took some trial and error before successfully landing first upon parkour and then scent work–based games.

Since Beans was more comfortable in the natural world, Kate started practicing basic parkour during their walks in the park. Two paws on a tree stump? No problem. Circling a shrub? Totally fine. From there, Kate gradually introduced man-made elements into their training games. Over the course of many months and several mini-breakthroughs, Beans became significantly more confident in the world around her.

The scent work–inspired games in Chapter 7 also played a role in Beans' confidence-building. In particular, recreational barn hunt became her obsession. Searching for a rat (safely hidden inside a tube) among hay bales brought out the natural hunter buried inside Beans, and she proved to be a methodical, determined ratter. Kate then helped Beans apply her rat-hunting skills to container searches and other indoor scent work activities.

Though Beans will always be a sensitive dog, Kate focuses on the things she can do. As it turns out, she can do quite a lot!

anything that your dog is too stressed or too excited to handle appropriately.

The strategies in the Attention Behaviors section go a long way toward building clear communication with your dog. The behaviors in this section can be applied specifically to the moments when your dog spots a trigger and needs your help to deal with his reaction. Think of yourself not just as your dog's teacher, but as his therapist. Your primary role is not exactly to teach him to *do* something, as in the previous section; rather, you will teach him to *feel* differently about the trigger. While the exercises in this section are indeed training activities, there is a major emotional benefit to doing them. The more you practice these exercises, the more your dog will learn to control his impulses, even in the presence of a trigger.

We recommend that you start with the first game, You Found One!, to help your dog change his emotional reaction to his triggers. This will lay a solid foundation for the other training behaviors that follow. When doing any activities to help your dog overcome his stress, work extremely methodically and avoid skipping steps. This kind of training is a marathon, not a sprint. Your success will usually be measured in terms of weeks or months, not days, and you may have setbacks along the way. (It sounds a lot like therapy for humans, doesn't it?) Celebrate your dog's victories, however small they may seem in the beginning. Duke didn't bark at that skateboard half a block away? Hooray! It might not be even close to your end goal, but any progress should be rewarded greatly to set your dog up for more success in the future.

If your dog's reactivity is still a challenge despite your best efforts, contact a qualified force-free trainer or behavior consultant who can tailor a training plan to your needs.

YOU FOUND ONE!
Basic • Games

This technique is very simple in principle, but it takes practice and patience to implement. The You Found One! game is a lighthearted interpretation of what's known as *desensitization* and *counterconditioning*. The goal of this technique is to make a new, positive association with a trigger, such as another dog, a cyclist, an ambulance siren, or a squirrel. For instance, Lola gets so anxious around other dogs on the sidewalk that she barks and lunges at them. She currently makes the association of the dog (the trigger) with intense anxiety (the emotional response). Desensitization and counterconditioning will help her make a new association, so when she sees another dog on the sidewalk, she looks to you as if to say, "Oh boy, I found one!" You will reward her for "finding" the dog, which creates happy and relaxed feelings, rather than hyperarousal or stress, about the trigger.

Dogs with a high prey drive can also benefit from this technique.

Does your dog lose control at the sight of a squirrel?

Rather than Buster seeing a chipmunk (the trigger) and getting maniacally excited (the emotional response), he can learn to see a furry critter and cheerfully look at you instead. In every case, it creates a pleasant emotional response toward the trigger, while simultaneously putting the focus on you, the giver of the treats, rather than on the trigger itself. By playing this as a game together, you become a valuable part of the game, whereas before, your dog forgot you even existed when he saw that squirrel or dog.

Counterconditioning refers to the process of teaching your dog to develop a different emotional response to a trigger. You'll do this by pairing the trigger with a delicious treat. Over time, the trigger will not produce a feeling of "oh no" but rather "oh yes!" And since you're the one delivering the treat, your dog will be able to see the trigger and then turn his attention to you, which gives you much greater control over the situation.

Desensitization is a concurrent process that makes counterconditioning possible; it requires you to manage the intensity of the trigger so that your dog stays *under threshold*. By exposing your dog to the trigger at a manageable level, he doesn't get overwhelmed and tip into overexcitement, fear, or frustration. How do you keep him under threshold and receptive to counterconditioning?

- Make sure that the distance between your dog and the trigger is sufficiently far.
- Avoid exposing your dog to one trigger after another after another. Repeated exposure can push a dog over threshold.
- Keep the exposure to each trigger short. Your dog may only be able to handle one second of exposure at first.

As time goes on, your dog's threshold will increase, and he'll be able to handle a higher intensity of the trigger.

You Found One! is useful for dogs who:

- appear aggressive when confronted with triggers

- get overly excited when confronted with triggers
- cannot focus on their owners in the presence of triggers
- cannot respond to simple cues in the presence of triggers

HOW TO DO YOU FOUND ONE!

1. You're walking your dog on the sidewalk. Be prepared for a trigger to confront you at any moment. Keep your eyes open and your treats handy.

2. Desensitize. Once you spot a trigger in the distance, watch your dog carefully for the first sign that he notices it.

   TIP: If your dog goes over threshold and starts reacting, turn around and give him more distance. Try again when you are sufficiently far away.

3. Countercondition. As soon as your dog notices the trigger, immediately and cheerfully say "yay, you found one!" and treat generously before he has the chance to bark or lunge. If the trigger lingers, such as a dog walking down the street, continue treating rapid-fire until that trigger is gone.

   TIP: If your dog starts barking or lunging during this process, walk him away from the trigger. It's too late to train at this point, so give him distance to cool off.

   TIP: Struggling? Consider 1) using higher-value treats, such as deli meat or cheese, and 2) feeding even more rapid-fire. This is hard work for your pup, especially in the early stages.

4. Once the trigger has passed, stop feeding the treats and resume your walk as before. It is best to walk away from the trigger, not toward it.

Repeat this game every time your dog sees the trigger. You will always have two choices:

"Yay Beans, you found a dog!" This game may seem silly, but Beans is proof that it works!

- When the trigger is at a reasonable intensity, countercondition with You Found One!
- When the trigger is too intense for your dog to stay under threshold, give him more distance by walking away. Don't try to countercondition a dog who is already barking or lunging.

From There

At a certain point, your dog will see a trigger and think to look at you before you reward him. This is his way of saying "hey, I found one!" When he looks at you by his own will, throw him a party with cheering and a lot of treats. He has learned the game and is choosing to focus on you instead of the trigger. This is a major breakthrough. From this point on, you can very gradually heighten the challenge.

High school: Increase the intensity of the trigger. For instance, let your dog get closer to the skateboard and wait for him to tell you "I found one!" When he looks to you, cheer and reward generously. If he goes over threshold, it tells you he's not ready for that intensity yet.

TIP: Have a notebook to record your dog's progress as well as his setbacks. How close did he get to a trigger today? How many triggers can he handle per walk? This information is essential to increasing the difficulty methodically.

College and beyond: Continue increasing the intensity of the trigger, making sure that your dog is always able to play the game and does not get overwhelmed. Simultaneously, when your dog tells you that he's found a low-intensity trigger (such as a skateboard a block away), you can cheer and pet him, but he does not need treats anymore.

Once your dog is showing high-school-level proficiency with this game, you can start doing some of the other activities in this section. The following activities are actually asking your dog to *do* something in the presence of a trigger, which is no small task. Therefore, practice them when the trigger is sufficiently far away so that your pup can easily focus on you. No animal can properly focus on learning when under stress. Just as it would be hard for you to do long division if you felt you were in danger, it is unfair to ask an emotionally overwhelmed dog to perform a trick or other behavior.

  FRONT CROSS
Basic • Sports

Used in: Freestyle

Imagine you're on a walk, with your dog on your left side, and you spot a cat up ahead that's also on your left. Avoid confrontation by teaching your dog to cross in front of you and end up in Heel position on your right side. (The reverse, from right to left, is also possible.) This handy exercise, drawn from freestyle, can help you get past all kinds of distractions. Our version was inspired by the Front Cross technique by trainer and freestyle competitor Jenn Michaelis of SassyT Canine Academy. Jenn says, "In the sport of canine musical freestyle, we teach our dogs to heel not only on the left side but also on the right side; they might even heel behind us or going backward! In a freestyle routine, I would use a Front Cross to keep my dog in direct view of the judge while moving around the ring, allowing me to show off my dog's best moves in the best possible way. A Front Cross is also a very handy skill for everyday walks."

Front Cross is useful for dogs who:

- bark or lunge defensively when confronted with triggers
- get overly excited when confronted with triggers
- have already shown some success with You Found One!
- can turn their attention to their owners in the presence of mild triggers

To start, teach your dog Front Cross when there are no triggers present. Use an imaginary trigger, such as a box or fire hydrant, to practice your timing.

HOW TO DO FRONT CROSS

1. Choose one side to start from. Let's say your dog is on your left, in Heel position. Have a few tiny treats hidden in your right hand.
2. Keep your feet planted. Lure your dog from the left, sweeping your hand slowly in front of you and to your right side. Swing as wide as your arm allows, especially for big dogs.

    TIP: If your dog is hesitant, you may mark and reward for each step he takes toward your right side.
3. Now your dog is on your right, but he's facing backward! Use the treat lure to loop him 180 degrees in a U-turn toward you. This is the same motion as Finish Left.

    TIP: For large dogs, you can take a step back and then a step forward as you lure, to help your dog circle around 180 degrees into Heel position.
4. Now that he's safely being body-blocked from the trigger, hustle past the trigger. Use your Walk with Attention or Heel technique to keep your dog focused on you.

5. Repeat Steps 1–4 until you get four-for-four smooth ones. Next, do the same sequence but with an empty hand. Treat at the end from your pocket or pouch. Make sure to treat from your right hand. Get four-for-four.
6. Add a verbal cue, such as "cross," before you start the sequence. Continue practicing this in various low-distraction settings.

Step 2: Lizzie slowly lures Phineas toward her right side.

Step 3: Then she steps back with her right foot...

Play Your Way to Good Manners

...and lures Phineas in a U-turn toward her.

Step 4: Now that he's in Heel position, he can have the treat. Lizzie will now heel past a distraction.

7. Switch to the opposite side. Starting with your dog on the right and the treat in your left hand, lure him to the left Heel position. Repeat Steps 1–6. When ready, you can add the same verbal cue, "cross," for this direction.

From There

High school: Practice in the presence of very mild distractions, such as stationary objects. In urban areas, garbage day is a good time to practice, as stinky garbage cans may beckon your dog but aren't likely to scare him.

College and beyond: Practice in the vicinity of triggers, starting with very mild triggers. Keep in mind that your dog may find it especially hard to focus around triggers that are in close proximity, are moving, or are making noise.

It will take a bit of practice until you can pass by a trigger that is simultaneously close by, moving, *and* noisy. (If your dog is triggered by other dogs, think "excited, barking Labradoodle crossing your path.") Work up to each criterion gradually.

AVOIDING CONFRONTATIONS: ADVANCED

  ## LEFT ABOUT TURN
Advanced • Sports

Prerequisite: Making Turns, particularly 180-Degree Right Turn
Used in: Rally, freestyle

This visually impressive version of the basic turns in the Attention Behaviors section is a creative way to give your dog more space between him and the trigger. Both you and your dog turn 180 degrees, but your dog turns clockwise while you turn counterclockwise. Both useful for changing directions as well as eye-catching for audiences, Left About Turn is used in rally and makes an appearance in many freestyle routines.

Left About Turn is useful for dogs who:
- bark or lunge defensively when confronted with triggers
- get overly excited when confronted with triggers
- need extra space when distracted

HOW TO DO LEFT ABOUT TURN

1. Have a treat in both hands. Your dog is on your left, in Heel position.
2. Put a treat in front of your dog's nose with your right hand.
3. Lure the dog in front of you and around to your right side. Mark and reward there.
4. Quickly, turn 180 degrees to your left (counterclockwise). At the completion of your turn, put a treat in front of your dog's face with your left hand. This will encourage him to continue moving into Heel position and to not be worried about your opposing movement.
5. When he's found Heel position again, reward there with your left hand and walk on, away from the trigger.
6. As you practice this, the movement will become more fluid, and you can fade out the right hand lure and reward.
7. You can use the same verbal cue, "around," and sweeping hand signal as Right Finish because it effectively means "circle around me."

From There

High school: Once your dog understands the mechanics of this maneuver, practice in the presence of distractions.

College and beyond: Practice in the presence of mild triggers, then more intense triggers. If your dog can't respond to Left About Turn at any point, it may mean the trigger is too intense.

Step 3: With her right hand, she lures Hank to her right side.

Step 4: Sarah turns her body 180 degrees to the left. Hank is still chomping a treat in her right hand...

Step 1: Hank is on Sarah's left, and she has treats in both hands.

Play Your Way to Good Manners

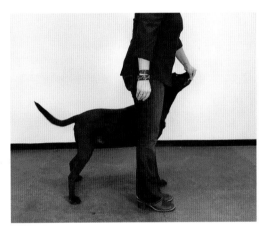

...but Sarah quickly switches hands. Hank is chewing a new treat in her left hand, which keeps him in place while she turns.

Step 5: Now they're facing the new direction in Heel position, and ready to move on.

  CALL FRONT RETURN TO HEEL
Advanced • Sports

Prerequisite: Heel
Used in: Rally, freestyle

Like the Left About Turn, this exercise allows you to remove your dog from a hairy situation up ahead. In a couple of simple steps, you can swing your pup (and then yourself) around 180 degrees and walk in the opposite direction, away from danger. The instructions here assume that the dog is starting on your left side, but you can do this exercise on your right as well.

Call Front Return to Heel is useful for dogs who:

- bark or lunge defensively when confronted with triggers
- get overly excited when confronted with triggers
- need extra space when distracted

HOW TO DO CALL FRONT RETURN TO HEEL

1. Stand with your dog at your side in Heel position. Have a few treats in both hands.
2. With your right hand, use a treat to lure your dog in front of you, so he's facing you. You may take a step or two backward so he can straighten out his body to face you.
3. Mark and reward when your dog is facing you.
4. Ask for a Sit. This completes the Call Front.
5. Now you will walk around the dog counterclockwise. Move to your right (the dog's left) and pass behind him, circling until you find yourself back in Heel position with the dog on your left.

Step 4: Batman is in the Call Front position.

Step 5: Kate walks around Batman counterclockwise. If your dog is still learning this, let him chew on a treat as you walk.

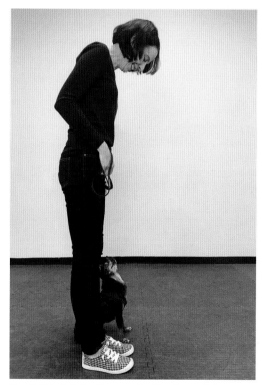

Step 6: Kate is facing the opposite direction, and they can walk off.

TIP: If your dog can't handle you moving around and behind him, use a treat to keep the dog stable, as in Sit/Walk Around in Chapter 2.

6. You're now both facing the opposite way together and can heel away from the distraction.

From There

High school: Once your dog understands the mechanics of this maneuver, practice in the presence of distractions.

College and beyond: Practice in the presence of very low-level triggers, for instance, a dog that is far away. As your dog gets comfortable with triggers at a distance, you can allow the trigger to get gradually closer before asking for the Call Front.

  WALK BACKWARD
Advanced • Sports

Used in: Rally, freestyle

You see your dog's nemesis up ahead. Don't panic! Instead, you can teach your dog to back away from a trigger. For this exercise, your dog is standing facing forward, and you will move around to face him. You walk forward and he walks backward, away from the trigger.

Backing up is a skill that comes up frequently in dog sports. It is used in rally and can be found in many freestyle routines. Dogs don't always realize that they have control of their back paws, so it's useful to gradually teach them hind-end awareness through this and other exercises. You may benefit from starting this exercise in a narrow hallway or using barriers to create a straight pathway.

This behavior takes some dogs longer to pick up than others. If your dog is struggling, practice each step over multiple sessions, getting four-for-four several times, before proceeding to the next step.

Walk Backward is useful for dogs who:

- bark or lunge defensively when confronted with triggers
- get overly excited when confronted with triggers
- need extra space when distracted
- need to build hind-end awareness

HOW TO DO WALK BACKWARD

1. Stand in front of your dog. Take a step toward him.
2. As soon as he rocks back or takes a step back, mark and reward. A clicker is useful for catching the moment, before he potentially rocks into a Sit. Continue until you get four-for-four single steps back over several sessions.

   TIP: Toss the reward between your dog's front paws. That way, he is continuing to think about moving backward, and he does not learn to rely on your presence for the reward. (This is helpful if, later on, you choose to teach your dog to walk backward while you stay stationary.)

3. Add a visual cue with your hand right before you step toward your dog. It could be an underhand wave that slightly "pushes" into his face, as in the photos for Backward Heel. Get four-for-four over several sessions.
4. Give the cue to get your dog to back up one step and then repeat the cue for another step back. Mark and reward after the second step. Get four-for-four over several sessions.
5. Continue this process until you get four or more backward steps in a row. Straight steps are more important than the number of steps, so take your time and reward for straightness.
6. Add the verbal cue "back" if you choose. Say it before you begin the sequence.
7. Vary how many steps back you ask for.

Step 1: Sarah takes a small step toward Hank, and he backs up in response.

Step 2: Sarah has tossed the reward a little behind his front paws.

8. Follow Walk Backward with another cue, such as Finish Right or Finish Left. This will allow you to change direction and walk your dog away from the trigger, if necessary.

From There

High school: Once your dog understands the mechanics of this maneuver, practice in the presence of distractions.

College and beyond: Practice in the presence of very low-level triggers. As your dog gets comfortable with triggers at a distance, you can allow the trigger to get gradually closer before asking for Walk Backward.

HALT/180-DEGREE PIVOT/HALT
Advanced • Sports

Prerequisites: Side Sit, Heel

Used in: Rally

This is another way to teach your dog to turn away from whatever is bothering him up ahead. The completed behavior chain involves a Side Sit, a 180-Degree Pivot so that you're facing the opposite direction, and a final Side Sit. (For pivots in rally, aim to keep your feet inside a paper-plate-sized space.)

Halt/180-Degree Pivot/Halt is useful for dogs who:

- bark or lunge defensively when confronted with triggers
- get overly excited when confronted with triggers
- need extra space when distracted

HOW TO DO HALT/180-DEGREE PIVOT/HALT

1. Start by heeling with the dog on your left. Cue your dog to do Side Sit as you stop moving.

2. Cue the dog to move with "let's go" (or similar encouragement) and pivot your body clockwise 180 degrees. When you step, start with your right foot and then bring your left foot to meet your right. You may take a final mini step or two to straighten your feet out.

Step 1: Kate and Batman start from a Side Sit.

Step 2: Kate brings her right foot back first, while luring Batman around. . .

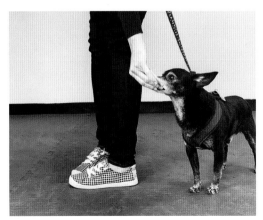

. . . and the left foot comes next.

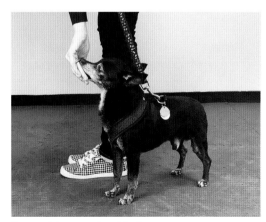

Kate straightens out her right foot.

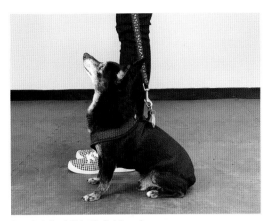

Step 3: A final Side Sit finishes the sequence.

TIP: Use a food lure in your left hand to encourage the dog to move with you, if needed.

3. When you get to your new position, cue the dog to sit again. Mark and reward.

4. Because this behavior has several components, you can mark and reward several times while your dog is learning it. Some dogs may need a treat for sitting, for moving 180 degrees, and for sitting again. Other dogs may be able to do the entire behavior chain for a single treat.

From There

High school: Once your dog understands the mechanics of this maneuver, practice in the presence of distractions.

College and beyond: Practice in the presence of very low-level triggers. As your dog gets comfortable with triggers at a distance, you can allow the triggers to get gradually closer before cuing Halt/180-Degree Pivot/Halt.

SOLVE SIDEWALK SNACKING: BASIC

Sidewalk snacking isn't just gross; it can be dangerous. You can tackle your dog's snacking tendencies directly (by teaching Drop It and Leave It) and indirectly (by practicing the Attention Behaviors presented earlier this chapter). After

all, a dog who ignores you is likely to focus his attention on sidewalk snacks, whereas a dog who's interacting with you is having too much fun with training to bother with anything else.

  LEAVE IT
Basic • Manners

To us, Leave It is no joke. It can literally save your dog's life. But, when teaching Leave It, you want to make it fun and rewarding for your dog. Kate's two dogs think Leave It is a game, and they actually try to play it while on walks. Batman will occasionally prance over to a piece of garbage and then swerve directly toward Kate as if to say, "Hey! I left it! Did you see?"

Leave It is different from Drop It. When your dog is approaching something forbidden—garbage, your sock, a cat—your cue to "leave it" tells him to stop approaching this item and return to you. It is a preventative measure. On the other hand, Drop It is the cue you use when your dog already has that forbidden item in his mouth and must release it. It is damage control. The goal should always be to prevent a problem, and practicing Leave It will greatly reduce your need to use Drop Its for dangerous objects.

Impulse control is not inherently fun for dogs, but you can make it fun by asking your dog to leave a low-level temptation (think "kibble") and be rewarded with a much higher-level treat (think "hot dogs"). Suddenly the idea of leaving an item is pretty awesome, and your dog will actually look forward to his Leave It training sessions. Another way to keep it fun is to increase the difficulty very gradually so your dog can easily "win" his hot dog. You'll see that we have outlined several levels of Leave It here to ensure that your pup will become a Leave-It addict.

Leave It is useful for dogs who:
- sidewalk snack

SEE IT IN ACTION

To see the different levels of Leave It in action, check out Kate's Leave It video at *bklnmanners.com*.

5. Get four-for-four and take a break. Be patient, as it may take many reps for your dog to realize what's earning him the reward.

6. Repeat this in several different locations until your dog has caught on to the Leave It game and purposefully backs away from the temptation.

- chase animals or other moving objects
- steal items
- counter surf
- lack impulse control, especially around food

HOW TO DO LEAVE IT: LEVEL 1

1. Put some dry food or a low-value treat in one hand and make a loosely closed fist. This will be the "temptation" hand, symbolizing the forbidden garbage. Your dog will never get the temptation, just as you would never let him eat the garbage as a reward. In your other hand is an even tastier treat. This becomes your "reward" hand, which will stay hidden behind your back for now.

2. Say "leave it" once, in a natural, firm voice, and then immediately put your temptation hand in front of your dog's nose.

    TIP: The purpose of the firm tone is to imitate what your voice actually sounds like when your dog is approaching a chocolate bar and you forget to use your bubbly "training" voice. If you're not comfortable with a firm voice, however, feel free to use a cheerful tone.

3. Hold your hand still while your dog tries to get the temptation treat out of your hand. Avoid saying anything or moving your hand.

4. Eventually he will take a pause, look away, or back up in frustration. Mark and reward at the very moment he does this. Yes, even if he simply got distracted and looked away! Reward with the tastier treat from your other hand as a surprise.

Step 3: Beans wonders, "What's this in your hand?" But having already said "leave it," Kate holds still.

Step 4: When Beans backs away, Kate marks it.

She rewards from her other hand, never with the temptation treat.

HOW TO DO LEAVE IT: LEVEL 2

Now your dog will be exposed to the sight of the temptation.

1. The setup is the same as in level 1. Say "leave it" and present your temptation hand as before, but this time your fist is ever so slightly open.

   TIP: Hold the temptation treat at the dog's eye level and off to one side. This gives a few feet of distance between the dog and temptation treat. Don't tease your dog by putting the treat in front of his face.

2. If your dog doesn't approach it, mark and reward from your reward hand. But if your dog moves toward the treat—even just a step—quickly pull your temptation hand away and start over. Get four-for-four Leave Its with a barely open fist.

3. Open your fist a hair more. If your dog leaves it, mark, reward, and proceed to Step 4. If he doesn't, practice until you get four-for-four at this level.

4. Continue opening your temptation hand until your palm is totally flat. If your dog struggles at any point, revert to an easier step and get four-for-four to ensure you're not pushing him too fast.

5. Gradually lower your temptation hand after every correct Leave It. The lower your hand gets, the more impulse control it takes for your dog. Repeat this until your hand is lying on the ground. If your dog struggles at any point, revert to an easier step and get four-for-four.

6. Practice this indoors and out with a variety of temptation treats. Make sure your reward is equal to or better than the temptation.

Step 2: Bad dog or bad handler? Kate should have snatched her temptation hand away before Beans got this close to it.

Step 4: This time, Beans does not approach it. (It doesn't matter if the dog is standing, sitting, or lying down.) Kate will reward with her other hand.

HOW TO DO LEAVE IT: LEVEL 3

This level gets you to the point where your dog can leave a piece of food you've dropped or other stationary challenges (meaning that your dog is standing still, not walking).

1. Your body position is similar to that of level 2, with a temptation in one hand and a reward in another. Ensure that your dog is a few feet away.

2. Say "leave it" as you drop the temptation treat on the floor from a few inches above. If he does not take any steps toward the temptation, mark and reward from your reward hand. If he goes for the temptation, block his access by covering it with your hand or foot. Get four-for-four.

3. With each successful Leave It, increase how far the treat drops. This means you'll gradually elevate your hand and body until you can drop the treat from your waist level.

   TIP: If your dog struggles once you're standing, you can throw the treat slightly behind you at first. Body-block him or put him on leash so he can't outrun you for it.

4. Practice at this level in many locations, especially in the kitchen and outside.

Step 3: She goes to Beans to reward her for staying still.

If Beans tries to dash for the treat, Kate can use her foot or a leash to block.

Step 2: Kate drops the temptation slightly behind her.

HOW TO DO LEAVE IT: LEVEL 4

Now we add motion, simulating a leash-walking scenario. You can practice indoors or out, but always on leash. Leave It will now have an element of recall, as you'll teach your dog not only to leave an item but also to happily run toward you.

1. With your dog elsewhere, put a very low-level temptation on the ground. An empty bag, uninteresting toy, or even a book will do. Have a high-value treat in your hand or pocket.
2. Walk your dog toward the temptation, keeping your body between the dog and the temptation.
3. The moment your dog's ears perk up or his head turns to see the temptation, say "leave it" once. Immediately pick up your pace. You can even run past it.
4. If your dog jogs past it with you, mark and cheer enthusiastically. This will encourage him to follow you, as in Chase Me. Reward once you are safely past the temptation so he doesn't turn back to grab it. On the other hand, if he tries to steal the temptation, just keep walking forward and give an NRM, such as "oops." Next time, don't walk so close to the temptation.

   TIP: If you have to pull on the leash to keep him from getting the temptation, he has not left it. You want your dog to leave it because you've asked, not because the leash is restraining him.
5. Get four-for-four Leave Its while body-blocking as you walk by.
6. Switch positions so that your dog is closer to the temptation than you are (as in the photos). Now you can't body-block.

From There

Leave It may have numerous intermediate steps before your dog can respond in all situations.

High school: Use increasingly valuable temptations, ensuring that your reward is always equal to or better than the temptation. Get four-for-four with each temptation before increasing to a higher one.

College: Add a higher level of recall. Allow your dog to walk close to a mild temptation while you

Step 3: Kate has just told Beans to "leave it," and Beans stops approaching the temptation. Kate will now encourage Beans to jog past it.

Step 4: Safely past the temptation, Kate rewards. (Note that this setup is for photo clarity. At first, you should be between the temptation and dog.)

are at the other end of the 6-foot (1.8-m) leash and then cue him to "leave it."

Grad school and beyond: Practice Leave Its with real-life distractions, such as actual garbage or a squirrel nearby.

DROP IT DURING PLAY
Basic • Games

Drop It is one of the first things we recommend teaching to new puppies. Because there are so many potentially dangerous things that your dog can put in his mouth, it's worthwhile to teach him how to spit something out on cue. The basic version of Drop It focuses on playing with toys. It aims to teach your dog that dropping an item actually begins, rather than removes, the fun. Once this level is going smoothly, proceed to the Drop It with Food in the Solve Sidewalk Snacking: Advanced section.

Here, Drop It will be the way you initiate any game involving toys: tug, chase, fetch, and so on. This teaches your dog that dropping something is his ticket to getting the game started. Once he sees Drop It as a part of the game, it will be easier to apply this technique to sidewalk snacks.

Drop It during Play is useful for dogs who:

- steal items and run off
- don't like to give up toys once they have them
- sidewalk snack
- need to learn more polite play behavior
- lack impulse control around toys or food

HOW TO DO DROP IT DURING PLAY

1. Hold out a toy that is long enough for both of you to share. (A short toy can lead to an accidental bite.) Wait for your dog to sit as laid out in Chapter 1.
2. When your dog puts his mouth on the toy, do not let go. Immediately say "drop it" *once* in a firm but friendly voice.
3. Let your dog spit it out. If he continues to hold onto it, gently remove the toy from your dog's mouth.

   TIP: If your dog really fights to keep possession of the toy, trade him the toy for a treat. Don't let it escalate into a fight.
4. Once the toy has been removed, praise him for a job well done and reward him by starting the game right away.
5. As you play, ask for a Drop It every once in a while. Reward by continuing the game.

From There

Practice this every time you play with your dog, so he learns that Drop Its are part of the fun.

Step 1: Trevor politely sits to start the game.

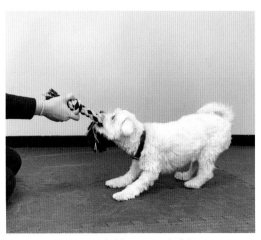
Step 2: Lizzie continues holding one end of the toy.

SOLVE SIDEWALK SNACKING: ADVANCED

  DROP IT WITH FOOD
Advanced • Manners

Prerequisite: Drop It during Play

When you teach your dog to drop something that he considers delicious, you want to make it a rewarding experience for him. If he learns that Drop It is no fun, he will only become sneakier and faster with his sidewalk snacking. The better course is to show him that when he drops an item, he gets something even better in return. Arm yourself with super-tasty treats or a very high-value toy.

While we focus on food here, this technique applies to anything your dog wants to put in his mouth. On walks, this could include sticks, leaves, or other objects that you come across; at home, this could be articles of clothing, kids' toys, and so on.

Drop It with Food is useful for dogs who:

- sidewalk snack
- steal items and run off
- counter surf
- lack impulse control, especially around food

HOW TO DO DROP IT: LEVEL 1

1. As in Drop It during Play, share a mildly interesting object with your dog. It could be a forbidden item, like an old piece of clothing, or a relatively flavorless chewy, like a plain rawhide. You will not let go.

2. As soon as your dog's mouth is on the object, firmly say "drop it" *once*.

3. Your dog may not spit it out at first, so be ready to make a trade. As you remove the object from your dog's jaws, simultaneously give him a surprise treat or favorite toy from your pocket. *This is a cool game*, your dog thinks to himself.

4. Repeat this two or three times maximum and

Step 1: Kate shares a rawhide with Beans. She does not give Beans full possession of it.

Step 5: Beans gets a piece of chicken for dropping the rawhide. Score!

then take a break. Practice occasionally until it's smooth.

5. Now, delay the reward. After you say "drop it," pause and let him spit the item out. Mark and reward with a jackpot of several treats because he just chose to drop it without any help from you!

6. Practice this in short sessions, indoors and out.

BUT MY DOG WON'T DROP IT!

Som dogs initially resist the whole concept of Drop It. Others have made unpleasant associations with being asked to drop items and, as such, have learned to grab the forbidden items and run for their lives. In these cases, start teaching Drop It without even presenting a toy or chewy to drop. Sound crazy? Actually, this technique uses classical conditioning to teach your dog that the words "drop it" mean "yay, treats!" This creates a happy emotional response in your dog when he hears the words. You will build from there. Here are the steps.

1. Say "drop it" once and immediately give your dog a treat. Repeat this many times until he clearly gets excited at the words.
2. Present a household object in which your dog has no interest. He shouldn't even put his mouth on it. Show him the item, say "drop it" as you remove the item, and give him a treat. Repeat several times with various objects.
3. Present an object in which your dog has mild interest (perhaps a rope toy). Allow him to put his mouth or nose on it for a split second. Say "drop it" as you remove the object. Give a treat.
4. Once your dog understands this sequence, proceed to level 1.

If your dog shows resource guarding tendencies (such as a hard stare, growling, snapping, or other "stay away from me" displays), contact a force-free trainer or behavior consultant to help you develop a safe plan for teaching Drop It.

7. Introduce new, more interesting objects for him to drop. Remember to increase the difficulty in baby steps. Don't ask him to drop a piece of steak yet! In addition to forbidden items, you can practice with toys and long chewies.

HOW TO DO DROP IT: LEVEL 2

1. Go back to your level 1 forbidden item. Now, with your dog on leash, you will give him full possession of the item. Give him just a second or two with it. Hold the leash with just a little slack, in case he tries to walk off with the item.
2. Say "drop it" and pause for him to spit out the toy. Mark and reward as before.

   TIP: If he does not willingly drop it, practice with more items at level 1.
3. When he is happily dropping the toy,

gradually increase to higher-level toys, chewies, and forbidden items.
4. Practice this in short sessions of one to three responses, indoors and out.

From There

Once your dog understands Drop It, you can set up training challenges for him. Here are some examples.

High school: On your walk, bring a toy or chewy with which you've already practiced. As you're walking—oops!—"accidentally" drop the item in your dog's path.

College and beyond: Generally, these challenges include high-value food, so use an especially tasty chewy or goodie. While you're busy in the kitchen—oh no!—the goodie falls to the floor right in front of your dog.

Once your dog can respond to advanced-level Drop Its, you can fade out treats for the easy Drop Its.

  FAST PACE AND SLOW PACE
Advanced • Sports

Prerequisite: Heel

Used in: Rally, freestyle

In rally, participants may be asked to heel at a slow, normal, or fast pace. A freestyle competitor may also include changes in speed. Practicing heeling at different paces, particularly the fast pace, is useful when passing delicious garbage, the neighbor's cat, or other distractions. With your dog happily focused on the Heel, that distraction won't beckon him in the same way.

Fast Pace and Slow Pace are useful for dogs who:

- sidewalk snack
- get distracted while on leash
- chase animals or other moving objects
- lack impulse control on walks, especially around distractions

HOW TO DO FAST PACE

1. Start from a normal-paced Heel and then pick up your pace so that both you and your dog are comfortably hustling. To give your dog a helpful visual cue, you can lean your torso forward as you hustle.

2. As you increase the speed, happily encourage your dog to match your pace. You can talk excitedly and/or pat the side of your leg to motivate him.

   TIP: If your dog is struggling to keep up with you, mark and reward more frequently when he is in the correct position next to you. Be sure to place the reward firmly at your side; avoid reaching back to reward.

3. Bring your dog back to a normal pace before either of you gets tired.

HOW TO DO SLOW PACE

1. Start from a normal-paced Heel and then slow your pace down to a stroll. You can lean your torso back a little, using your posture as a visual cue for your dog.

2. Continue engaging with your dog verbally to keep his interest. You may have to reward your dog more frequently when he is in the Heel position.

From There

High school: Practice Fast Pace and Slow Pace in the presence of various distractions, starting with low-level distractions.

College and beyond: Add Fast Pace and Slow Pace to your very own rally or freestyle sequence by performing other exercises before and after it.

ADVANCED WALKING GAMES TO BUILD TEAMWORK, BURN ENERGY, AND IMPRESS NEIGHBORS

The exercises in this section are drawn from various dog sports and tricks. Adding sports- and trick-training techniques to your walks has a number of general benefits that go far beyond the walks themselves. First of all, you and your dog will develop better communication, which in turn will strengthen the bond and trust between you. Secondly, you'll maximize your dog's walks, burning extra mental and physical energy by asking him to do new things. Additionally, your dog will never act out during walks due to boredom, so his behavior will naturally improve. He'll no longer have a reason to sidewalk snack, pull you, or engage in other rude behaviors. Finally, you will become the envy of all of the other dog people in your neighborhood!

  TRICK ON A PLATFORM
Advanced • Sports

Prerequisites: Four Feet On, any trick where at least two paws stay on the ground

Used in: Parkour

This one is open to a lot of interpretation and can draw on a number of the tricks from other chapters. For Trick on a Platform, you'll ask your dog to hop onto an object, like a tree stump or stair, and then perform a trick he already knows well. Parkour has some safety guidelines for this activity:

- The width of the platform should be no smaller than the dog's dimensions.
- The dog should be supported with a secure back-clip harness and leash throughout, in case he loses his balance.
- The trick should be "stable," meaning that at least two paws are on the platform at all times. No flips!

Start with a small, defined area on the floor, such as a yoga mat or dog bed.

Trick on a Platform is useful for dogs who:
- love doing tricks
- get bored on walks
- struggle to stay focused on their owners while on walks
- need confidence boosts
- like to play, either with their owners or with the environment

HOW TO DO TRICK ON A PLATFORM

1. Ask for Four Feet On on a very low, wide object like a towel, dog bed, or flattened piece of cardboard.
2. Once all four paws are stable on the object, ask for a safe trick your dog already knows. Mark and reward.

    TIP: Get your dog comfortable with being supported by the harness now, before he progresses to performing the trick on higher or smaller platforms. Hold the leash above the dog and apply gentle pressure while he's on the platform and especially when dismounting.
3. Say "OK" to release. Support your dog as he dismounts.

From There

High school: Once your dog is nailing it, switch to a platform that is slightly more challenging by being 1) a little higher, 2) a little smaller in diameter, or 3) located in a more distracting area.

College and beyond: Continue increasing the difficulty by one criterion at a time. You don't need to always get four-for-four, but ensure that your dog is totally comfortable with a 3-inch (8-cm)-high platform before increasing to a 6-inch (15-cm)-high platform. If you plan to do proper parkour, switch the reward to the end of the sequence, after you release.

The agility version of Balance Beam, as demonstrated by Hank, requires both speed and accuracy. Photo by Richard Knecht

 BALANCE BEAM
Advanced • Sports

Prerequisites: Walk with Attention, Four Feet On
Used in: Parkour, agility

This is a common parkour exercise, and you have likely seen versions of it in agility, including the teeter-totter, A-frame, and dog walk. This exercise encourages your dog to focus on the task at hand. He will learn to walk along a narrow, elevated surface such as a bleacher, log, stone wall, or stair of a public building. To do this safely, he will have to pay attention not only to your cues but also to what his paws are doing. If following parkour guidelines, you should gently support him with a secure back-clip harness and leash as he performs this exercise, including mounting and dismounting, if the "beam" is higher than the dog's elbow.

Balance Beam is useful for dogs who:

- need to pay more attention to their feet
- have energy to burn
- need to learn how to channel their energy
- need to learn how much fun it is to spend time with their owners
- need to build trust in their owners
- like to play, either with their owners or with the environment

HOW TO DO BALANCE BEAM

1. Find a surface that is slightly elevated and wide enough for your dog to comfortably walk along. A step leading to a library or museum (think the steps from *Rocky*) is a good starting point.

2. Tap on the surface and either use your voice to encourage him to hop up or cue him to do Four Feet On on the object.

3. Once he's on the object, assuming he isn't showing any signs of fear, encourage him to walk along it as you walk next to him.

   TIP: Unlike Walk with Attention, you don't want your dog looking at you; he should be watching where he's going.

4. At the end of the object, encourage him to hop off or use a cue such as "off."

   TIP: If he has gained too much speed on the object, either ask him to do a Stop and Stay (Chapter 2) before jumping off or hold your palm in front of his face to indicate that he should stop, after which you can release him.

From There

Practice walking on various objects but avoid pushing him to balance on surfaces that make him nervous or unsafe. The whole point is for him to have fun and build trust.

High school: Decrease the width of the object. Gradually look for narrower "balance beams."

College: Increase the height. Always support him throughout, and never ask him to get on an object that is too high for you to spot him.

Grad school and beyond: Combine narrow and higher objects, taking into account the level of distraction in your surroundings.

  SERPENTINES
Advanced • Sports

Prerequisites: Heel, Making Turns
Used in: Rally

This leash-walking activity gets you and your dog negotiating obstacles together. If you've practiced Making Turns earlier in this chapter, you'll find it quite easy. You and your dog will weave in and out of several objects in a row, such as shrubs, construction cones, or street signs, in a serpentine pattern. In the beginning, it is easiest to set up your own serpentine pattern using the following guidelines.

Serpentines is useful for dogs who:
- need fun ways to build the Heel
- need mental challenges
- get bored on regular walks
- need to build better communication with their owners
- are easily distracted by things in their environment

HOW TO DO SERPENTINES

To prepare, have four items that can be used as markers, such as cones (as used in rally), paper towels, 2-liter plastic bottles, or something similar. Place the "cones" in a single row, approximately 6 to 8 feet (1.8 to 2.4 m) apart.

1. With your dog on leash, approach the line so that the first cone is directly in front of you, with the second cone behind the first, and so on.

2. Start walking with your dog in a Heel. You will enter the serpentine from the right, so the first cone will be on your left as you pass it. Your dog will be between you and the cone.

   TIP: Engage with your dog as you walk, to keep his focus on you.

3. Once you have passed the first cone, veer left until you are on the opposite side of the second cone. Pass cone 2 with the cone on your right.

   TIP: Plan your route so neither you nor the dog hits the cones.

4. Veer right until you are on the opposite side of cone 3 and have passed it on your left.

5. Lastly, veer left again until you have passed cone 4 on your right.

From There

High school: You can double the size of the pattern by looping around cone 4 and walking in a serpentine pattern back to cone 1.

College and beyond: Practice this exercise in increasingly distracting areas. Playgrounds and public parks may provide you with objects to swerve around.

  ## SPIRALS
Advanced • Sports

Prerequisites: Heel, Making Turns
Used in: Rally

This rally exercise is similar to Serpentines in that you are looping around a series of obstacles together; in this case, three cones (or similar objects) placed in a row about 6 to 8 feet (1.8 to 2.4 m) apart. You and the dog, in a Heel, will make three loops. The first loop is large and circles all three cones, the second loop circles around cones 1 and 2, and the final loop circles only around cone 1. So you will be walking in sequentially smaller circles, in a shape that resembles a paperclip.

Spirals is useful for dogs who:
- need fun ways to build the Heel
- need mental challenges
- get bored on regular walks
- need to build better communication with their owners
- are easily distracted by things in their environment

STEPS FOR SPIRALS: CLOCKWISE

In this case, your dog will be in a Heel position on your left, so he will be to the outside of the circles. You will be between the cones and the dog.

1. Stand facing the line of cones with cone 1 in front of you, cone 2 behind the first, and cone 3 behind the second. Your dog is in Heel position.

2. In a Heel, pass to the left side of all three cones. After you pass the third cone, make a U-turn and walk back to the starting point. You have just made the first, and largest, clockwise circle.

   TIP: In the beginning, you may reward your dog as often as necessary.

3. When you get back to the starting point, don't stop. Keep walking, this time circling around cones 1 and 2 but not cone 3. You will make the U-turn right after cone 2, passing between cones 2 and 3. Get back to the starting point again.

4. Keep walking and make your final circle, only around cone 1. You will pass between cones 1 and 2 before getting back to the starting point. Reward your dog for completing the sequence.

Clockwise

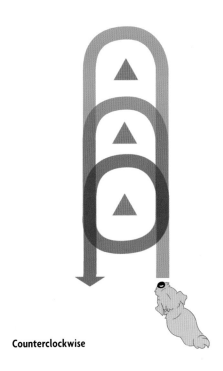

Counterclockwise

STEPS FOR SPIRALS: COUNTERCLOCKWISE

In this case, your dog will be in a Heel position on your left, so he will be next to the cones. You will be to the outside.

1. Stand facing the line of cones with cone 1 in front of you, cone 2 behind the first, and cone 3 behind the second. Your dog is in Heel position.
2. Make a large counterclockwise oval around all three cones.
3. When you get back to the starting point, don't stop. Keep walking, this time circling around cones 1 and 2 but not cone 3.
4. Keep walking and make your final circle, only around cone 1. You will pass between cones 1 and 2 before getting back to the starting point. Reward your dog for completing the sequence.

From There

While you could increase the difficulty by adding more cones, we don't recommend it, as it can make you quite dizzy. Instead, try these suggestions.

High school: Reduce the space between cones so that you will have to plan your path more carefully.

College and beyond: Practice these exercises in distracting areas. Even if you can't find three objects to circle, two will suffice.

  BACK ONTO A PLATFORM
Advanced • Sports

Prerequisite: Walk Backward or Backward Heel
Used in: Parkour, agility

This exercise requires your dog to take one or more steps backward until his back paws step up onto an elevated surface. It's essentially a Two Feet On but for the back paws. Back onto a Platform is used as both a parkour exercise and a technique for agility. In agility, this exercise can be used to teach a *two-on/two-off contact performance*, which is basically the dog targeting the obstacle he is about to leave with his back paws. People often teach the two-on/two-off to prevent their dogs from dangerously jumping off the A-frame, dog walk, or teeter-totter from the middle. Instead, dogs learn to run to the very bottom and target their back paws at the end.

As with other activities focusing on the back paws, this builds hind-end awareness. You'll start with an extremely low object, but the end goal is for your dog to back onto an object that is hock height or higher. If the object is higher than the dog's elbow, we recommend using a back-clip harness and leash, held with gentle support for safety.

Back onto a Platform is useful for dogs who:

- lack hind-end awareness
- need mental challenges
- get bored on regular walks
- need to build better communication with their owners
- are easily distracted by things in their environment

HOW TO DO BACK ONTO A PLATFORM

To start, place a very low platform, such as an unfolded towel or flat piece of cardboard, on the floor.

1. Walk your dog over the platform, heading forward (not backward yet). Stop him right after walking over the platform so that it's a step or two behind him.
2. Ask the dog to do Walk Backward or Backward Heel for one or two steps until both back paws are on the platform.

Step 2: Sarah cues Hank to do Backward Heel.

Step 3: He pauses once both back paws are firmly on the platform, and Sarah will now reward him.

3. Mark and reward with a few treats while his back paws are on the platform, and then release. Get four-for-four.
4. Gradually increase the height of the platform. Get at least four-for-four at every height.
5. Add a new verbal cue like "park it" before starting the backward sequence. Get four-for-four.

From There

Once your dog has gotten comfortable backing onto many different objects, you can add duration, distance, and distraction.

High school: Add duration. Ask for a short Stay while his back paws are on the object.

College: Add distance. Ask your dog to take more steps backward to reach the object.

Grad school and beyond: Add distraction. Practice in parks or other areas with distractions. If doing proper parkour, reward after the release, when all four paws are on the ground.

  ## BACKWARD BETWEEN
Advanced • Sports

Prerequisite: Walk Backward
Used in: Parkour, freestyle

Here, the dog walks backward between two objects. It is the reverse of the Between exercise from Chapter 3. Like the other parkour exercises, this one gives your dog a fun and more-than-a-little-tricky way to interact with the environment while simultaneously building his relationship and communication with you. The challenge of Backward Between is that it requires your dog not just to back up, but to do so in a focused, straight line.

Backward Between is useful for dogs who:

- need mental challenges
- get bored on regular walks
- need to build better communication with their owners
- are easily distracted by things in their environment

HOW TO DO BACKWARD BETWEEN

1. Warm up with a regular Walk Backward a few times.
2. Place two objects, such as cones, large boxes, or flowerpots, a few feet apart to start. Walk your dog up to the objects. With a treat, lure your dog forward so that only his head pokes between the two objects. Give him the cue "back." Mark and reward after his head has backed through.

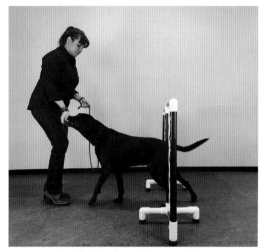

Step 4: Sarah, walking backward, lures Hank forward until most of his body is through the gates.

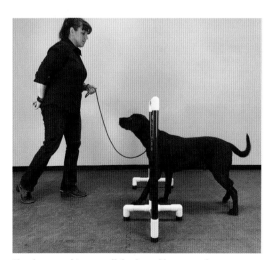

She then cues him to walk backward between the gates.

TIP: If your dog is hesitant, create a very wide space between the objects. You can always close the gap later.

3. Next time, as you approach the objects moving forward, lure the dog so his head and shoulders go between the objects. Give him the cue "back." Mark and reward after he has fully backed through.
4. Continue until the dog's whole body can back up between the objects.

From There

High school: Outdoors, practice with objects that are set several feet apart, such as two trees or street signs. Indoors, you can practice narrowing the space between the two objects, provided it is safe and continues to be fun for your dog.

College and beyond: Continue with objects that are closer, so the gap is narrower than before. You can also ask your dog to back up slightly farther each time in order to reach the objects, keeping in mind that this is hard work for your pup!

  COP COP
Advanced • Tricks

Prerequisite: Peekaboo
Used in: Freestyle

This cool trick, also called Your Feet on Mine, teaches your dog to walk on your feet, as small children sometimes do with adults. The dog starts by standing directly under you, then he puts his two front paws on top of your feet, and finally you walk forward together.

If your Heel needs a little extra flair, this trick will certainly get the job done. You are your dog are moving forward perfectly in line, and, at the same time, he is learning how fun it is to be very close to you. A dog-and-handler team who can do this trick clearly have a lot of trust and communication with each other.

Step 3: Benah lures Mojo as she takes a tiny step forward.

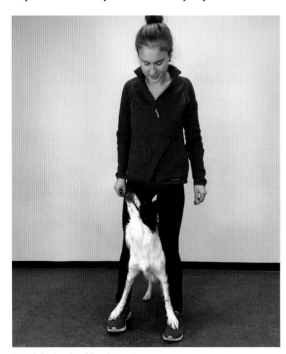

Mojo's high-school level Cop Cop.

Cop Cop is useful for dogs who:

- need to build confidence around their owners' bodies
- need mental challenges
- get bored on regular walks
- need to build better communication with their owners
- are easily distracted by things in their environment

HOW TO DO COP COP

1. Cue Peekaboo and then use a food lure to guide your dog to take a small step forward.

   TIP: Turn your toes to the inside, pigeon-toe style, to make an easier platform for your dog's paws.

2. Use the lure to encourage your dog to get closer and closer to your feet. Shape the behavior by marking and rewarding each time your dog gets closer to having both paws on top of your feet. Practice until your get at least four-for-four repetitions of his feet landing on yours.

3. Add motion. Put a treat in front of your dog's face as you take a single step. If your dog stays on your foot, mark and reward.

   TIP: If your dog doesn't stay on your foot, shape it. Mark and reward just for staying on your foot as you lift it slightly. Proceed toward bigger and bigger lifts.

From There

High school: Ask for two, then three, steps before giving a single reward.

College and beyond: Practice in increasingly distracting areas. Indoors, you can perform this for friends; outdoors, you can perform for neighbors or passersby.

MIRROR IMAGE: SIDE PASS
Advanced • Sports

Used in: Freestyle, parkour

Have you ever seen a comedy sketch in which two actors stand facing each other, one imitating the other as if they are reflections? In this activity, you and your dog will act like mirror images of each other, sidestepping to the left or right in sync. This could be a fun behavior to break up your walk, as well as an adorable element in a freestyle routine. There is also a version of this exercise in parkour.

Mirror Image: Side Pass is useful for dogs who:

- need mental challenges
- get bored on regular walks
- would benefit from building better communication with their owners
- are easily distracted by things in their environment

HOW TO DO MIRROR IMAGE: SIDE PASS

For this activity, start with a jump bar, broomstick, or similar bar. Ensure that your dog isn't afraid of the bar. You may have to do several sessions for each of the following steps, as this is a new way of moving for your dog.

1. Start with your dog facing you. Hold the bar in your right hand, extended next to your dog on his left. Have a treat in your left hand, in front of the dog's nose.
2. Take a small side step to the left. As you move, the treat will naturally move with you. Simultaneously put gentle pressure on the dog with the bar so that he sidesteps to his right.
3. If he takes any size step, even an itty bitty one, mark and reward. Then, take another side step.
4. Once your dog can do small steps, continue by rewarding for increasingly larger steps. Get four-for-four over several sessions.

Step 2: As Sarah steps to the left, the lure and bar encourage Hank to side-step to his right.

5. Add a verbal cue such as "mirror" or "side" right before you start the sequence.
6. Fade the bar. Rely on it less and less, and eventually drop the bar. You can keep your right hand extended a little as a visual cue.
7. Remove the treat from your left hand. Mark and reward from your pocket or treat pouch.

From There

High school: Once your dog is proficient in Mirror Image: Side Pass, you can start in the other direction, following the same steps.

College and beyond: As time goes on, gradually increase how many steps your dog can take. Separately, ask for Mirror Image: Side Pass in distracting places.

WEAVE THROUGH YOUR LEGS (WALKING FORWARD)
Advanced • Tricks

Used in: Freestyle

This exercise is a favorite in freestyle, as it looks impressive and allows you to walk forward while your dog is performing the trick. Weave through Your Legs involves you walking forward with large, deliberate strides while your dog weaves in and out of the space between your legs. Once your dog has learned how to weave, it's a great canine workout without being tiring for you.

Weave through Your Legs is useful for dogs who:

- need mental challenges
- get bored on regular walks
- have a surplus of energy to burn
- would benefit from building better communication with their owners
- are easily distracted by things in their environment

HOW TO DO WEAVE THROUGH YOUR LEGS

1. Stand with your right leg a little in front of your left. Bend your right leg so your knee is pointing forward. (This looks snazzier than the A-frame leg position, and, with time, the bent knee becomes a visual cue, telling your dog to weave.)

2. Have a treat in your right hand. Lower your hand so it rests a little behind your right knee. Let your dog bring his head between your legs to get the treat, and then lure him through and into a right Heel position. Mark and reward as he's moving into the Heel position. (You're rewarding the movement, not the standing still.)

TIP: If your dog is hesitant to walk through your legs, shape it. First, mark and reward his head behind your right knee, and then extending his head through to your right side, and then his shoulder through, and then his full body. Go at your dog's pace.

TIP: If your dog appears confused, help him by looking at your treat hand. This will direct his eyes in the correct direction.

3. Now, do the mirror image, with your left leg forward and knee bent, and lure through with your left hand. Mark and reward when he's in Heel position on the left side.

4. Repeat these steps until your dog is comfortably weaving through your legs several times in a row.

5. Add the verbal cue "weave" each time, right before luring the dog in between your legs.

6. Remove the food lure. You will simply do the leg-forward-with-knee-bent position and gesture with your hand behind each leg. Reward from your pocket or treat pouch. Repeat until it's a smooth pattern of right leg forward and "weave"/the dog weaves through/ left leg forward and "weave"/ the dog weaves through/and repeat.

From There

High school: Ask for more repetitions of weaving before rewarding, which will build your dog's endurance.

College and beyond: Focus on distraction. Practice in places that are mildly distracting.

Step 2. Lizzie lures Phineas between her legs, from left to right.

Rewarding him here sets him up for the next step.

Step 3: She repeats the sequence from right to left.

Step 6: Phineas has learned that a bent knee cues "weave."

05
CUTE TRICKS

ith tricks, there is so much more than meets the eye. A cute trick can also function as a way to keep your dog's impulses in check, particularly when those impulses are directed at dog-friendly passersby or guests coming into your home. If your dog gets overly excited at the sight of new friends, you can use tricks as a way for him to communicate with such people politely.

There are different ways of dealing with dogs who can't control their excitement around people, especially visitors. You can employ a number of management techniques, covered in detail in Kate's *BKLN Manners*™ book, to guide you through sticky social situations in a pinch. In some cases, such as when the doorbell rings or when a lively person is petting your dog, management is the best starting point. But to really teach your dog polite greeting behavior, you can't beat tricks. Tricks allow your dog to interact with people, but those interactions are controlled by you. A dog that can give high-fives or do other cute tricks is a dog who isn't jumping up or barking, so he gets the opportunity to be a part of the group. This will take some effort in the beginning but has an invaluable payoff in the end.

BASIC TRICKS

The basic tricks and games in this section are generally easy to teach. Keep in mind that different dogs are attracted to different kinds of behaviors: naturally "pawsy" dogs will probably love giving their paws to friends and family, coordinated dogs can quickly learn to catch cookies in the air, and dogs who love cuddling up to people will surely enjoy Chin Rest. Beyond just looking cool, these behaviors are practical. They can encourage polite interactions with people as well as keep your dog's mind focused when he

would otherwise be looking for trouble. As an added bonus, he's burning extra energy and, in some cases, stretching and working muscles.

While most of the behaviors in this chapter are primarily considered tricks, you will find many of them in freestyle routines. This is because freestyle is a particularly flexible sport that allows for creative applications of tricks.

 PAW
Basic • Tricks

Prerequisite: Sit
Used in: Freestyle

Is your dog a social butterfly, happily greeting every passerby on the street or guest in your home? Paw is the perfect simple trick, as it is inherently rewarding for your dog. By being polite and "shaking hands" with a person, he gets to have the physical contact he craves. (It is also extremely rewarding for the person. Who could pass up such a polite greeting?) If, on the other hand, he chooses to jump on the person, he will be removed and "lose" the reward of attention. It won't take him long to realize which choice is better.

Paw is useful for dogs who:

- tend to jump on people, especially during greetings
- are generally excitable around people
- have trouble holding the Sit
- are antsy during nail trims (see Paw for Nail Trims sidebar on page 156)

Paw should not be used for dogs who are fearful of strangers. Avoid forcing your dog to interact with people against his will; he may dutifully respond to the "paw" cue but concurrently be fearful (and, if sufficiently stressed, even bite).

HOW TO DO PAW

While there are many ways to teach this behavior, try this method first, as it encourages your dog to think for himself.

1. Ask for a Sit. No treat yet.
2. Hide a treat in your hand, palm up and knuckles down, and make a loose fist. Extend the fist to your sitting dog, at his elbow level or lower.
3. Your dog will probably lick or chomp at your hand. Ignore it. When he lifts his paw, even a little, mark with "yes" or click. Immediately open up your fist and let him eat the treat.
4. Continue this until your dog is reaching his paw up and actually touching your fist. Get four-for-four paw-to-hand touches.
5. Remove the treat from your "paw" fist. Put a few tiny treats in your other hand, which is hidden behind your back. Now present the empty fist as you say "paw." When he paws at it, give him a jackpot: one treat after another

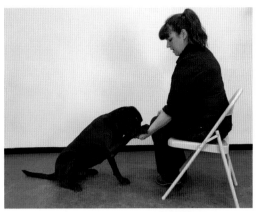

Step 3: Hank paws at the treat in Sarah's fist. This is the moment she will open her hand and let him eat the treat.

Step 7: Such a polite boy!

from the hand that was hidden behind your back. *Cool surprise!*, he thinks. Get four-for-four.

6. Add the cue "paw" right before you present your fist. Get four-for-four.
7. Unfurl your cue hand gradually. If you immediately switch from a closed fist to a flat palm, your dog probably won't understand this dramatically different cue. Open it slowly, flattening your palm an inch or two (2 to 5 cm) more each time. You probably don't need four-for-four anymore, but if your dog gets stuck, go to the previous step (a tighter fist) and get four-for-four.

PAW FOR NAIL TRIMS

If your dog is mildly uncomfortable having his nails trimmed, Paw can help him make a more positive association with the clippers. This is the kind of training that takes a lot of baby steps over time to achieve your end result, but it's worth the effort. Here's how.

1. Have extra-tasty rewards for this activity. Bits of real meat or cheese usually do the trick.
2. Cue "paw" and, once his paw is in your hand, gently pick up your clippers with the other hand. Put the clippers down a moment later and reward with an extra-tasty treat.
3. Repeat this sequence until your dog is totally comfortable with the presence of the clippers.
4. Repeat the same sequence but, this time, gently tap the clippers to your dog's paw. Work at this level as many times as needed until your dog thinks it's no big deal.
5. As time goes on, gradually intensify the interactions with the clippers to the point where you can actually clip a nail (just a tiny bit at first!).

What about the back paws? Rather than Paw, you can use Chill to condition your dog to having his back paws handled and trimmed.

For the dog who never thinks to raise his paw, you can do this method.

1. With your dog sitting in front of you, extend one hand, palm up, in the "paw" position. Meanwhile, with your other hand, gently tap the back side of his front leg.
2. When he feels the tap and lifts the leg up, let his paw briefly touch your outstretched palm. Mark and reward. Get four-for-four.
3. Add the cue "paw" before you show your palm. Get four-for-four.
4. With each repetition, reduce the tap on the back of the leg until you don't need to tap at all.

From There

High school: Once your dog can consistently give one paw, teach him to give the other paw. Have a different cue for the second paw, such as "other paw." This will make more advanced tricks like High Ten easier.

College and beyond: Practice with friends, family, and, ultimately, willing strangers. Make sure your dog is on leash so that, if he goes to jump on someone, you can remove him.

MEERKAT
Basic • Tricks

Prerequisite: Sit
Used in: Freestyle

The common name for this one is Sit Pretty or, sometimes, Beg. But we think Meerkat really gives you a sense of the end product of this trick, in which the dog rocks back on his haunches, back erect, and gives the impression of a meerkat on the lookout for predators. It is a useful trick because it doesn't require the dog to actually touch the person cuing the behavior; therefore, your dog can interact with people from a distance, making it useful for people who are afraid of or allergic to dogs, or for dogs who aren't yet ready to handle close interactions.

Maintaining the Meerkat position takes a good deal of core strength. Initially, your dog may not be able to hold this position on his own or do more than a few repetitions. You can build his strength slowly over time, being careful not to push it. (Think about how crunches at the gym feel.)

Meerkat is useful for dogs who:

- tend to jump on people, especially during greetings
- are generally excitable around people
- are better off not touching people

HOW TO DO MEERKAT

1. Start with the dog in a Sit.
2. Hold a treat over the dog's head, just out of his reach.
3. When he lifts either paw, even a little, mark and reward right there. (It's OK if the paw has hit the ground already, but his head should still be reaching up.) Get four-for-four.
4. Now, when you hold the treat up, wait for a higher paw lift or a two-paw lift. Mark and reward. Get four-for-four.

   TIP: You can help him balance as you build his strength. Offer your forearm under his front legs, at about his shoulder height.
5. Build on your dog's success. Once he can confidently balance, wait to mark and reward

Step 3: A paw lift is a great start for Meerkat. Reward it!

Step 4: Sarah holds out for a double paw lift. She rewards Hank while his paws are still in the air.

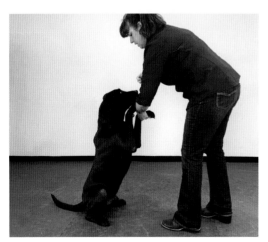

Support your dog if he needs it. This is a physically demanding behavior for some dogs.

Hank shows off his high-school level Meerkat, with Sarah cuing from a distance.

for higher front-paw lifts until he is fully rocking back on his haunches.

6. Once you have the final behavior, say the cue "meerkat" right before luring with the treat.

7. Get rid of the lure. Make the same gesture with an empty hand, and reward from your other hand or pocket.

From There

High school: Very gradually move your cue hand away from the dog, so you can cue Meerkat without being directly in front of his face.

College: Incorporate distractions by using it as a "party trick" with guests in your home or people on the street. At first, the other person can say "meerkat," but you show the visual cue and reward.

Grad school and beyond: Combine Meerkat with Wave, so your dog sits up and then waves.

 TAKE A BOW
Basic • Tricks

Used in: Freestyle

This behavior involves your dog's front end stretching to the ground, as in a Down, but his rear is still standing upright. As the inspiration behind yoga's "downward dog" moniker, this position looks like the dog is bowing. Not only is this a cute trick, but it's used among canine athletes to stretch and condition. This is also a useful trick when you don't want your dog to physically touch guests or strangers, as you can cue it from a distance.

Take a Bow is useful for dogs who:

- tend to jump on people, especially during greetings
- are generally excitable around people
- are better off not touching people

HOW TO DO TAKE A BOW

1. Start with your dog in a standing position.

2. With a treat in one hand, slowly lure his nose diagonally down and back, aiming for a spot on the floor between his front legs, just behind his front paws.

3. You may need to place your other arm under your dog's hips to prevent him from lying down all the way. Don't prop him up; rather, your arm is just there as a physical guide.

TIP: Your dog may find your arm under his hips distracting. In this case, mark and reward quickly before he slumps into a full Down.

4. When he is in the bowing position, mark and reward. Get four-for-four or practice until it's happening easily.

TIP: If your dog will not go into a full bow right off the bat, shape it. Reward him for slightly bending his elbows. Start holding out for deeper and deeper bends until his elbows are resting on the floor.

5. Add the cue. Say "ta-da!" (or another cue, but avoid "bow" because it sounds like "down") and then lure your dog as before. Get four-for-four.

6. Fade out your arm from under his hips, removing it a little more with every successful repetition.

7. Remove the food lure. Make the same hand movement but reward from your pocket or treat pouch.

Step 2: Sarah drags the treat a little behind Hank's paws.

Step 3: If your dog slumps into a Down, place your free hand under his hips.

Hank's college-level Take a Bow.

From There

High school: Gradually, you can turn the hand signal into a sweeping gesture toward the dog, as if you are presenting him to an audience. To do this, you will slowly begin standing up straight with your own body. You're no longer pointing to where your dog should aim his nose.

College and beyond: Increase the challenge: practice in distracting areas, such as when guests come over; gradually distance yourself from your dog; and/or teach the exercise from a Heel position.

CHIN REST
Basic • Tricks

Asking your bouncy dog to interact calmly with a guest can be difficult, so put the behavior on cue! For this trick, your dog will learn to rest his chin in a person's hand. It is an inherently calm behavior, so by training your dog to take a relaxing posture, his body will, in turn, naturally relax itself. He gets the extra reward of being able to have physical contact with anyone who wants to pet him.

Chin Rest is also an integral component of *cooperative care*, which refers to training methods that teach animals to tolerate blood draws, nail trims, toothbrushing, and so on. It is used for zoo animals as well as companion animals. By teaching your dog a very solid Chin Rest, he can rest his head in your hand while your vet does her job, all without a struggle.

Chin Rest is useful for dogs who:

- need help calming down around people
- like to be touched
- are excitable during grooming, vet visits, and the like

HOW TO DO CHIN REST

1. Face your dog. Gently place your palm on your dog's chest. While your hand is on his chest, mark and reward.
2. With every repetition, inch your hand gradually up your dog's neck. Mark and reward.

   TIP: If your dog appears uncomfortable or restless at any point, go back to a lower spot on his neck or chest and get four-for-four.
3. Cradle your dog's chin in your palm. Mark and reward.
4. After practicing many repetitions of resting his chin in your palm, test your dog's proficiency. Hold your palm a few centimeters under your dog's chin, and see if he lowers his head onto your hand. If he does, jackpot! (If

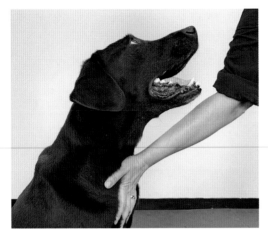

Step 1: Sarah starts at Hank's chest and slowly works her way up.

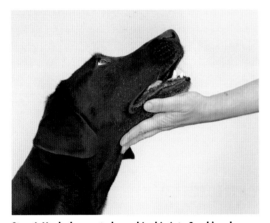

Step 4: Hank chooses to lower his chin into Sarah's palm.

he doesn't, go back to Step 3.)

5. Once your dog intentionally lowers his head onto your palm, get four-for-four.

6. Add the verbal cue "chin" before you offer your palm. Get four-for-four.

    TIP: The hand gesture looks similar to Paw and may confuse your dog at first. If your dog offers his paw, ignore it. Reward generously for correct Chin Rests.

From There

High school: Add duration. Using the rule of four-for-four, very gradually extend how long your dog's head is resting in your palm.

College and beyond: Add distractions. By practicing this trick in the presence of distractions, you will help teach your dog to focus and relax, even when exciting things are happening around him. Start with mild distractions, like friends or family making noise in another room, and build all the way up to large distractions, like practicing Chin Rest at the vet's office or having guests do Chin Rest with your dog.

  KISS ME
Basic • Tricks

Used in: Freestyle

This simple trick involves your dog touching his nose to your cheek (or even licking your cheek, if you're into that kind of kiss). It is a variation of targeting in which the dog will target your cheek. If your dog loves getting up close and personal with people, this is a controlled way to let him express his affection without ending up in the person's lap. When you cue it from a distance, it can even be used as a recall.

A safety side note: Not all dogs are comfortable having a person's face close to theirs. Never put your face in a dog's personal space unless you are certain that it is safe to do so.

Kiss Me is useful for dogs who:

- need help focusing their energy around people
- are safe and happy to approach people
- need more help with recalls

HOW TO DO KISS ME

1. Bait the location of your "kiss" with something tasty. For example, if you want your dog to kiss your cheek, put a dab of cream cheese on the spot.

2. Offer your cheek to your dog and wait for him to go in for a sniff.

3. As soon as your dog has made contact with your cheek, mark and reward with a treat from your pocket or treat pouch.

Step 2: Batman has taken the bait (literally) and kissed Kate in the process.

TIP: In the beginning, reward any contact. Perhaps you ultimately want a nose touch, but your dog is actually licking your cheek. Reward the licks at first, and you can shape the behavior later on.

4. Get at least four-for-four and then fade out the bait as quickly as possible.

5. Tighten the criteria, if necessary. If your dog is zealously licking your face, but your end goal is a gentle nose touch, start ignoring the most offensive licks and rewarding the more delicate ones. With repetition, you can get pickier about which touches you reward.

6. Add the verbal cue. Stay very close to your dog and say "kiss me" right before your dog touches your face. Mark and reward.

From There

High school: Try a recall to do Kiss Me. Once your dog knows the cue well, stand several inches farther from him and ask for a Kiss Me. As time goes on, you can add more and more distance until your dog can run to you for a kiss.

College and beyond: If your dog is neither shy nor dangerously enthusiastic around other people, friends and family can do Kiss Me as well. What a cute way to greet people!

  ## GO TO YOUR PLACE
Basic • Manners

Prerequisite: Down

True, this is neither a trick nor a game, but if your dog will stop pestering the guests and go to his bed on cue, you are sure to get compliments on how cute and well-behaved he is.

Go to Your Place is useful for dogs who:
- get underfoot when their owners are eating meals
- get excited when guests come into their homes
- door dash when their owners open doors
- need alternatives to sleeping on the couches or beds
- accompany their owners to friends' houses or dog-friendly cafes

Practice Go to Your Place on something portable, such as a towel. When you go out, you can bring the towel and drape it anywhere you want your dog to remain. This gives him a home base to securely park himself, even at an agility trial, in a hotel room, or at a party. Having a comfortable place to lie can ease stress for anxious dogs and reduce the excitement of bouncy dogs who don't know what to do with themselves.

For the early stages of Go to Your Place, you can use either some treats or a food-stuffed hollow rubber toy.

HOW TO DO GO TO YOUR PLACE

1. Stand next to the dog's bed. Point to the bed or lead him to it with a treat. (Don't give him the treat until the completion of Step 3.)

2. When your dog gets all four paws on the bed, ask him to lie down and then pause for one to five seconds, depending on how animated your dog is.

A TRICKY SOLUTION TO ANXIETY AND FEAR

Zuri, a three-year-old Bolognese, proves that tricks are more than just fun and games. From the start, Zuri struggled with overwhelming anxiety and fear; it caused her stress on walks and led her to shut down during training classes.

Her owner, Anita, took Zuri's training in a different direction. Anita explains, "I learned to use tricks to get Zuri focused and engaged. Little by little, I started to see a change. By allowing Zuri to do tricks she knew well, she didn't let her anxiety get the better of her." Zuri can now successfully perform tricks in the presence of new people, which lets her break the ice from a distance until she's comfortable enough to get closer. On walks, turns from rally (as in Chapter 4) have "come in handy when I need to redirect my dog from reacting to another dog," says Anita.

Zuri now boasts an impressive repertoire of tricks and several trick titles (AKC TKP, Do More With Your Dog ETD, and counting). With the help of tricks, she's been able to overcome hurdles that Anita originally thought would be impossible. Zuri has even started trialing in rally, using tricks as a way to warm up and get focused before her run. From here, the sky is the limit!

3. Place some treats or the food-filled toy on the bed. Let him eat it on his bed.

   TIP: If your dog tends to carry his goodies off the bed, practice this on leash.

4. As soon as your dog has finished eating, release with "OK" and encourage him to get off the bed. Pick up the food toy, if you used one. Get four-for-four.

5. Add the verbal cue "place" before you point to the bed. Get four-for-four.

6. With each successful repetition, slightly increase the duration of your pause before giving the food. The sequence will be: say "place" and point to the bed/ask for a Down/ pause for five to ten seconds/give treats or a food toy on the bed/release with "OK."

   TIP: If your dog struggles at any point, go to an easier duration and get four-for-four.

From There

High school: To advance your dog's Go to Your Place skills, you want to isolate the three Ds:

- **Duration:** Keep your dog on his bed for longer and longer periods before you release him.
- **Distance:** Ask your dog to walk to his bed himself, without you leading him.
- **Distraction:** Practice Go to Your Place while there is activity in the room.

Step 1: Sarah points (even with her foot, in true agility style) to tell Fever where to go.

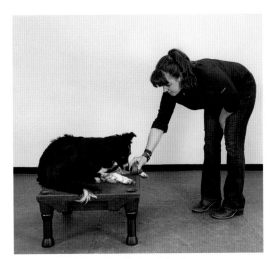

Step 3: Fever gets a toy stuffed with food.

Step 4: Fever has finished the food and is waiting for Sarah to release her.

Each D should be increased in very small increments over time.

College and beyond: Once your dog has mastered each D separately, you can combine them. For instance, ask your dog to stay on his bed for several minutes (duration) while you eat dinner with a few guests (distraction). Also, consider practicing with different towels, mats, and dog beds. This helps your dog generalize Go to Your Place, so you can use the cue even when your dog's special bed isn't available.

ADVANCED TRICKS

 BALANCE AN OBJECT
Advanced • Tricks

Ah, the dog who can balance a cookie on his head. He's the envy of nearly every dog owner, and rightly so. A dog with this skill has the ability to control his strongest impulse—the urge to eat—until the owner gives a release word. An excited or bouncy dog won't be able to accomplish this task. The activity here will get you started on teaching your dog to balance any item on his head. (This means that even Pugs and other brachycephalic breeds can do it, whereas they're out of luck with the "balance on your nose" trick.)

The end product is a visually impressive crowd-pleaser, but don't be tempted to start piling rawhide chewies on your dog's head from the get-go. That would be setting your dog up for failure. Rather, you'll start from a step that's so simple that almost any dog can do it. From there, each subsequent step is a tiny increase in difficulty, imperceptible to anyone but you. By "thinly slicing" this trick, your dog will feel that each step is easy because it is only slightly more challenging than the previous step. Slow and steady progress will yield faster results than trying to skip steps, which ultimately only confuses and frustrates your dog. Once your dog gets the hang of the game, you'll be amazed by how he is able to remain still, quiet, and focused during the activity. It's a great life skill for him to practice, neatly packaged as a trick. The steps for Balance an Object come compliments of Frankie Joiris at Total Team.

Balance an Object is useful for dogs who:
- struggle to stay still
- could benefit from more focus
- need indoor hobbies

Step 2: Sarah lays the towel on Fever's head and simultaneously gives her a treat.

Step 3: She lays the towel on Fever's head, but pauses before treating.

HOW TO DO BALANCE AN OBJECT

1. Start with a paper towel, tissue, or similarly thin, floppy object that can be momentarily draped on the dog's head. Have the paper towel in one hand and some treats in the other.

2. With your dog sitting in front of you, momentarily lay the paper towel on your dog's head with one hand for about half a second while simultaneously feeding one or more treats with the other hand. Don't let go of the paper towel. Remove the paper towel and the treats at the same time. This is conditioning the dog to enjoy the otherwise strange sensation of having something on his head. Practice this until you get four-for-four.

3. Place the paper towel on your dog's head for half a second but do not treat yet. After a half-second of the paper towel on his head, reward with a treat and immediately remove it. Get four-for-four repetitions.

4. Increase the duration to one second and then reward and remove. Get four-for-four.

5. Increase the duration to three seconds and then reward and remove. Get four-for-four.

You can balance all kinds of humiliating objects on your dog's head!

6. Now, fold the paper towel in half lengthwise, so it is long but thinner and heavier. Repeat Step 3, and then Step 4, and then Step 5. (If this is too difficult, go back to Step 2.)

7. Now, here is the catch: if the object falls off his head for any reason, even human error, he does not get the treat. You want to teach him

that only a successful balance will earn him the reward. This motivates him to stay extra-still.

From There
High school: Gradually practice this with slightly more difficult objects, such an envelope or a folder.

College and beyond: Practice with tempting items, like a toy or a cookie. The reward can be getting that toy or treat.

  ## WAVE
Advanced • Tricks

Prerequisite: Paw

Used in: Freestyle, agility

This trick is essentially a Paw from a distance, which gives the appearance of waving hello or goodbye. It's a real crowd-pleaser! Wave also has practical applications in sports, as it is used for conditioning work in agility.

Wave is useful for dogs who:

- have any type of energy level, including low energy
- have trouble focusing around people
- are better off not touching people

HOW TO DO WAVE

1. Ask for a Sit. Show your dog a new hand signal, such as waving your hand back and forth, and then immediately give the verbal and visual cue for Paw.
2. When your dog's paw is reaching toward your hand, slip your hand away so you do not make contact. (This creates the dog's waving motion.) Mark and reward. Get four-for-four.
3. Eliminate the verbal cue "paw" from the sequence, which is now: new hand signal (waving)/old hand signal (holding out your hand in front of the dog)/mark and reward. Get four-for-four.
4. Add the new verbal cue "wave." The sequence is now: new verbal cue "wave"/new hand signal (waving)/old hand signal (holding out

When your dog is as big and bouncy as Hank, teaching Wave is a great way to greet people!

your hand in front of the dog)/mark and reward. Get four-for-four.
5. Continue fading the old "paw" hand signal by presenting your hand for a shorter and shorter time.

From There
High school: Increase the distance between you and the dog. Very gradually, with each successful repetition, inch yourself farther away from the dog. How cool will it look when you can secretly cue your dog to "wave" from far away? Your guests will love it!

College and beyond: Practice with other people giving your dog the cue. You are still welcome to be the one who gives the reward.

  ## HIGH FIVE AND HIGH TEN
Advanced • Tricks

Prerequisite: Paw

Used in: Freestyle

Like giving paw, a High Five or a High Ten allows your dog to interact with other people in an active but controlled way. It's inherently rewarding for both a human-friendly dog and a dog-friendly human, and it encourages polite behavior in times of excitement. It's also super-easy to teach, provided your dog already knows Paw fluently.

High Five and High Ten are useful for dogs who:

- are active
- enjoy close contact with people
- are motivated by attention
- need calm alternatives to jumping on people

HOW TO DO HIGH FIVE

1. Start by asking for Paw and offering your outstretched hand. Get four-for-four, marking and rewarding after each one.
2. Change your hand position. This time, offer a flat palm facing your dog (just like a high five) at the same height and give no verbal cue. The dog will naturally throw his paw at your hand, so mark and reward.
3. With each correct High Five, gradually offer your flat palm higher and higher so that your dog will lift his paw higher as in a real high five. Keep in mind that the height should be relative to the dog's size.

TIP: If your dog can't perform at a certain point, it may mean that you've increased the

Gimme some skin, Hank!

height too much too quickly. Go back to a lower height and get four-for-four.

4. After four-for-four at your ideal height, say "high five" and then offer your flat palm. Mark and reward.

From There

Once your dog can do High Five, try High Ten.

High school: To teach High Ten, offer both hands up, a little too high for your dog to reach. Let him think about it. Even if he only hits one paw at first, reward him. With encouragement and repetition, he will naturally think to throw both paws at you.

College and beyond: Practice High Five and High Ten with friends and family, or in distracting situations.

  ## CRAWL
Advanced • Tricks

Prerequisite: Down
Used in: Freestyle

Crawl involves your dog starting from a Down position and army-crawling close to the ground for several steps. It's a pretty cute way for him get from point A to point B.

Crawl is useful for dogs who:

- like showing off for their owners and guests
- are agile and like challenges

HOW TO DO CRAWL

1. Have six or more treats in your hand. Ask for a Down but do not reward yet.
2. Drag one treat on the floor, starting from your dog's nose and moving it out in front of him in a straight line.
3. If your dog moves forward a tiny bit without standing up, mark and reward with the treat. Reward any forward motion, even the smallest microstep, at this stage.
4. Using your second treat, continue to lure forward to encourage your dog to crawl another small step. When he does, mark and

Even long, leggy dogs can learn to crawl.

reward. Continue this sequence until you need to reload your treats.

> TIP: If you dog stands up at any point, remove the treat and begin again. Make sure that you are only rewarding for forward crawling motion.

> TIP: If your dog is having difficulty, put your other hand on his rear and apply gentle downward pressure if he starts to stand up. Your dog may need to learn how to physically do what you're asking. Preventing him from standing up may help him get the idea.

5. When your dog is able to crawl a couple of feet at a time, add the verbal cue. Say "crawl" and then lure, mark, and reward as before

6. Remove the food lure. Say "crawl" and use the same hand motion (which is now your hand signal) but without the treat. Mark and reward with a treat from your other hand or pocket.

From There

High school: Gradually fade your hand signal. Ultimately, you can use just your verbal cue.

College and beyond: Increase the distance your dog crawls, a little at a time. Alternatively, you can ask for Crawl during mild distractions, such as when a guest has come over. Make sure to reward generously when your dog performs a Crawl that is harder than usual.

I'M SO EMBARRASSED
Advanced • Tricks

Prerequisite: Meerkat

Used in: Freestyle

For this trick, your dog will start from a Meerkat position in front of you. If he doesn't know or isn't comfortable doing Meerkat, he can stand taller on his hind legs, as Mojo demonstrates in the photos. In either case, the dog will then put his front paws on your arm or another object in a begging gesture, and then duck his head between his front legs. The end result is the look of "I'm so embarrassed," "I'm really sorry," or "pretty please."

I'm So Embarrassed is useful for dogs who:

■ like to get close to people

■ need calm behaviors to do with others

HOW TO DO I'M SO EMBARRASSED

1. Cue Meerkat and offer your forearm under the dog's front paws. Your dog should naturally land his paws on your arm as support.

   > TIP: Instead of your arm, you can use an object like a chair, stepstool, or box, especially if your dog already knows a front paw target behavior. Just make sure that the object is at least as tall as your dog's shoulders.

2. With the dog in this position, offer a food lure under and in between the dog's front legs.

3. When your dog reaches his head down between his front legs to get the treat, mark and reward right there. Get four-for-four.

4. Eliminate the "meerkat" cue. Use a new cue, such as "duck," right before you offer your forearm. Get four-for-four.

5. Remove the lure. Have a treat ready in your pocket. Give the verbal cue, show your arm, and wait for your dog to duck his head. When your dog lowers his head, quickly grab the treat so you can mark and reward in that position.

Step 3: Benah marks and rewards Mojo when his head has ducked below his paws.

Step 5: The finished product!

TIP: You may have to shape this behavior. Point your (formerly luring) hand under the dog for shorter and shorter durations until it is no longer necessary.

From There

High school: As you continue to train I'm So Embarrassed, you can fade out the hand motion under his legs so that the dog performs this behavior on a verbal cue alone. If you train this on a forearm, you can also later transfer the behavior to other objects.

College: Let family and friends try this trick, too! You may have to be there to reward in the beginning.

  CRISSCROSS APPLESAUCE
Advanced • Tricks

Prerequisites: Down, Paw Target
Used in: Freestyle

This adorable trick involves the dog crossing his front legs while lying down. First, he puts his left paw over his right, and then right paw over left, as if dancing. It builds upon the Paw Target activity (as in Chapter 7). You can imagine how seamlessly this fits into a freestyle routine, with the dog tapping back and forth to the beat of the music.

Crisscross Applesauce is useful for dogs who:

- like showing off for their owners and guests
- like to use their paws
- are better off not touching people

HOW TO DO CRISSCROSS APPLESAUCE

1. With your dog lying down, place the paw target item on the floor, in between his paws, closer to his left paw.
2. Cue "hit it." Mark and reward as long as he uses his left paw to touch the target. Place your reward on the outside (to the right) of the right paw. This will eventually be in line with where his balance should be for the behavior.

Step 2: Fever puts her left paw on the target...

3. Pick up your target after each repetition.

4. When he is consistently using the left paw to touch the target, move the target item incrementally closer to the right paw. Cue "hit it" as before and continue to place the reward on the opposite (right) side of the right paw.

5. Eventually, you will move the target to rest on top of his right paw. Continue to place the reward to the outside of the right paw. Get four-for-four.

6. Move the target to the outside (right side) of the right paw and cue "hit it." Continue to place the reward to the right of the right paw. Get four-for-four.

   TIP: If he tries to target with his right paw, ignore it.

7. Add the verbal cue "crisscross" and then present the target to the right side of the right paw.

8. Eventually, your dog will anticipate the sequence and will respond after the verbal cue. You no longer need the target.

   TIP: If necessary, fade out the target by cutting it into a progressively smaller size.

9. Repeat Steps 1 through 8, reversing left and right. The verbal cue for this side is "applesauce."

10. Once you have both behaviors, you will chain them together. Cue "crisscross" and then mark and reward on the outer side of his right paw. Then cue "applesauce," marking and rewarding on the outer side of his left paw.

    TIP: Always ask for the behaviors in this order so that your dog will begin to expect that one follows the other.

From There

High school: Eventually your dog will learn the full behavior chain, so you can reward just once at the end of the "applesauce" portion.

College and beyond: Practice this sequence for other people, adding mild distractions.

...and gets a treat to the far side of her right paw.

Step 6: The target is now to the right of her right paw.

Step 8: Fever no longer needs the target.

Step 9: Don't forget applesauce!

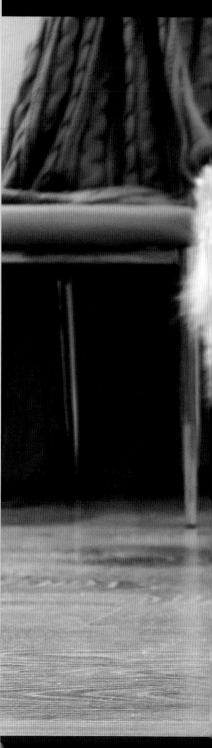

06
ACTIVE TRICKS

Fever's success in the agility ring is largely due to her foundation training. Photo by Barry Rosen

Not all tricks have to be low-key. While Chapter 5 aimed to give you techniques to help your dog relax, this chapter has tricks that encourage him to jump, run, and spin. Active tricks are an effective way to channel a dog's physical energy toward a focused activity. His body and mind will be working together, which in turn teaches him that, yes, it is possible to burn off steam and listen to his human at the same time. Win-win!

As with the tricks in Chapter 5, many of the tricks in this chapter can be applied to a freestyle routine.

BASIC TRICKS

  JUMP OVER
Basic • Sports

Used in: Agility, parkour, rally, freestyle

This is an essential agility exercise that teaches dogs to jump over obstacles in a safe, controlled manner. It also turns up in parkour, rally, and freestyle. The jump could be a DIY jump set up in your home (see Chapter 7), or you can utilize the natural or urban landscape. When used outside,

Jump Over is a super-fun way to get your dog to focus on you, all the while building his trust in you and reinforcing the bond you've developed. This activity can be done on a leash or long line or, if in a safe area, off leash. Remember that dogs whose growth plates haven't yet closed (roughly less than eighteen months old) should jump no higher than hock height and should avoid repeated jumping. Most older dogs can jump as high as 2 inches (5 cm) below the withers.

Jump Over is useful for dogs who:

- are healthy and active
- need to learn how to channel their energy
- need to build trust in their owners
- like to play, either with their owners or with environmental elements

Note that in the instructions that follow, you will toss a treat on the ground as is done in agility training. By placing the reward on the ground, your dog will learn to look where he's jumping. This is critical for safety and will come in handy when your dog is jumping on uneven surfaces. Conversely, if you reward from your hand, the dog learns to jump while looking up at your hand, and he is much more likely to injure himself this way.

HOW TO DO JUMP OVER

1. Find or create a very low, stable object for your dog to jump over. You can add height later; for now, start easy to build his confidence.
2. Approach the low jump with your dog. Before you reach it, toss a treat to the other side of the jump, onto the ground.
3. Allow your dog to jump over the obstacle and get the treat.

    TIP: If your dog is going around rather than over the jump, move your body to the landing side of the jump (while your dog stays on the takeoff side). Put the treat right in front of his nose and lure him over the jump and to the ground. It is still important that the treat is delivered on the ground. Alternatively, you can put his leash on to prevent him from swerving around the jump. Avoid pulling him over the jump, as that is a sure way to make your dog afraid of this exercise. It has to be his choice.

4. Once your dog is happily clearing the jump, you can add the verbal cue. Say "jump" right

Many dogs are natural jumpers and will enjoy using these skills.

before you toss the reward to the other side of the obstacle.

From There

You can increase the jump height gradually as your dog builds confidence in his abilities and trust in your handling skills. (Remember, pushing him to jump too high will have the opposite effect!) While your Jack Russell can probably scale a stone wall, there is no reason to put his physical or emotional health at risk by asking him to do so. Agility organizations such as the United States Dog Agility Association (USDAA) and American Kennel Club (AKC) have set limits for jump height, which you can find online.

TURNING WHILE JUMPING

In agility, the course is full of twists and turns. In many cases, the dog will sometimes make a turn while jumping over an obstacle. The agility handler's position is one of the cues that tells the dog to turn while taking a jump. When Sarah sends Hank to a jump but does not run past the jump herself, Hank should know to turn toward her while taking the jump. By the time he lands, he has already completed a large part of the turn.

To start teaching this, Sarah did her dogs' foundation jump training by teaching them to go around traffic cones, as in Go Around (in Chapter 3). She didn't use a jump bar at all in the beginning, partly because her dogs were not old enough to do any real jumping. When Sarah practiced Go Around, she always stepped with the foot closest to the dog and extended the hand on the same side, aiming toward the outside of the cone. (See the photos for Go Around.) She continued to practice, cuing the behavior from farther and farther away. By the time Fever was old enough to take jumps, Sarah could already send her to jumps from up to 10 feet (3 m) away.

 **JUMP OVER YOUR LEG**
Basic • Sports

Used in: Freestyle

Active dogs sometimes just need a channel for their energy. Does your dog get underfoot or jump on people when you're trying to have a conversation? You don't need a yard full of agility jumps to keep him engaged while you chat. Instead, while you're talking to a neighbor on the sidewalk, or while you and your guests are hanging out on the sofa, your dog can jump back and forth over your outstretched leg. Not only does this entertain everyone, it also burns enough of your dog's energy that he won't be nearly as motivated to jump on your guests or behave inappropriately afterward. This is a common exercise in freestyle routines, too!

Jump over Your Leg is useful for dogs who:

- are healthy and active
- need to learn how to channel their energy
- need to build trust in their owners
- like to play, especially when there's an audience

HOW TO DO JUMP OVER YOUR LEG

1. Sit on the floor with one leg stretched out in front of you. Your other leg should be out of the way—either bent at the knee and held close to your chest, or curled up under your rear.

2. With the dog on one side of your leg, show him a treat. Toss the treat or lure him to the other side, as in Jump Over. Be sure to allow enough room for the dog to land all four paws on the opposite side of your leg.

   TIP: If your dog keeps going around your leg, do this exercise in a hallway or with your foot against a piece of furniture so that he has no choice but to cross over your leg.

3. Reward him at ground level when he gets to the opposite side, even if there was no actual "jump."

4. Repeat until your dog is confidently crossing over your leg.

5. Add the verbal cue "jump." Get four-for-four.

6. Begin to lift your leg. Put your outstretched foot on a book or box to add a little height. Repeat until your dog is enthusiastically and confidently jumping.

From There

High school: Vary your position. Sit on the couch and place your outstretched foot against the coffee-table leg (but not too high!). Stand and hold out your leg in front of you or even out to the side or behind you. The possibilities are only limited by your imagination.

College and beyond: Practice during times of distraction, such as when guests are visiting or while waiting at a crosswalk.

  SPIN
Basic • Tricks

Used in: Freestyle, agility

If your dog is active, Spin is a simple trick to teach. It doesn't involve jumping, running, or physical contact, so it's safe to use around kids, too. This is one trick that Kate taught Batman in her building's elevator, as it only requires a few seconds and a few feet of space. Spin, along with variations of it, makes its way into many freestyle routines. It may be used in agility training, too; for example, handlers might teach their dogs to turn 180 or 360 degrees on a 12-inch (30-cm)-wide board to build their confidence for the teeter or dog walk. If a dog knows he can maneuver all four paws in a tight space, he'll be more comfortable when the obstacle is 4 feet (1.2 m) high.

Spin involves your dog rotating 360 degrees in a tight circle. (He is not circling around an object; that is Go Around.) He can spin in front of you or to your side in a Heel position. Note that some dogs prefer spinning in one direction over the other; this is fine, and it simply means that you'll need to take it slowly when teaching the more difficult direction.

Spin is useful for dogs who:
- just can't contain themselves around people
- are active or bouncy by nature
- are better off not touching people

HOW TO DO SPIN

1. Face your dog. Have at least four treats in one hand.

2. Start luring your dog's nose in a wide circle. Pop a treat into his mouth when he completes each quarter turn. When he's almost completed his spin, mark it with "yes" or click before he gets that final treat. Practice until your dog is moving smoothly, which may take several sessions of four-for-four.

   TIP: Move your lure hand slowly enough for your dog to follow the scent. If his nose becomes detached from your hand, you're moving it too fast.

   TIP: Be aware of your dog's comfort level as your arm moves above his head. Some dogs may find this intimidating and will need a slow introduction to this trick.

3. Continue to lure, but now you'll mark and reward with only one treat when the Spin is fully completed. Gradually turn your hand into

a recognizable visual cue, like a pointing finger, as this will help your dog ease into the next step. Get four-for-four or practice until smooth.

   TIP: As your dog gets better at this, you can move the lure more quickly for a faster Spin.

4. Once your dog can make a relatively small, quick Spin, remove the lure. You will draw the circle with an empty hand. Mark and reward at the end from a pocket or other hand. Get four-for-four.

5. Add a verbal cue, such as "spin," before starting the sequence.

Step 1: Batman starts by facing Kate, ready for his treat lure.

Step 2: Kate slowly lures, treating when the turn is 25 percent, 50 percent (as shown here), 75 percent, and 100 percent complete.

From There

High school: Repeat the steps in the other direction. Choose a different cue for this direction, such as "twist."

College: Teach him to spin from a Heel position on your left or right. Since you're changing the context, start from Step 1 and work your way up. (You will likely find that it goes much faster than the first time.)

Grad school and beyond: Indoors, use this as a trick to show off to your guests. Outside, practice Spin as a fun way to burn some energy while waiting at a crosswalk.

CATCH A COOKIE
Basic • Tricks

Used in: Agility

The beauty of this trick is that it can be done at a considerable distance. If your guests or their kids aren't comfortable around dogs, you can encourage them to toss a treat in the air for your dog to catch. On the flip side, if your dog is too excitable or shy to calmly interact with new people, this trick is likely a great fit. You can hold your dog on leash if you have any concerns about him getting too close to your guests. Catch a Cookie has a practical purpose in sports such as agility, where the handler needs to reward the dog from a distance.

Prior to teaching your dog, you might need to practice your throws. Aim your throws just above your dog's nose. Sarah finds it easier to throw underhand, but you should experiment to see what works for you. Additionally, choose your treats wisely. Your dog should be able to easily see the treat, so be sure to choose a goodie that is large and colorful. When you're ready to practice with your dog, have a partner who can help.

Catch a Cookie is useful for dogs who:

- love treats
- have any type of energy level
- need to be given extra space between them and your guests

HOW TO DO CATCH A COOKIE

1. Start with your dog on leash, being held by your training partner. At first, your dog is allowed to go anywhere within the radius of his leash. Your partner should stand still, as though your dog's leash is tied to a post.

2. Toss a treat to your dog. Whether he catches it or not, allow your dog to eat the treat for the first six tosses.

3. On the seventh toss, your training partner will prevent your dog from getting the treat unless he catches it mid-air. If the treat hits the floor, your dog can't have it. Your partner can use the leash to restrain the dog, put her foot over the treat, or block with her body. This will build your dog's desire to catch the treat.

4. As soon as your dog catches a treat for the first time, celebrate! Throw him a party and cheer.

   TIP: Be patient. It might take a while to get a successful catch. If you see your dog opening his mouth while the treat is in the air, he's starting to get the idea!

5. Once your dog is reliably catching, say "catch" right before you throw the treat.

From There

High school and beyond: Begin to practice without the leash. Invite others to throw a treat as well, provided they can throw accurately! You can also play "catch" with other items, such as balls.

 RUN THROUGH YOUR LEGS
Basic • Sports

Used in: Freestyle

Here, you will stand still with your legs spread far enough for your dog to fit through. Your dog, facing you, will run between your legs from front to back. This can easily be applied to a freestyle routine, and it also teaches your dog to trust you as he moves close to your body.

Run through Your Legs is useful for dogs who:

- are high energy
- prefer active tricks to stationary ones
- need a fun recall refresher
- struggle with more complex behaviors involving their owners' legs
- are short enough to fit under people's legs

Run through Your Legs is a good bonding activity for smaller dogs and their owners.

HOW TO DO RUN THROUGH YOUR LEGS

1. Face your dog with only a little space between you.

2. With your legs spread wide enough for him to fit through, reach down and toss a treat between your legs, aiming for just a little behind you.

   TIP: If your dog is uncomfortable running through your legs, start with a less intimidating position. Sit in a chair with your legs propped up on another chair and drop treats directly below you. Shape the behavior so, with time, he has to walk a little farther under you to get the treat. Eventually, he will trust you enough to walk under your legs to get the treat.

   TIP: If your dog is darting around you to get the treat (but is otherwise comfortable), do this exercise with barriers, such as two chairs, at your sides, or put your dog on leash, using the leash to restrict him only if he tries to swerve around you.

3. Continue tossing the treat farther each time until he is able to get his whole body through your legs without backtracking after eating the treat. Get four-for-four over several sessions.

4. Practice the same sequence, but with your dog a little farther in front of you. Now he will have to make a more conscious decision to go through your legs and not around you. Get four-for-four over several sessions.

5. Fade the treat by making the pointing gesture through your legs, but no treat. As soon as your dog runs through your legs, give him a jackpot of several treats from your hand.

6. Add a verbal cue, such as "through."

From There

You can increase both distance and distraction, as well as combine Run through Your Legs with other behaviors, as in a freestyle routine.

High school: Work on increasing the distance your dog has to run to you before doing Run through Your Legs. This is great for building recall skills.

College and beyond: Increase distraction gradually, both indoors and out. Also consider combining this behavior with other tricks and behaviors.

 CLOSE THE DOOR
Basic • Tricks

Prerequisite: Nose Target or Paw Target

Sometimes you just need a little privacy. This trick will teach your dog to approach an open door and close it with his nose (or paw). While a cute trick, it is also the kind of daily task a service dog might do for his owner.

Close the Door is useful for dogs who:

- need extra engagement in the house
- like to do targeting activities

HOW TO DO CLOSE THE DOOR

The instructions here use a Nose Target. (Don't know what that is? Check out the What's a Nose Target? sidebar.) However, you could just as easily do this with a Paw Target, as outlined in Chapter 7.

WHAT'S A NOSE TARGET?

Any behavior that teaches your dog to touch an object with his nose is a form of nose targeting. This includes Hand Target in Chapter 3, Close the Door in this chapter, and Kiss Me in Chapter 5. Start with these steps, which can then be applied to any object you'd like your dog to target.

1. Rub a treat on a sticky note. With one hand, hold out the sticky note, right in front of your dog's nose.
2. Your dog will reach his nose over to sniff it. Mark and reward the moment he touches the note. After he touches it, remove the note. Get four-for-four nose touches.
3. Add the verbal cue "target" right before you present the note. Get four-for-four.
4. Gradually increase the difficulty by moving the note in different directions and heights. Then, stick the note to other objects (like a door) and cue "target."
5. If you plan on using Nose Target to teach a new behavior, such as Close the Door, you'll be changing the cue and fading out the sticky note. The steps for this are listed for each behavior.

1. Choose a door that your dog can comfortably close. Start with the door ajar.
2. Place a sticky note on the edge of the door at the dog's nose height.
3. Cue "target," and mark and reward when your dog makes contact with the target.
4. Repeat until the dog is offering to target before you can even ask.
5. Now, only mark and reward if the door moves, even a tiny bit, when he targets it. Repeat until he is comfortable with (and not startled by) the door moving in this way.
6. Shape the behavior. Only reward for progressively stronger pushes until he closes the door all the way. When he closes it, jackpot!
7. Start rewarding him only when he fully closes the door.
8. With each repetition, open the door a bit wider. It will require more effort to close it.

TIP: If your dog struggles at any point, go back to an easier step and get four-for-four.

9. Add the verbal cue "close the door" right before he starts pushing it.
10. Remove the sticky note.

TIP: If your dog has become reliant on the sticky note, you can fade it gradually. With each successful rep, shave off the edges of the paper to make it smaller.

From There

High school: Continue working on longer closes, meaning that the door ultimately starts from a fully open position.

College and beyond: Apply this to other doors and low-level cabinets.

  RING A BELL
Basic • Tricks

Prerequisite: Paw or Nose Target

Has your dog ever had an accident simply because you forgot to take him out on time? Teach your pup to get your attention by ringing a bell! That unmistakable jingle is sure to prevent future accidents.

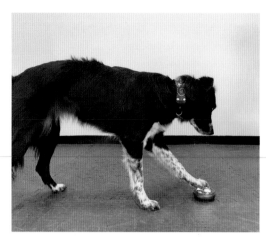

Step 2: Fever does a Paw Target on the sticky note attached to the bell.

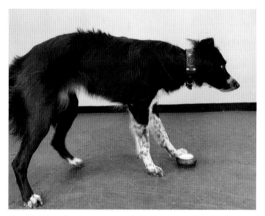

Step 3: Now, she doesn't need the sticky note.

There are numerous kinds of bells that you can make or purchase: hanging jingle bells, a hotel-style call bell, an electronic bell designed specifically for potty training a dog, and so on. Consider what your dog would be the most comfortable with, and whether he would prefer to touch the bell with his nose or paw. In the photos we're using a push light, so you can see it illuminate when Fever has performed the correct behavior. Therefore, our steps will use a Paw Target (see Chapter 7).

While ringing a bell is typically used for going potty, you could teach your dog to ring it to request any other event, too. Keep in mind, though, that if you teach your dog to ring a bell when he's hungry, he might be ringing it from morning until night.

Ring a Bell is useful for dogs who:
- don't give clear signals when they need to go out to potty
- have forgetful owners
- have urinary or bowel issues

HOW TO DO RING A BELL

1. Use the sticky note with which you taught Paw Target (or Nose Target). Adhere it to the bell.
2. Ask your dog to target the bell until you get four-for-four.
3. From there, make the sticky note smaller and smaller until your dog will touch the bell without the sticky note at all.
4. Add a verbal cue, such as "bell" or "ring it," right before you present the bell. Practice several sessions of this, aiming to get four-for-four touches.
5. If you haven't already done so, put the bell in the spot where you will keep it long-term. Practice "bell" from a very short distance at first, with your dog standing next to it. After each successful repetition of "bell," you and your dog should take one step away before beginning the next rep. Repeat "bell" from a slightly longer distance each time. This teaches your dog to both approach and touch the bell.

   TIP: If your dog struggles with distance, go back to a shorter distance and get four-for-four solid reps before proceeding.
6. Once your dog is a "bell" expert, ask him to touch the bell right before you take him out to go potty. The sequence is: do "bell" and reward/immediately snap on the leash (if needed)/go outside.

From There

High school: Fade the food reward. Going outside is rewarding in itself, so ultimately you will not need the treats. As an intermediate step, for several reps you can do the following sequence: do"bell"/leash up and walk out the door/reward.

College: Your dog will take it to college level, when he's ready, by thinking to ring the bell on his own when he needs to go out. (At this point, you won't need the verbal cue "bell" anymore.) The tricky part is ensuring that your dog connects "bell" to potty breaks, not to general playing or walking outside. You will have to make an effort to teach him this point. First, make sure he goes potty right away before he gets his walk or playtime. If he doesn't go potty right away, he goes back in the house. Also, be ready for false alarms. If he rings the bell, and you're certain he's doesn't have to go potty, have a consistent expression such as "not now" to tell him that you won't take him out.

ADVANCED TRICKS

INFINITY WEAVE THROUGH YOUR LEGS
Advanced • Sports

Prerequisite: Run through Your Legs
Used in: Freestyle

With your legs spread, you will teach your dog to weave in and out in an infinity-shaped pattern. It is similar to Weave through Your Legs, except you will remain stationary. It's a great trick for times when you would like to stand still but your dog is itching to move around: while chatting with a friend, waiting at a crosswalk, or even in the vet's waiting room. It's also a simple way to expend your dog's energy in a small space, without working up a sweat yourself.

Infinity Weave through Your Legs is useful for dogs who:

- have extra energy to burn
- get frustrated when standing still for too long
- benefit from doing exercises close to their owners' bodies

In Weave through Your Legs, pictured here, the handler walks forward; in Infinity Weave, the handler stands still.

HOW TO DO INFINITY WEAVE THROUGH YOUR LEGS

1. Have a few treats in both hands. Your dog can start by facing you.

2. Take your right hand (holding a treat) and tuck it behind your right knee.

3. Let your dog bring his head between your legs to get a nibble of the treat. Then, slowly lure him between your legs from front to back and then all the way around your right leg.

   TIP: If your dog is hesitant to walk through your legs, shape it. First, mark and reward when his head is behind your right knee, then when his shoulder is behind your right knee, and so on. Go at your dog's pace.

4. When he has finished wrapping around your right leg and is in front of you again, reward with the treat from your right hand, as in the photo.

5. Quickly tuck your left hand behind your left leg and lure your dog in between your legs, from front to back. Continue to lure him around your left leg until he is in front of you.

   TIP: If your dog appears confused at any point, help him by looking at your treat hand. This will focus his eyes in the correct direction.

6. Mark and reward from your left hand. Quickly bring your right hand behind you as in Step 2. Continue this pattern for a few weaves.

7. Get four-for-four repetitions of smooth weaves.

8. Add the verbal cue "weave" right before luring the dog in between your legs. Repeat the cue for each weave.

9. Ditch the food lure. You will simply sweep your empty hand outward after you say "weave." Reward from your pocket or treat pouch.

Step 1: Sarah has treats in both hands. Ready, Schoffie?

Step 3: She slowly lures Schoffie around her right leg.

Step 5: Sarah has rewarded from her right hand and then quickly tucks her left hand behind her left leg.

She lures Schoffie around her left leg.

Step 6: Sarah rewards Schoffie when she's finished the figure eight.

From There

High school: Extend the behavior so that you ask for two (and eventually more) Infinity Weaves in a row for a single reward. Also, if you're still leaning down to "pull" your dog through your legs, slowly fade how far down your torso bends.

College and beyond: Ask for the behavior in increasingly distracting areas. At first, ask for only one full sequence during a distraction. You can increase the duration of the weaves with time.

  JUMP THROUGH YOUR ARMS
Advanced • Tricks

Prerequisite: Hula Hoop Jump
Used in: Freestyle

This trick has lot of circus-dog appeal, and it can be a great workout for your pup. Jump through Your Arms is when the handler makes a hoop-shaped jump with her arms, and the dog jumps through. It incorporates some skills from agility and, when used in freestyle routines, gets a big reaction from the crowd.

Jump through Your Arms is useful for dogs who:

- have a surplus of energy to burn
- need extra engagement in the house
- prefer active tricks

HOW TO DO JUMP THROUGH YOUR ARMS

1. Warm up with several reps of Hula Hoop Jump (Chapter 7) at a low height.
2. Wrap your arms around the hula hoop, ensuring that your head is not in the way. Cue "jump" as before and get four-for-four jumps.
3. Remove the hula hoop so that only your arms will be creating the hoop. Your hands do not need to connect at this point.

Jump through Your Arms develops skills that you and your dog may use later in agility.

TIP: If your dog is large, for safety, your hands might never connect. In fact, you can practice this using only one arm as the jump bar and do away with the second arm hovering above.

From There

High school: Gradually increase the height of your arms, keeping safety in mind. You can also change the shape of your outstretched arms, for instance, one arm as a horizontal bar.

College and beyond: Try using your legs as jump bars, too, as in Jump over Your Leg.

JUMP INTO YOUR ARMS
Advanced • Tricks

Used in: Freestyle

How would you like it if, on cue, your dog could jump into your arms? This trick provides a classic ending to a freestyle performance. Not only is it a huge crowd-pleaser, but it can serve a practical purpose, too. One day while Sarah was walking Fever, a neighbor's passing dog started barking

furiously at them. Seeing that Fever was becoming increasingly stressed, Sarah cued "fly," and Fever jumped into her arms. This handy trick allowed Sarah to avert a canine crisis by getting her dog out of harm's way in less than a second.

Jump into Your Arms is useful for dogs who:
- are active
- might need to be picked up quickly

Before starting, decide how you can most comfortably catch your dog. It could be with your right arm holding most of the weight at the torso and your left arm supporting the dog from below, or the reverse. The following steps assume that your right arm will take the weight.

HOW TO DO JUMP INTO YOUR ARMS

1. Start by sitting on the floor with your legs outstretched and with your dog on your left.
2. With a treat in your right hand, lure your dog across your lap.
3. When your dog is centered, lift him slightly with your left arm. While holding him with your left arm, feed him with your right hand.

4. Release your dog toward your right. Get four-for-four or practice until your dog is comfortable being suddenly held.

5. Sit on increasingly higher objects as you repeat Steps 2–4. Start with items like a thick book, then a stepstool, then a plastic storage container, then a chair, and so on.

   TIP: If you don't have something to sit on, use a wall as support while you position yourself in higher and higher squats. It's a great workout!

6. Add the verbal cue "fly" when your dog is reliably hopping up rather than just climbing. Get four-for-four.

7. At a certain point, you'll stop luring because the dog won't be able to follow the lure all the way up. You can gesture with an empty hand and reward once the dog is in your arms.

   TIP: If you ask your dog to jump, it's imperative that you catch him. If you let him fall, your dog might begin to distrust you and become reluctant to jump.

Step 2: Sarah lures Fever across her lap.

Step 3: Sarah is supporting Fever with one arm while feeding with the other.

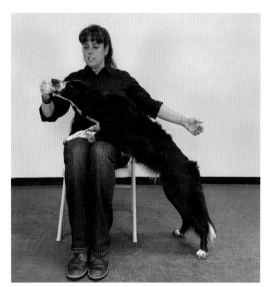

Step 5: Sarah increases the height gradually, over several practice sessions.

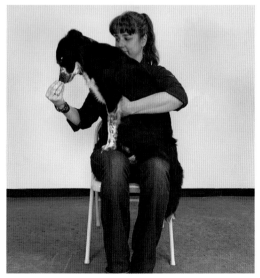

You can see Fever isn't anxious or stressed.

Step 7: "Fly!"

Success!

From There

High school: Work your way up until you're in a standing position (or the highest level at which your dog can safely jump). Remember to reward the dog as you are holding him.

College and beyond: Practice in distracting environments.

  OPEN A DRAWER
Advanced • Tricks

Prerequisite: Tug for Polite Play

This trick could prove very useful, especially if you combine it with the following trick (Go Get Your...). You could have your dog open up a drawer and then bring you an item from it! To do Open a Drawer, you'll have to tie one of your dog's longer rope or tug toys to a drawer so he will be able to open it by pulling on the toy.

Open a Drawer is useful for dogs who:

- need extra engagement in the house
- like to use their mouths
- are curious about their surroundings
- enjoy Tug

HOW TO DO OPEN A DRAWER

1. Show your dog the tug toy hanging from the drawer. Encourage him to "take it," meaning that he should put the tug toy in his mouth, as if playing. Revisit Tug for Polite Play in Chapter 1 if necessary.

   TIP: He may be uncomfortable taking the toy in this context, so hold the toy to make it move, and encourage him to take it. Be patient and keep the energy fun.

2. Once he's comfortable tugging on the toy, open the drawer slightly with one hand. Continue holding the toy with the other hand.

3. While he's tugging, let go of the toy. This will cause him to pull the drawer open a little more. When the drawer opens, even a tiny bit, mark and reward with a treat. (The treat

will make him release the toy, so he won't continue tugging.) Get four-for-four.

4. As your dog gets the hang of it, fade out how much you play with the toy in Step 1.

5. Eventually, you will offer the toy and then release it the moment your dog takes it. If your dog moves the drawer as this happens, mark and reward with a jackpot!

    TIP: If he doesn't move the drawer, go back to playing Tug.

6. Once your dog is reliably opening the drawer, add the verbal cue "open" and then offer the toy to your dog.

From There

High school: Practice the same sequence but with the drawer fully closed. It might take a little more force for your dog to open it now. You'll say "open," offer the tug toy, and wait until he's cracked the drawer open to mark and reward.

College and beyond: With practice, you can fade out your presence. Eventually, you will be able to just say "open," and your dog will grab the tug toy on his own.

  ## GO GET YOUR…
Advanced • Tricks

Prerequisite: Fetch
Used in: Freestyle

You may have noticed that your dog has learned the name of several things on his own. Most dogs learn what "treat" means pretty quickly, and they may respond to questions like "Where's your teddy?" by running and grabbing their favorite teddy bear toys.

You can formalize this natural behavior by teaching your dog the names of different toys and objects and then asking him to find or even retrieve them. Can't find your leash? If you've taught your dog what "leash" is, let him do the searching for you. First, you'll teach your dog the names of different items, and,

after that, he can learn to find or fetch them. This is an ongoing process that takes time and practice, so enjoy the journey.

This practical trick also has sports applications. Since props are used in some Freestyle routines, the handler can cue the dog to retrieve a specific item.

Go Get Your… is useful for dogs who:

- like toys
- like putting things in their mouths (though this is not a requirement)
- misplace things
- need extra engagement in the house

HOW TO TEACH OBJECT NAMES

1. Choose an item with which your dog will interact. A favorite toy is a good starting point.

2. Place the item right in front of your dog. When he reaches his nose to sniff it and touches (or nearly touches) the object, mark and reward. If you have done the free-shaping exercises, using a clicker is advised.

3. Practice targeting the item until your dog gets four-for-four legitimate nose touches.

4. Name the object. So, if it's a rope toy, say "rope" as you place the object on the ground. Mark and reward for touching it. Practice several sessions with four-for-four before proceeding to the next step.

5. Introduce a second novel object, for instance, a candle in a jar. Place both the candle and rope in front of the dog. If he investigates the candle, ignore it. Then say "rope" and mark and reward when he touches the rope toy. Get four-for-four.

6. Change the position of the two objects so that when you say "rope," your dog has to take a few steps to touch it. We're priming him for the next part.

7. Add a third item, such as an empty takeout container, and repeat Steps 5 and 6.

8. Teach the names of other items using the same steps.

HOW TO DO GO GET YOUR...

1. Warm up with a few repetitions of Fetch, using a toy that you have already named.

2. Now, before you throw the toy, add the cue "go get your [rope, ball, teddy]!"

3. If your dog picks it up and brings it to you, mark and reward. You can play with the toy or reward with a treat.

From There

High school: Practice this with several named items, toys at first.

College and beyond: Gradually introduce named items that resemble toys less and less, starting with soft or floppy items. A leash or

Step 2: "Schoffie, go get your ball!"

Schoffie takes her fetching very seriously.

She brings the ball back to Sarah.

Step 3: Sarah rewards her with a treat. It's also fine to play with the toy.

articles of clothing are good intermediate steps, rather than going straight to something like a set of keys.

  PUT YOUR TOYS AWAY
Advanced • Tricks

Prerequisites: Drop It, Go Get Your...

This is one of the most requested tricks. Who wouldn't want a dog who can clean up his own toys at the end of the day? Put Your Toys Away will teach your pup to tidy up by putting his toys into a designated toy box. If it were only this fun to teach human family members the same thing!

Put Your Toys Away is useful for dogs who:

- like toys
- make a mess with their toys
- like putting things in their mouths (though this is not a requirement)
- need extra engagement in the house

HOW TO DO PUT YOUR TOYS AWAY

1. Stand next to your dog's toy box. Place a named toy on the floor nearby.
2. Ask your dog to fetch an item, as in Go Get Your....
3. When he returns to you, hold your hand over the toy box. Then cue "drop it."
4. Reward with a treat (not the toy).

   TIP: Once he's dropped it, your dog might try to grab the toy out of the box. Be ready with a few treat rewards and, if necessary, reward him with one treat, and then another, as you lure him away from the box.
5. Repeat with the next toy.

From There

High school and beyond: With time, your dog will learn the game and require less explicit cuing for each toy. When he sees you approaching the toy box, he'll know it's time to put all his toys away, one after the other. As you walk to the box, you can also add a verbal cue, such as "time to clean up!"

Step 2: "Trevor, go get your monster."

Step 3: Trevor brings it to the toy basket. For your dog, hold your hand over the basket and ask for Drop It.

Step 4: "Where's my treat?"

07
GAMES TO BEAT BOREDOM

A bored dog can easily become a naughty dog. Oftentimes, walks around the block are simply not enough, or perhaps outdoor exercise isn't possible due to weather conditions or your dog's health. That doesn't mean you should relegate your dog to just loafing around the house all day (or, worse, making his own fun by destroying anything with stuffing). There are plenty of activities you can do, even indoors, to keep your dog's body and mind engaged. Sometimes just a few minutes of training games can stave off boredom and give your dog a healthy outlet for his energy. The games in this chapter can engage any dog, even if you have only a small space and limited tools. Some of these activities include a lot of participation from you, while the dog can do others independently.

FREE-SHAPING GAMES

Free-shaping games are most successful when you use a clicker to mark the desired behavior. Make sure you've done the basic clicker exercises in Chapter 1 before starting the games that follow.

Free-shaping games are useful for dogs who:

- are not satisfied by only physical exercise
- are cooped up indoors due to bad weather or injuries
- make their own "fun" when their owners aren't looking
- like to problem-solve or need challenges
- have independent streaks
- are needy
- would benefit from confidence-building activities

 **PAW TARGET**
Basic • Games

Prerequisite: Clicker Training: Free
Shaping 101
Used in: Agility, parkour

In the general sense, paw targeting is used
in canine sports to teach a dog to put his front
paws, back paws, or all four paws on a certain
surface. (Two Feet On, Four Feet On, and
Back onto a Platform are all versions of such
targeting.) In this trick-related version, you'll
teach your dog to target an object with his front
paw. Once your dog learns how to target, you
can apply it to fun and useful scenarios, such as
Crisscross Applesauce in Chapter 5 and Ring a
Bell and Close the Door in Chapter 6.

HOW TO DO PAW TARGET

1. Choose an object that your dog can easily
   see on the floor, such as a sticky note or
   plastic container lid.
2. Place the item on the floor, a few feet
   away from your dog. When your dog
   walks over to the item and touches it
   with either front paw, click and treat.
   Toss the treat away from the target item
   so his paw comes off it.

   TIP: If your dog is tentative, shape it.
   Click and treat whenever a paw approaches
   the target. Click for closer and closer paw
   movements toward the target.

   TIP: If your dog gets "stuck," pick up the
   target item and place it in a new spot.
3. Repeat this until your dog clearly
   understands that he has to paw target, not
   just hover over, the item.
4. Put the behavior on cue. Say "hit it" right
   before your dog starts walking toward the
   item. Get four-for-four at one location,
   and then place the item in a new spot and
   start over.

Step 2: Fever will get a click and treat for touching the sticky note with her paw.

Cute—but no click and treat for this creative interpretation (unless you want a Paw Target with flair!).

From There

High school: Move the target onto a vertical
surface. Adhere it to a wall or a piece of stable
furniture at the lowest point. With time, you can
elevate it higher and higher.

College and beyond: Apply paw targeting to
new objects. See Crisscross Applesauce in Chapter
5, Ring a Bell in Chapter 6, and Balance Work on
Inflatable Objects in this chapter.

This game rewards the dog for showing off his repertoire of behaviors.

SHOW ME A NEW TRICK
Advanced • Games

Prerequisite: Clicker Training: Free Shaping 101

This free-shaping game requires only your dog, some treats, and a clicker. (If your dog doesn't know a ton of tricks, you can modify it by incorporating a tool, such as a cardboard box.) Even though the rules are simple, this game requires a lot of thinking on your dog's part. Your dog will get a click and treat whenever he offers a new behavior that he hasn't already offered during the game. This means that if he just "waved" for a click, he won't get a click for waving again during the session. Show Me a New Trick allows your dog to get creative and really think for himself.

HOW TO DO SHOW ME A NEW TRICK

1. Have treats in your hand or pocket, and a clicker in the other hand.
2. As soon as your dog offers any behavior or trick without being asked, click and treat.

In most cases, he'll sit as soon as he sees that it's training time, and a Sit is a great first behavior.

3. Say "show me a new trick" and wait. If your dog continues sitting (or stands up and sits again), gently say "nope" and continue waiting. As soon as he offers any behavior, from a Down to a Spin to anything in between, click and treat.
4. Continue this game for three or four repetitions and then take a break.

The alternate version of this is to ask your dog to engage with a box or other dynamic object. Each interaction can only be clicked once, pushing him to come up with a new interaction each time.

From There

High school and beyond: As your dog increases his repertoire of tricks, the game can take fun twists and turns. Maybe he'll even come up with new tricks you'd never thought of!

PUSH A BALL
Advanced • Sports

Prerequisite: Nose Target
Used in: Treibball

This is a targeting game, but with a twist. Here, you'll teach your dog to push a beach ball or balance ball with his nose. (You can teach a Paw Target instead, if your dog prefers.) This game is inspired by treibball, a sport in which dogs "herd" large balls between goalposts. Your dog doesn't need herding genes to enjoy it, though; the first dog Kate taught to push a ball was her Chihuahua mix, Batman!

Push a Ball is useful for dogs who:

- tend to herd family members or other animals
- are active with their mouths or paws
- enjoy independent activities

For this game, you'll need a beach ball or balance ball that your dog can reasonably push with his nose. Have your clicker and tons of tiny treats ready. Expect this process to take several sessions.

HOW TO DO PUSH A BALL

1. Put down the ball. Anytime your dog interacts with it—a look, a sniff, or a touch—click and treat.
2. Start to shape it. Click and treat for closer approximations of the goal: facing the ball, approaching the ball, touching the ball, and ultimately pushing the ball.
   TIP: Give a jackpot whenever your dog has a "breakthrough."
3. Continue raising the criteria so that he is pushing the ball, ultimately hard enough to move it, and then pushing it twice: once to start it rolling and again as it rolls.
4. Once your dog is reliably pushing it, add the verbal cue "push" before he starts the sequence: cue "push"/he pushes/click and treat.

Shape this behavior by rewarding your dog's interactions with the ball.

If your dog struggles with free shaping this behavior, you can alternatively do Nose Target with a sticky note on the ball at nose level. Over several repetitions, fade out the sticky note.

From There
High school and beyond: Want your dog to push the ball in a certain direction? Ask him to stay and then place the ball in front of him, setting him up for the direction in which you'd like the ball to go, and then give him the cue to "push."

  ## SCENT GAMES
Basic • Sports

It's no mystery that a dog's sense of smell is exponentially more developed than ours. Scent games can benefit and entertain all dogs, not just those genetically predisposed to having their noses to the ground. These games provide motivating mental challenges for nearly every canine, without the excitement that accompanies more active sports.

PICK A HAND

This is a simple scent game that any dog can do. Pick a Hand involves holding out both of your fists, one containing a treat, and letting the dog guess which fist is holding the goodie. This game allows the person to work in close proximity to the dog, but both are focused on the game, so neither the dog nor the person is going to be too pushy or jumpy.

Pick a Hand is useful for dogs who:

- like food
- need games to play with children
- are comfortable being close to people
- do not resource-guard or take food too intensely
- have any energy level, including low energy

HOW TO DO PICK A HAND

1. Put a super-smelly treat (think bacon, not dry food!) in one hand. Make a loose fist so that the smell is easily detectable. Also make a loose fist with your empty hand.
2. Turn to your dog and present both fists at dog level. Say "pick a hand" as you present your fists.
3. If your dog chooses the fist with the treat by sniffing, licking, or pawing at it, or even intently staring at it, mark "good dog!" and let him eat the treat.

   TIP: In the beginning, if your dog isn't able to choose the correct hand based on the scent, you can wedge the treat between two fingers so he can see it.
4. If he focuses on the wrong hand, mark it with an "oops" or "nope" and open your hand to show him that it is empty. Step away or turn your back before trying again.

From There

High school and beyond: As you practice, switch hands frequently so the dog learns to use his nose rather than simply assuming that the treat

Batman makes an incorrect choice.

The next time, Batman chooses the correct hand.

The taste of victory!

GAMES FOR THE GOLDEN YEARS

Kate's dog Batman is a perfect example of a dog who might not need a lot of engagement but absolutely loves playing sports and games. Due to some physical and cognitive issues, not all activities are appropriate. Scent work-based games, such as the container searches in this chapter, have provided an ideal outlet for this feisty fifteen-year-old. Here's why.

- Scent work allows Batman to focus on a task and burn mental energy without overdoing it physically. His searches provide a short, highly rewarding break between naps.
- When doing searches, Batman can work independently, with minimal input from Kate. As his hearing and vision are declining, activities like rally, which depend on Kate's visual and verbal cues, have become somewhat more challenging. With scent work, Batman lets his nose do all the work. It's stress-free for everyone.
- Scent work can be done indoors, even in small urban spaces. As Batman grows intolerant of less-than-perfect weather, indoor activities have become more important. Since scent work allows for flexible setups, Kate can create simple searches or more complex ones, based on Batman's health and his mood that day.

is always in the same hand. Wash your hands between repetitions so that you don't confuse the dog with lingering odor.

CONTAINER SEARCHES

The three games here are based on typical recreational scent work searches, which start by teaching a dog to search for a treat hidden inside a container. The food, when used in this way, is called the *primary* (or *primary reinforcer*), as it is inherently rewarding for your dog to find it.

Recreational scent work provides a challenging and instinctively fun activity for any dog. Consequently, your participation is minimal. Though you will set up each search, once you release your dog to search for the treat, it's his time to work independently. That means not pointing out the *hides* (the treats) if your dog looks to you for help. It also means not

hindering your dog by blocking the hides, making unnecessary noises, and so on.

It's hard for us humans to understand that sniffing out an odor is an incredibly complicated task. Odor moves in various ways, depending on the temperature, humidity, airflow, and even

types of surfaces in the room. As a result, avoid the temptation to test your dog beyond his limits. (Remember, it's a game, not the MCAT. It should be fun.) Your dog should be able to reach the hide on his own, so avoid placing treats above your dog's eye level or in places that are difficult to reach.

Container Searches are useful for dogs who:

- are cooped up inside
- need more hobbies
- are predisposed to using their noses
- need to learn how to use their noses
- have independent streaks
- need to be reminded how fun their owners are

The following searches are inspired by Dianna L. Santos, a professional trainer, Certified Nose Work Instructor (CNWI) through NACSW™, AKC Scent Work Judge, Unites States Canine Scent Sports (USCSS) Judge and Chief Search Designer (CSD), and owner/lead instructor at Scent Work University. If your dog enjoys these activities and you'd like to learn more about the sport, check out Chapter 8.

HOW TO DO BASIC CONTAINER SEARCHES

All the materials you'll need for entry-level scent work are probably already in your home. To get started, collect six or more cardboard boxes with dimensions that allow your dog to stick his head in comfortably. (A shoebox will work for many dogs.) If you don't have the space for multiple cardboard boxes, opaque plastic containers with open tops will also work. Label half of them with the word "treat," and the other half with "empty." From now on, put treats only in the "treat" boxes, so as not to contaminate the "empty" boxes and confuse your dog. As for the treats, choose something soft and stinky that your dog will be able to smell easily and eat quickly.

1. With your dog in another room (or tethered or in a Stay), place the six boxes in a row in the middle of a room, alternating between "treat" and "empty" boxes. The boxes shouldn't be more than a few feet apart at first. Drop a few treats into the three "treat" boxes.

Advanced scent work training teaches the dog to identify various scents placed in tubes.

TIP: If your dog appears stressed or confused while searching, it is fine to start with just one "treat" box and one "empty" box.

2. Bring your dog into the room, held by the collar or harness. Say "search!" and release him. Let your dog investigate in whatever way he pleases, without interfering.

3. Any time he finds a hide, praise with "good dog!" You can then verbally encourage him to keep going. Otherwise, remain quiet.

4. Once he's found the last hide, tell him "all done" and cheer. Use a treat to lure him away from the search area.

From There

You can play a few repetitions of this game, with the "treat" boxes switching places each time. If he is nailing it, here are some modifications to increase the difficulty and further hone his searching skills.

- Change the position of the boxes. You can put them into two rows and, following that, a more disheveled pattern.
- Add more boxes. You can gradually add both "treat" and "empty" boxes into the mix, and you can vary how many boxes have treats and how many are empty.
- Move the boxes farther apart. A little at a time, spread out the boxes in the room.
- Push the boxes closer together so that they are almost piled on each other. Make sure that there is always a clear path to each hide so that your dog can access it without having to push or step on other boxes.

HOW TO DO INTERMEDIATE CONTAINER SEARCHES

There are many ways to increase the difficulty of searches. One is to partially cover the opening of a box. If you're using cardboard boxes, you can use the flap of one box to cover the opening of another box. If using a plastic storage container, you can lay the lid halfway over the opening.

1. With your dog in another room (or tethered or in a Stay), place the six boxes in the middle of a room. Drop a few treats into the three "treat" boxes. Partially cover the opening of one "treat" box with the flap of another box.

2. Bring your dog into the room, held by the

Any dog, not just scenthounds, can enjoy scent work.

collar or harness. Say "search!" and release him. Let your dog investigate in whatever way he pleases, without interfering.

TIP: If your dog is struggling to find the treat in the half-covered box, make the opening bigger—that is, only cover about a quarter of the opening, not half.

3. Anytime he finds a hide, praise with "good dog!" You can then verbally encourage him to keep going. Otherwise, remain quiet.

4. Once he's found the last hide, tell him "all done" and cheer. Use a treat to lure him away from the search area.

From There

Once your dog is comfortable with this new search, there are several ways to increase the challenge.

- Cover the "treat" boxes more fully, so only a quarter of the opening is exposed. Do not fully cover the opening, though.

- Change the position of the boxes so that the treat boxes aren't always in the same position. Move boxes slightly farther apart or closer together.

- Add more boxes and vary how many of the openings are covered.

HOW TO DO ADVANCED CONTAINER SEARCHES

The advanced search incorporates elevation into your scent game. This means that you will place the hide in a box that is resting on top of a book, stool, or other object, but take care not to elevate it higher than the dog's head.

Another tricky point about elevated hides: when elevating one box with treats in it, make sure to have an empty box diagonally underneath it. This is due to the nature of odor, which tends to roll over the top of the treat box and cascade in a diagonal fashion downward. By having an empty box in this position, it can capture the odor and allow it to pool in the empty box. Your dog is likely to locate the odor in the floor-level empty box first and then follow it up to the elevated hide. Pretty cool, right?

1. With your dog in another room (or tethered or in a Stay), place the six boxes in the middle of a room. Drop a few treats into the three "treat" boxes. One of the "treat" boxes should be elevated on a book, chair, or stool. The box height is determined by your dog's height; do not elevate it higher than his head, so he can get to the treat with minimal help from you. Place an empty box diagonally under the elevated hide.

2. Bring your dog into the room, held by the collar or harness. Say "search!" and release him. Let your dog investigate in whatever way he pleases, without interfering.

    TIP: If your dog is struggling to find the treat in the elevated box, consider reducing the elevation. Also make sure the air current isn't affecting the odor's ability to pool in the empty box below.

    TIP: If he is tentative about reaching up to the treat box, help him out by bringing the box down to him to eat the treat. The objective is simply to find the treat, not to push himself to reach it.

3. Any time he finds a hide, praise with "good dog!" You can then verbally encourage him to keep going. Otherwise, remain quiet.

4. Once he's found the last hide, tell him "all done" and cheer. Use a treat to lure him away from the search area.

From There

Once your dog is comfortable with this elevated search, you can get creative.

- Include some covered boxes in addition to elevated boxes.
- Add more boxes, vary the boxes' positions, and change how many contain hides.

TRACKING GAME

This game is based on the principles of tracking, which is a favorite canine hobby as well as a structured sport and even a canine job. Tracking involves your dog following a scent path left, usually, by a human or other animal. When you see your dog furiously sniffing out the route that

Search and rescue dogs train and develop their tracking skills on all types of terrain.

a chipmunk traversed, that is tracking. It is also used in search-and-rescue efforts to find someone who is lost. In all cases, the individual has left behind olfactory evidence of his presence as he moves, which your dog can pick up on and follow to the source.

This game will let your dog track something that he will be highly motivated to find: a hot dog or a similarly delicious, stinky food item. This is an outdoor activity for which you'll need a friend to help, plus several pieces of hot dog. To prepare, attach a chunk of hot dog to a string, at least 6 feet (1.8 m) long, which you will drag on the ground behind you. Have your dog in a back-clip harness and on a long line. Set your dog up for success by choosing a day with no breeze or just a slight breeze that blows from the hot-dog source toward your dog.

Tracking Game is useful for dogs who:

- are predisposed to using their noses
- need to learn how to use their noses
- have an independent streak
- need to be reminded how fun their owners are

HOW TO DO TRACKING GAME

1. Hold your dog's long line or harness while your helper drags the hot dog a short distance through the grass and slightly out of sight,

such as behind a few bushes. Your dog can watch the hot dog bouncing away.

2. Once your helper has stopped moving, she should stay in that spot with the hot dog. If she returns to you, it will affect the odor picture.

3. When it looks like your dog has a whiff of the hot dog (which might be immediate), tell him to "search" and let him follow the scent.

4. As he follows it, stay behind him so as not to interfere. You can use the leash to prevent him from getting too far off the track or to slow him down if he starts barreling toward the hot dog dangerously fast.

   TIP: If your dog veers off the track, you should stand still and not let out any more of the long line. Avoid reeling him in, which would be doing some of the work for him.

5. When he reaches the hot dog, celebrate and let him have several pieces of hot dog.

From There

You can increase the difficulty in a couple of ways.

- Lengthen the track. Ensure that every time you play the game, you use a new spot so that there is no confusing overlap of old and new scents.
- Lay the track when the dog is not there to watch. When you bring your dog out, start relatively close to the beginning of the track so that he doesn't struggle to find it.

⭐ ⚽ AT-HOME AGILITY
Basic • Sports

While proper agility is practiced in a training facility on specific equipment, you can replicate the agility experience in your own home and backyard using regular household items. By practicing agility at home, you're exercising your dog's body and mind, all the while building a trusting dog-and-handler relationship that extends beyond just fun and games.

At-Home Agility is useful for dogs who:

- need more than walks around the block to feel satisfied
- like to run, jump, and explore
- enjoy mental challenges
- would benefit from more indoor or backyard activities

DIY JUMP POLES

If you're handy, it's easy to build jumps with pieces of PVC. You can buy strips that attach to PVC with premeasured jump cups to hold a jump bar. You'll need two uprights, two feet, one crossbar to connect the feet, and one jump bar. Jumps are usually either 4 or 5 feet (1.2 or 1.5 m) wide. Using PVC glue on the couplers will keep it all together. Or, if you're not handy, grab a broomstick and two stacks of books.

Choose a location that allows your dog to make a sufficient running start and finish. The surface should not be slippery or super-hard; if you're unsure about the surface your dog is jumping on, put down a yoga mat for safety.

Once you've got your jump(s) ready to go, follow the steps for Jump Over in Chapter 6 to teach your dog how to properly jump over an object.

HULA-HOOP JUMP

Add to your circus-dog repertoire with this one. A hula hoop could be part of a freestyle routine, and it also resembles the tire jump used in agility. This indoor or outdoor activity is sure to burn some canine energy and put your dog's mind to good use. You'll need a hula hoop, but choose one that doesn't make noise (or remove the internal beads). Follow the same safety guidelines as DIY Jump Poles.

HOW TO DO HULA-HOOP JUMP

1. Hold the hula hoop so it is between your body and a wall. Rest the bottom of the hoop on the floor. At first, your dog will simply walk, not jump, through.

2. Toss a treat through the hoop so your dog will have to walk through the hoop to get the goodie. Get four-for-four. As with other jump skills, it's important to toss the treat on the floor to teach the dog to look where he's going.

From There

Vary the height and location of the hoop, ensuring that you follow the safety guidelines.

DIY TUNNEL

The tunnel isn't just a crowd-pleaser; it's often a dog's favorite obstacle because it's fast and easy to do correctly. But it doesn't always start that way, as the idea of stepping inside a dark tunnel doesn't come naturally to many dogs.

In beginner agility classes at Brooklyn Dog Training Center, we ease the dog into this exercise by making the tunnel as short as possible. Sarah holds the dog, on leash, at one opening of the tunnel, while the owner goes to the other opening and encourages the dog to come through. The leash simply prevents the dog from going around the tunnel. Once the dog has chosen to enter the tunnel on his own, Sarah may drop the leash. Meanwhile, the owner, at the other end, is encouraging the dog to come

TIP: If your dog keeps going around the hoop instead of through it, practice this in a hall or doorway so the only path to the treat is through the hoop.

3. Add a verbal cue, such as "jump" or "tire," before you toss the treat. Get four-for-four.
4. Hold the hoop a tiny bit off the ground. Cue and toss the treat, same as before. Get four-for-four.
5. Using the rule of four-for-four, continue elevating the hoop until it is raised up to a maximum of your dog's hock height (for young dogs whose growth plates haven't closed) or 2 inches (5 cm) below the withers (for fully grown dogs).
6. Once your dog is enthusiastically jumping, ditch the treat lure. This can happen at any point in the process.
7. Now you can keep it at the same height, but start inching the hoop away from the wall. Get four-for-four before moving it farther from the wall.

You can start with a child's play tunnel for puppies and small dogs.

through, using her voice, clapping, or making any other sounds to motivate him. When he runs through, he gets a jackpot with treats or a toy.

Here are a few tips to consider when practicing Tunnel at home.

- If your dog tries to go around, rather than through, the tunnel, it's important not to correct him. He doesn't understand the game yet, but he will with practice.
- Never use the leash to pull the dog through the tunnel, as that can easily make a dog fearful of this new obstacle. The dog must choose to go through it on his own.
- Only make eye contact with your dog through the tunnel. If you make eye contact from around the sides of the tunnel, it unintentionally cues him to go around it. While your head will be looking at the dog through the tunnel, take care that your body does not entirely block your dog's exit.
- As he goes through the tunnel, continue encouraging him until all four paws have exited the obstacle. Then, once he's fully through, reward.
- Avoid throwing food into the tunnel. You want your dog to run through it as quickly as possible, not stop to hunt for snacks.
- When your dog gets four-for-four solid runs through the tunnel, increase the length of the tunnel a little bit. Continue lengthening the tunnel in this way until it is fully expanded.

To practice the basics at home, you don't need to buy an actual agility tunnel. All you need is a large towel or sheet, and a chair or coffee table that your dog can easily fit under. Drape the sheet over the chair so that the left and right sides are covered but the dog can walk under it from back to front. If you prefer an actual tunnel, you can buy an agility tunnel for dogs online; alternatively, a children's play tunnel can work for small dogs. If you use a tunnel, be sure to secure it so it doesn't roll around when the dog is inside. Do this by placing sandbags, gallon jugs of water, or similar heavy objects to the sides of the tunnel.

  PARKOUR
Basic • Sports

The parkour exercises starting from Chapter 3 can all be done indoors. Whether a sprawling mansion or a "cozy" studio, your home affords you limitless parkour opportunities. Even something as simple as a book or an empty box can allow you to do numerous exercises in a small space.

FIVE USES FOR A CHAIR

If you have a standard straight-back dining chair, you've got yourself at least five parkour exercises. You can modify these for other kinds of furniture. Be creative!

1. **Go Under.** Your dog can crawl under the chair in its regular position. Or, turn the chair upside-down, creating a more challenging space to squeeze under.
2. **Go Around.** Your dog can loop around the chair both clockwise and counterclockwise. Short dogs can even circle one leg of the chair.

3. Figure Eight. Weave in a tight figure eight around two legs of the chair by asking for a circle around one leg and then a circle around another leg. If your dog is too tall for this, he can do Figure Eight around two chairs.

4. **Two Feet On.** Place the chair in any position you like, such as on its side or upside-down, and ask your dog to put two paws on it.

5. **Backward Between.** Short dogs can walk backward under the chair. Taller dogs can back up between the chair and the wall.

This is just a start. See what other items you have at home to build a whole amusement park for your pup.

 ## MEALTIME GAMES
Basic • Games

Feeding meals from a bowl is so outdated. Mealtime games are the simplest way to keep your dog entertained without much effort on your part. Your dog has to eat anyway, so why not use his food to reduce his surplus energy? The goal is to find a food-dispensing toy or game that is mildly challenging for your dog—not too easy but not too frustrating.

Mealtime games are useful for dogs who:
- are mouthy or teething
- need to build independence (because they can play these games in a separate room from their owners)
- need to burn energy and beat boredom when they can't get sufficient exercise
- need to be entertained so they don't get underfoot when their owners are cooking, greeting guests, or doing other activities
- need diversions as their owners leave the house to reduce mild separation anxiety

If you have multiple dogs, we recommend separating the dogs while playing mealtime games. One dog will inevitably finish faster than the others and be tempted to "help" his siblings with their games, too. This can lead to resource-guarding displays.

FOOD-DISPENSING TOYS

The options are seemingly endless when it comes to food-dispensing balls, cubes, tubes, and other toys, ranging from DIY to expensive. We recommend having a variety of toys for each dog, so you can rotate the toys. Also, after your dog masters how to use one toy, consider getting new ones that are increasingly harder. Some toys actually have multiple difficulty levels built into their design, so you can start with the easiest setting and build the challenge with time.

Consider the following types of toys:
- Basic *hollow toys* have a hole for inserting dry food, and the food can tumble out of one or more holes. This type of toy might be in the shape of a ball, a cube, or another shape. Some are quite easy, while others require great effort from the dog to get the food out. There are also

You can fill hollow treats with pieces of kibble or a soft food, such as peanut butter.

Play Your Way to Good Manners

toys that can be filled with wet food, which the dog has to lick out.

- *Puzzle toys* usually hold food in several compartments, and your dog has to figure out how to open them up to release the food.
- *Remote* or *Bluetooth-controlled toys* allow you to dispense food from a distance or have the toy dispense food automatically when the dog interacts with the toy in a certain way. In some cases, this means the dog can play the game while home alone. (Naturally, these toys have high price tags.)
- *Slow feeders* (bowls with raised designs on the inside) are not technically toys, but their unusual shapes make it harder for the dog to inhale his food, so there is a playful aspect to these items.

"FIND IT" SCENT GAME

This scent game is easy to set up, requires little space, and can keep your dog engaged for several minutes. You'll start by hiding a number of treats or a serving of dry food in a rumpled-up blanket, sheet, or towel. Your dog will have to sniff, dig, and push to reach the pieces of food. Depending on how tightly you rumple or fold the blanket, the game can either be very easy or extremely challenging.

HOW TO DO FIND IT

1. Tether your dog or ask him to stay. Let your dog watch you sprinkle several treats or pieces of dry food into a blanket, sheet, or large towel on the floor. Don't rumple the blanket yet.
2. Say "find it" and let him find the treats on his own. You may verbally encourage him, but don't help him find the treats.
3. When you think he's found all of the treats, say "all done" and pick up the blanket.
4. Once your dog can find all (or most) of the treats without asking for your help or giving

Your dog will love to use his nose to find a tasty reward.

up, you can rumple the blanket a little bit next time. Increase the challenge slowly.

From There

Increase the challenge by:

- rumpling, twisting, or folding the blanket more
- using a larger blanket
- using more treats or food

OTHER EASY GAMES

Does your dog *still* have energy to burn? Not to fear! These games will surely tire him out.

AUTOMATIC BALL THROWER

If your dog loves fetching balls, consider purchasing an automatic ball launcher to keep him busy for as long as his doggie heart desires. If you teach him how to load the ball himself (see following instructions), you don't even need to participate. Some launchers have distance and angle settings, making them appropriate for both indoor and outdoor use. They may also include sensors for safety, emit sounds to help the dog learn how the machine works, and feature a rest setting that shuts the machine down after several minutes to ensure that your dog doesn't overdo it.

HOW TO TEACH THE DOG TO RELOAD THE BALL

Prerequisites: Fetch, Drop It

1. Your dog has fetched the ball. As he is bringing the ball back, place your hand, palm up, over the opening to the ball reloader.
2. Cue "drop it" into your palm.
3. As soon as you have the ball in your hand, drop it into the ball reloader. Repeat every time your dog brings the ball back for another throw.
4. Incrementally, move your palm farther away from the center of the ball reloader and angle your fingers down so that when your dog drops the ball, it naturally rolls into the reloader.
5. Continue gradually moving your hand away from the reloader. Cue "drop it" when he is close to the reloader so he can release the ball without your hand guiding it.

6. Eventually, you can remove your hand from the equation. Then, at some point, your dog will understand how to reload the ball on his own, without the "drop it" cue.

FLIRT POLE

A flirt pole is a great way to tire out your playful dog without expending a ton of your own energy. While running or playing Fetch with your dog every morning sounds like a great idea, it may not be feasible in the dead of winter or when you are sick with the flu. For dogs with a high play drive, having a flirt pole on hand can make for a great Plan B.

A flirt pole looks like a fishing rod with a toy dangling on the end. You may have seen versions of this for cats. The idea is for your dog to chase the plush toy but not catch it. If he does catch it, just stop playing and ask your dog to drop it. Then, reward the Drop It by starting the game again immediately. You can stand in one place, and, by moving the toy, your dog will dart, change direction, jump, and stalk. As you move the flirt pole back and forth, aim to drag the toy on the ground. This is for safety reasons as well as to prevent your dog from learning to jump up to grab what he wants.

BALANCE WORK ON INFLATABLE OBJECTS

Using inflatables is a fantastic way to increase your dog's strength, balance, coordination, and confidence. Sarah regularly guides her senior dog, Hank, through a variety of exercises in order to keep him fit. Hank doesn't run as much as he used to, but, being a large dog, he needs to retain his muscle strength to avoid failing joints. Balance work has practical benefits not only for older dogs but also for active dogs, dogs with limited access to exercise, and those living in small spaces.

You can purchase 12-inch (30-cm) balance discs for humans online for a reasonable price;

they work just as well for dogs. You can also shop around for dog-specific balance items, which come in a variety of shapes and sizes. The more you inflate the disc, the more challenging it will be. There are numerous different exercises that you can do with your dog, so you'll never get bored. The exercises are mainly paw targets on the inflatables, so if your dog has practiced paw targeting, such as Two Feet On, Four Feet On, and Back onto a Platform, he will catch on quickly. Look for a dog trainer in your area who can show you how to get started with balance work, or you might consider an online conditioning class. Here are some tips for working with inflatable stability discs.

- Have your dog in a back-clip harness in case you need to support him or hold on to him in a pinch. You'll be by your dog's side the entire time he's balancing himself.
- If the disc slides on the floor, support it with your hand or foot.
- Go at your dog's pace. Use treats to lure the dog to put his paws on the disc, but don't push him past his comfort level. If your dog is nervous, reward every interaction he has with the disc to slowly increase his confidence.

- If your dog is bold and gets all four paws on, great! But if your brave pup is trying to do things he's not physically ready for, support him to ensure that he is both safe and comfortable.
- Reward your dog as often as necessary to keep him motivated to continue working. The rate of reinforcement will depend on the dog.
- If your dog's legs get wobbly and shaky on the discs, that means he's working really hard—well done! Remember, this is a workout for your dog, so don't push him past his physical

Navin guides Ella to do Two Feet On, Back onto a Platform, and Four Feet On, all on the inflatable object.

08
TAKE IT FURTHER

GETTING INVOLVED IN DOG SPORTS · 212

GETTING INVOLVED IN DOG SPORTS

Interested in getting more involved in a canine sport? Whether you want to participate recreationally or competitively, this chapter will point you in the right direction. The resources at the end of this book provide useful websites for all of the sports mentioned.

AGILITY

These days, there are myriad ways to get more involved in agility. Most dog-training facilities offer an agility-for-fun class. If you would like to get involved in competitive agility, search for clubs in your area that offer classes and host trials. You can search for local clubs online via numerous organizations: AKC, USDAA, UK Agility International (UKI), Canine Performance Events, Inc. (CPE), and the North American Dog Agility Council (NADAC). Online schools, such

as OneMind Dogs, Agility University, and Dog Sport University, bring agility workshops and courses straight to you. As described in Chapter 7, you don't necessarily need a lot of equipment to get started.

Even if you're just looking for a recreational class, keep safety in mind. For instance, on what flooring does the class take place? Avoid hard or slippery surfaces, such as concrete. How old is your dog? A young dog can still participate, but if his growth plates have not closed yet, he should not be jumping higher than his hocks, nor should he be doing much weaving. Likewise, don't push your older dog to jump higher than he's able.

Look for instructors who have, or whose students have, attained the types of goals you've set for yourself. It's best to begin with a foundation class, which may not even involve any obstacles. The importance of flatwork (that is, training that occurs without the dog leaving the ground) is an often-overlooked but vital component for future success.

Regardless of the program you choose, training in agility is a great way to participate in an activity that engages both you and your dog physically and mentally.

DOCK DIVING

Dock diving is a sport tailor-made for dogs that love water. While it may be a challenge to find a facility that offers it, a lot of the practice doesn't require an actual dock. Multiple-time national finalist Lindsay Hill says, "Teaching my dog how to swim and building a love for water, conditioning my dog so that he is physically fit to jump and swim, and increasing toy drive are all skills that can be taught away from the dock. If you're unsure if your dog will make the leap from dock to water in a dock-diving pool, try getting your dog acclimated to this in natural water first."

The agility course tests a dog's speed, balance, and accuracy.

Your dog may make a splash in the sport of dock diving!

Many of the organizations allow members to compete either live or by video submission. The video option "allows all types of dogs (and people) that get too nervous in new places or in front of people the opportunity to have an outlet for competition," says trainer and competitor Beverly Blanchard, KPA, of Periwinkle Dog Training. She also notes that video submission is appropriate for dog-reactive dogs or those who can't attend competitions in person. On the other hand, she says, "Live venues give you the opportunity to have you and your dog play off of a live audience as well as have the camaraderie of others who participate in this fun sport supporting you. Most freestylers participate in both live and video events because once you prepare a routine that is ready for competition, it is beneficial to have options in more than one or two live competitions in your area annually."

If you'd like to pursue dock diving further, Lindsay advises you to "search the national organizations that sanction dock diving events to find a club more local to you where you can attend training sessions to get your team more acclimated to working on the dock." Those organizations include DockDogs, North America Diving Dogs, and Ultimate Air Dogs.

FREESTYLE

Canine freestyle is one of the most fascinating sports to watch, as the handlers often create routines that are not only technically impressive but also imaginative and heartwarming. If you'd like to delve deeper into freestyle, you may be able to find a local instructor to guide you in a private lesson, group lesson, or seminar. Check the resources at the end of this book; some of the titling organizations have training clubs throughout the country. Online courses are also an option, as little equipment is needed to get started.

Canine freestyle is dancing fun for dog, handler, and audience.

Both parkour and agility involve obstacles that teach balance and focus.

PARKOUR

Parkour differs from the other dog sports in that, while you can earn titles, there are no trials. There are two titling organizations: the International Dog Parkour Association (IDPKA) and All Dogs Parkour (ADP). The exercises in this book are based on ADP, which has a wider variety of exercises from which to choose and allows modifications for senior or disabled dogs.

To get more involved in the sport, Jude Azaren, ADP's founder, says, "The best way for you and your dog to learn about parkour is by taking classes. You will learn how to keep your dog confident and safe as well as how to teach the parkour exercises to your dog." Jude emphasizes making sure that the instructor is qualified and focuses on safety. "If you don't find competent instruction near home, online parkour courses are a great choice… You work at your own pace and attend class when it is convenient for you." Poised for Success Freestyle offers several online classes in both IDPKA and ADP, and

Fenzi Dog Sports Academy offers an online class in IDPKA.

You can take your parkour practice a step further by earning titles. Jude explains, "Both IDPKA and ADP offer their titles through video submission. Teams are awarded titles based on their accurate and safe demonstration of various parkour exercises." There are several advantages to titling by video. "Each exercise is [recorded] separately, usually taking fewer than fifteen seconds to complete. Exercises may be [recorded] on different days, making it easy to do as much or as little as time permits on a particular day. You can take multiple videos until you are satisfied with the performance of each exercise. When you have videos of all the exercises you need, you put them on YouTube and submit your entry for judging."

RALLY

Rally obedience is a rewarding activity for dogs young and old. To find classes in your area, try searching the AKC and World Cynosport Rally (WCRL) websites, which list training clubs by area. As it grows in popularity, you'll find that rally is being offered at more and more training facilities. Since rally requires minimal equipment, it also lends itself to an online class format, such as those at Fenzi Dog Sports Academy.

To get familiar with what a rally course entails at each level, the two main titling organizations, the AKC and WCRL, have YouTube channels with videos that demonstrate all of the exercises. (Though generally similar, the rules and requirements of these two organizations differ at times.) You can also drop in to watch a rally trial in your area to familiarize yourself with the courses, the trial atmosphere, and the level of the competitors. As with all sports, you'll find a mix of seasoned professionals, anxious newcomers, and everything in between at most local trials. The AKC and WCRL websites list upcoming trials in each state. And if you are interested in earning titles in rally but aren't able to attend trials in person, not to worry! Cyber Rally-O is an organization that allows you to earn titles from home by recording and submitting your runs. (See the section on parkour in this chapter to learn more about how that works.)

SCENT WORK

If you'd like to build your dog's scent work skills, you have lots of options. All of the suggestions in this section come compliments of judge and instructor Dianna Santos. If you're looking for in-person training, "work with a CNWI instructor through the founding organization, NACSW [National Association of Canine Scent Work]. These instructors complete an intensive program where they learn all the tools necessary to help you and your dog on your scent work journey." Scent work also lends itself to being learned online, through schools such as Scent Work University, which offers numerous classes for both skill building and trial preparation, and Fenzi Dog Sport Academy. There are also in-person and online seminars, plus NACSW Nose Work Camp, "a week-long engrossing experience where you and your dog will focus on all things scent work."

If you'd like to trial, there are several organizations: NACSW, United Kennel Club (UKC), United States Canine Scent Sports (USCSS), AKC, and others. Dianna recommends volunteering for as many scent work organizations as you can. "This will help you see how that specific trialing organization works, [and] what you and your dog would be expected to do at a trial...volunteering can simply be an excellent learning experience." Then it's time to "train, train, and train some more!" She emphasizes taking your time and enjoying the journey, as rushing to grab titles at the lower

levels can catch up with you at the upper levels. "Titles and ribbons are wonderful, but the fact that you get to spend time with your dog and create memories is the most important part."

Scent work is unique because it has applications not only as a sport but also as a canine "job." As Dianna explains, "Professional detection dogs are used in a variety of capacities, including with police forces (finding contraband, weapons, explosives, and fugitives), the military (finding explosives), and search and rescue teams (locating victims of natural disasters or assisting police departments in working homicides or cold cases). There are teams who are contracted by hotels and private citizens in detecting bed bugs. One of the most exciting fronts is in the medical field, where research is underway to use dogs to help in the detection of a variety of diseases, such as cancer. Some dogs are even used to detect if gluten is in certain types of food. Basically, if it has an odor, it may be possible to train a dog to find it and help society at large!"

With scenting ability thousands of times stronger than that of humans, all dogs are candidates for scent work.

RESOURCES

Note that the online schools listed here may offer courses in a number of sports.

AGILITY

Agility University
www.agility-u.com

American Kennel Club Agility
www.akc.org/sports/agility

Canine Performance Events, Inc.
www.k9cpe.com

Dog Sport University
www.dogsportuniversity.com

North America Dog Agility Council
www.nadac.com

OneMind Dogs
www.oneminddogs.com

UK Agility International
www.ukagilityinternational.com

United States Dog Agility Association
www.usdaa.com

BARN HUNT

Barn Hunt Association
www.barnhunt.com

Happy Ratters
www.happyratters.com

DISC DOG

K9 Frisbee Toss and Fetch
www.tossandfetch.com

Skyhoundz
www.skyhoundz.com

UpDog Challenge
www.updogchallenge.com

US Disc Dog Nationals
www.usddn.com

DOCK DIVING

Dock Dogs
www.dockdogs.com

North America Diving Dogs
www.northamericadivingdogs.com

Ultimate Air Dogs
www.ultimateairdogs.com

FLYBALL

North American Flyball Association
www.flyball.org

FREESTYLE

Canine Freestyle Federation
www.canine-freestyle.org

Dogs Can Dance
www.dogscandance.com

Karen Pryor Academy Canine Freestyle
www.karenpryoracademy.com/courses/
canine-freestyle

Musical Dog Sport Association
www.musicaldogsport.org

Rally Freestyle Elements
www.rallyfree.com

The World Canine Freestyle Organization, Inc.
www.worldcaninefreestyle.org

PARKOUR

All Dogs Parkour
www.alldogsparkour.com

All Dogs Parkour Facebook Group
www.facebook.com/groups/AllDogsParkour

Dog Parkour Training Facebook Group
www.facebook.com/groups/dogparkourtraining

International Dog Parkour Association
www.dogparkour.org

Poised for Success!
www.poisedforsuccessfreestyle.com

RALLY

American Kennel Club Rally
www.akc.org/sports/rally

Cyber Rally-O
www.cyberrally-o.com

Fenzi Dog Sports Academy
www.fenzidogsportsacademy.com

World Cynosport Rally
www.rallydogs.com

SCENT WORK

American Kennel Club Scent Work
www.akc.org/sports/akc-scent-work

K9 Nose Work
www.k9nosework.com

National Association of Canine Scent Work
www.nacsw.net

Scent Work University
www.scentworkuniversity.com

United Kennel Club Nosework
www.ukcdogs.com/nosework

United States Canine Scent Sports
www.uscaninescentsports.com

TREIBBALL

American Treibball Association
www.americantreibballassociation.org

National Association of Treibball Enthusiasts
www.nationaltreibball.com

INDEX

ACKNOWLEDGMENTS

Sarah and Kate would like to thank everyone who contributed their time and expertise to this book: Lizzie Marks, Navin Sivakumar, Benah Stiewing, Stephanie Teed, Anita Ambani, Coco and Ben VanMeerendonk, Beverly Blanchard, Lindsay Hill, Dianna Santos, Jude Azaren, Jenn Michaelis, Barry Rosen, Richard Knecht, Kevin Johnson, Pat McGowan, and Joy Brewster.

Kate would like to thank chef and advisor Jun Naito, stylist Jamie Obijiski, photographer Erich Molloy, and horse trainer Janet Lawson, as well as Florence Valentino and Len Fox of Brooklyn College, for their incredible guidance; Bonnie and Jim Tully for nurturing her love of animals and reining in her love of semicolons; David Muriello of CATCH for encouraging her to pursue dog training as more than a hobby; and Sarah Westcott for hanging in there after hiring the world's most nervous trainer.

Sarah would like to thank her partner, Vincent Bova, for his encouragement and support; her mother, Suzanne Hall-Westcott, for sparking her love of dogs; her mentor and coach, Frankie Joiris, for her constant teachings, guidance, and friendship; the staff at Doggie Academy for their hard work and being so good at what they do; and David Muriello of CATCH for suggesting that she hire Kate Naito. Sarah would also like to thank Hank, her challenge dog. He passed away before this book was published, but he's the one that taught Sarah the value of these behaviors. Hank is deeply missed.

PHOTO CREDITS